A Woman Writing

A Woman Writing

A Memoir in Essays

What writing *about* writing taught me about
determination, persistence, and the ups and
downs of choosing a writing life

Mary Lou Sanelli

Sanelli, Mary Lou
A Woman Writing

ISBN: 978-0-912887-29-6

Library of Congress Control Number: 2015931138

Book design: VJB/Scribe

AEQUITAS BOOKS
About the Press: Aequitas Books is an imprint of Pleasure Boat Studio: A Literary Press. We are located in New York City. The imprint focuses on sociological and philosophical themes in non-fiction. Our books are carried by Baker & Taylor, Ingram, Partners/West, Brodart, and Small Press Distribution (SPD).

For more information,
Pleasure Boat Studio: A Literary Press
201 West 89 Street, New York, NY 10024

Email: pleasboat@nyc.rr.com
URL: www.pleasureboatstudio.com

PRINTED IN THE UNITED STATES

FIRST PRINTING

For Larry

⁓

For making dinner as I made my way through another book.

And for breakfast. And for lunch.

⁓

I met my husband on a Saturday on the Sol Duc Hot Springs Road. The air smelled of wood smoke. I'd just hitchhiked my way to Port Angeles. When the beat up Volkswagen van pulled over, I knew the man inside was the man for me.

He still is.

"Write what you experience and see, because what history needs more of is first-person testimony."

—WILLIAM SAFIRE, POLITICAL COLUMNIST & SPEECH WRITER (1930–2009)

I wish I could thank this writer in person. His words give me permission, pretty much on a daily basis, to keep at it. *Oh, the confidence you give to me, Mr. Safire!*

Contents

PART THREE

PART FOUR

Introduction

Back in November of 2009, Congresswoman Sheila Jackson Lee, a Texas Democrat (which has got to be a pretty sticky thing right there), echoed the point that it was funny to call health-care reform rushed, "America has been working on providing access to health care for all Americans since the 1930s."

I have often felt the same way about writing a book.

Not that I, for a minute, compare writing, mine or anyone's, to the crucial issue of health care. I'm just struck by how often there is this misconception of time, how long it takes to accomplish certain things, how slow and arduous writing really is.

For instance, you might think all my thoughts come to me as I write, and in one sense, they do. In another, they've taken all my life to uncover. All that comes to me now is an intensified need to get at them.

I've written a lot about being a writer, a woman, a wife, a daughter, a friend, and, I regret, what it feels like to be completely disillusioned about American politics as of late, and how I feel vulnerable about so many things because of it. And yet, in my earlier titles, I was writing from a younger perspective (a glorious deficit)! I was unable to crawl underneath and lift my work to where I can now.

I'll say this though: I tried. I was determined. I spent whole weeks at a stretch pruning a single poem. I not only wanted my work to be beautifully written, I wanted it to make sense of things, especially the unexplainable, and especially to me.

I no longer put that kind of pressure on myself.

Gradually, I came to realize something: Writing, the act itself, is enough. If questions are answered along the way, better still, but it's no longer my desire to make sense of so much. Isn't there something completely shady about people—religious, political—who talk as if they hold the key to the truth, as if they know the great secrets, as if they know at all?

I think so. And I can't tell you *why* people like this scare me so much. But they do.

It's as if I freed myself. I remember it as *the* moment that I knew I would spend the rest of my life writing, a pivotal distinction in my life, when, even though I'd already published several books, I would no longer think of myself as a woman trying to be a writer, but as a writer. A woman writing.

Gratefully, with age come many such distinctions.

For as far back as I can remember, I've looked to the wise guidance of women like Sheila Jackson Lee, women who swim against the tide, who have what it takes to make things happen. Risk-takers are my greatest influence. *If she can chip away at the glass ceiling, I can surely shape this book!*

Early on, May Sarton's *Journal of a Solitude* literally changed the direction of my life. Reading about a woman active in a life of her choosing, a writing life, when most of the women around her spoke of themselves with reference to what their children were up to, and then, as the years passed, grandchildren, well, even as a young woman still giving thought to having a child, I knew her solitary, writerly ways would become my own. I thought of her often while in the throes of these pages.

I also think of Edith Wharton, writing years before May Sarton, how she inhabited a 113-acre estate alone so she could have the "freedom from trivial obligations which was necessary if I was to go on with my writing." She wrote this in the late 1800s. Hard to imagine how strong the tide against her independence must have been.

I'm well into the late stages of revision here when one family invitation arrives, and, later, another, and I must choose not to attend both my husband's family reunion (not so difficult, really) and a wedding of a niece who lives across an ocean and a continent, a more difficult decision. I'm rather fond of the woman my niece has become.

Naturally showing up for neither didn't win me any points, but it was a choice I had to make. I'd given myself the year to write, a promise I had to keep, making it impossible to say *yes* to the many social obligations — wait, I'd go so far as to say *all* — that take focus away if I cave. To disrupt the continuity is the worst thing.

The voice of Nancy Reagan, of all people, comes to me now. I suppose because I was in my most vulnerable years when, in reference to drug use, she coined the catchphrase: "Just say no." On purpose, I applied her slogan to my own set of needs as a young writer.

Okay, Nancy, I *will*.

I'm not saying it's impossible to write between demands and duties, allowing a sliver of time here, another there. But I'd be lying if I didn't say that, for most of us, writing is just so all-consuming, such hard work, requiring so much energy and time and concentration that it has to be our only work. *It's amazing anyone wants to be a writer at all* is what I think when I'm tired, or when my confidence falters and I fall into the fear pit again. I remind myself how many times fear has turned into the teacher I need. When I think, *I stink; my writing stinks!* I allow myself a few hours of that, tops. Until I'm more determined than ever. And off I go.

I've never been the kind of writer who can define a book at the beginning. I write it page by page (no, it writes me, which may sound like a writer's cliché, but it's true) and this requires patience. It requires exacting work, and it requires lots and lots of time. You can't rush a delicate process.

Maybe this is why so many books nowadays seem forced. It's no secret that a writer's first book can take years to write. But the same writer can be asked to hand over a second title in under a year. And why I'm struck by some of the lesser-known European authors I've discovered, how they write without seeming to give much thought to the American bestseller list, how individually they tell a story, how originally they make the pages their own.

In the back of my mind, I store what Anne Lamott said about her book *Bird by Bird,* how her process began as separate essays, but as she got into them, they grew into a single theme.

Her saying so left me reassured, a confidence booster if ever there was one. Here I thought I was creating another collection of essays stemming from my various columns and commentaries, but, in the end, it didn't work out that way. Sure, I had to revise the tone from "column/commentary" into "book." I had to get in there and release each essay from the constraints of word count. Like a proud gardener, I had to stand back and let them flourish.

Writing is my greatest pleasure, all I ever wanted in terms of work. Still, I had to ask myself why I was determined to write a book about writing? Isn't *living* the writer's life enough?

The simplest answer is that a woman who writes her life is sooner or later going to write a book about the process. I know by now that writing honestly about writing and writing about my life are, pretty much, writing about the very same thing, inevitable to anyone who has made a stage of her life and given a backstage pass to her readers.

So here are a few things my mind kicked around during what I now look back on and fondly call the "Obama Years." But, really, it doesn't matter when they were written, because the issues remain the same.

And not simply because of the way they have driven me crazy over the years.

Part One

"Writing is like driving a car at night. You can only see as far as your headlights, but you can make the whole trip that way."

— E. L. DOCTOROW

Let's Begin Here

A new year is here, and it's just the kind of year I've been waiting for!

Sure, I've told just about everyone I know that I can't take much more of the way things have been going. I am not a silent sufferer.

But look around, we are in the throes of a new beginning. We are supposed to let go of the past; that's what I keep hearing.

But you know what? I can't.

Not yet anyway.

I'm trying. Professionally, that is. I'm fine with where my work is going.

Well, maybe not as fine as I thought I'd be by now. Honestly, I'm sort of struggling. Between sips of coffee, I sit here trying to find a new way into an old story, as if any part of it could surprise me by now, as if some new angle will suddenly come to me.

I would not have dreamed, could never have imagined, that I'd be back here writing about a friendship gone awry. I thought I'd covered everything there was to say on the subject in my last title. I wonder if there are just some things we need to live through again and again before they sink in. We are a stubborn species.

True, I am probably the last person who could tell you exactly what happens between friends. What's more, I don't want to travel down that road again. But last night I couldn't sleep. I tossed and turned. Because it wasn't just any old friendship; it was the kind of love that happens intensely between two straight women. And it's taken me forever to be able to admit just how shaken it left me. All the time we spent together, all our laughs and confidences coming to nothing? How does love amount to nothing? No more lasting than fumes of paint?

It took one search after another (books, magazines, and a particularly powerful reality check from a woman I hardly know who said,

"You need to know something: she did the exact same thing to me, checked me off like eggs from a grocery list.") to make me see that there are just some people who want to cream off the best of you and move on. They choose you for a while and then, poof, you are history, and they are *gone*.

For weeks, I was miserable. I grew to resent having to try to explain what happened to my friends, to my husband, even to myself, partly out of embarrassment, partly out of regret, mostly out of pure old friendship fatigue.

But today, after picking it apart for a while, I recognize a turning point.

In fact, these are not pathetic tears I'm shedding, but finality tears. Not whiny, but necessary. And necessary tears have the perfect view. They can *see*. I just had to write myself up here in order to see over the hump, where finally I can say, "No, *I* don't want a friend who would do this, who would decide in an instant she has what she needs so why continue."

Admittedly, there has been something a little haywire with me in the friendship department as of late. In the same way some women can't choose faithful men, I've had my share of wandering friends. And in the clear light of day, I can look at my pattern objectively, take responsibility for my part of the flubs, and promise myself to honor each red flag as I see them.

But then a new flag waves, red as all get out, and I follow along.

So, I decide, this is the reminder every writer needs, to get to the place where time raises perspective and perspective raises the bar. And my job is to climb over the bar.

Um, excuse me, but, no. Big mistake. Enough already! She's moved on, you've moved on. Snap! Crackle! Pop! Two new lives.

So you see, even if I wanted to write about a lousy ex-friend, which I don't, there is a better friend to contend with here, someone I need to introduce you to straightaway because *she* sticks by me no matter what.

I appreciate how her tone has matured over the years. It's more "sweetie-listen" and less "listen-or-else" which makes all the difference.

I'm proud of us for evolving so well together. The way she insists I get on with it while, at the same time grounding me, well, how many friends do you know who can pull off this balancing act?

But damned if I am not a little put off at times. Because even as my fingertips resist, I think about my other friend, the faithless one, her smile coming to me even now. And when I have about as much ability to learn from my mistakes as the military, it drives me nuts.

You needed a wake up call. Someone to wipe that heart off your sleeve.

So let's just say that when a friendship has breathed its last, no amount of writing about it can revive it.

And leave it alone.

And begin again.

Because this whole year feels more promising. Can you feel it?

Maybe it's how wonderful it feels to watch a woman run for president. How just saying this, I sense everything more fair than before, what a country that truly values women is like.

But it's taken so long!

Do I need to sing the Prince song to you again? "Maybe I'm just like my mother: she's never satisfied."

Or maybe it has more to do with the fact that this month, in every single way, is so much easier than October when Puget Sound fades from green to gray with no leafy-red in between. Better than drippy November by a long shot. And so much better than December, the most trying month because it's supposed to be the merriest. But we both know how much energy it takes, not to mention how ridiculous and unconvincing we sound, when we are faking it.

Then there's January.

January is about as bleak as it gets in the Pacific Northwest.

But there are days, merciful days, when the sun casts a stark light over Elliott Bay and I find myself staring out at the waves lit up like torches, until I, too, become lighter. Maybe that's what I'm feeling.

But when a brutal wind blows across Lake Washington and rips through town, it's just no fun to be outside. Maybe this is why we make resolutions this time of year, to give ourselves a new survival tool.

A new survival tool.

Come to think of it, I found one! Inspired by, for the sake of privacy, a man I will call Mr. P.

See, I wound up calling Mr. P a bad name, a very bad name, a name that is much too New York for Seattle, This time of year I'm prone to surliness, and I'm beginning to take it more seriously. Last year around this time I was *this* close to calling one of my editors the same bad name. Right after I told him he needed a wife. I didn't stop there. "I don't underestimate the perceptiveness of women readers and neither should you!" I yelled. "You just don't *get* it!"

"It" being me, us, *women*. He had (I am sure of this) no idea what I was talking about. I didn't want to lose my column in his paper, but neither did I want to dumb down my stories to the level he was suggesting. "It is better to respect my readers, right?"

It has to be better.

He, however, implied my readers don't give a damn. Which may be true, but the assumption that people don't care about reading anymore always sends me into a tizzy. What on earth am I supposed to write then? And for whom?

"I don't believe that," I said.

But, to be perfectly honest, I've been doubting myself lately. Not altogether, but maybe I should think about writing wine-pairing tips like everyone else, just so I don't feel a hop, skip, and jump away from total unemployment as yet another editor suggests I write less about "real life."

It was early in the month, the first week, the day our neighborhood newspaper comes out. Mr. P's eyes were fixed on the headline: "Seattle Center Axed? The Whole Park Developed Into Condos."

How can it be? I thought.

Though, now that I think about it, I am beginning to worry about Seattle with more and more frequency. Lately, I can't even walk down the sidewalk without worrying. I never used to worry all the time. And worry does crazy things to people, makes us say things we don't mean, explode into nutcase versions of ourselves. Take yesterday: I told a complete stranger sitting next to me on the bus that I was worried about all the new condos springing up that look exactly the same, how developers homogenize our neighborhoods, make them impersonal, bleak, how enormous push-up walls have lowered our expectations on so many levels and I have trouble forgiving us (me) for that.

"Just your average worry, or did something bad happen?" she asked, lowering her newspaper.

"No, no," I said. "I'm just surprised by how many new condos there are."

"I live in a condo," she said.

"So do *I.*"

Her newspaper popped back up. And, just like that, I was reminded how crazy the city can make me sometimes. *Please make this bus hurry.*

I'm more resistive, too. More so all the time. I don't believe anything I'm told about the wars in the Middle East. I've grown too jaded to think, even for a second, that anything will ever be better because of them, even when I'm feeling positive. I wanted to understand the insanity as soon as we headed into Afghanistan.

I still do.

Mr. P not only registered my arrival, he wanted to talk. Which can be one of the most comforting things you love about a neighborhood, or a huge pain in the ass, when the unavoidable encounter means face time with a ghost. *Oh, there he is! I'll just pretend I don't see him.*

What tipped me off that Mr. P wanted my attention? "Hey, Sanelli, I've got a bone to pick with you!" Right there in the corner coffee shop. Gossip central.

"Okay, fine."

The thing is, I've been a columnist for years so "bones to pick" doesn't level me as badly as it once did. The thing that does level me is when a reader doesn't understand that a column is only an opinion. What surprises me even more is when a reader feels the need to correct my opinion when it doesn't gel with their own. Something about this always reminds me of my teenage years, when my opinion was considered "talking back."

Mr. P went on about something I wrote a few columns back, after telling me for the umpteenth time how he used to be a professor, in the time-stealing, relentless way retired people do when they have nothing to get back to, nowhere to go, who get angry at columnists because we become their work and social life combined, their underling to admonish, their link to the outside, wage-earning world. (Twice I've had to call the cops on one of these guys, and decide whether to file a restraining order.)

Still, without question, Mr. P had every right to question me, to take issue. What I question is his right to call my take "unacceptable."

And in that moment I could not think of a person, not one, who I wanted to get away from more. I rubbed my hand on my head trying to think of a comeback, and finally, in a moment both adamant and resigned, I looked him in the eye, searched for anything good amidst all his dislike of my writing and, what felt like, *me*.

But nothing surfaced.

Except a little confidence surge. And I have to tell you, I have never felt so brave, not even the time I stood up to my dad for calling me stupid (I was only a kid); not even when I found the nerve to say, "look, any more lip from you and I walk" when a rude host of a reading series admonished me for suggesting we do without the lectern (I couldn't see over the top of it); as when I found the confidence, the absolute sureness to say the following unoriginal words to Mr. P: "You *@$#-ing idiot!"

To defend myself. To protect my sanity.

Now, you might think I ended there because if I was so confident, why act so defensively? I was fired up, that's why, and I like getting fired up now and again. It keeps me from shutting down. "If I nudge you to think about life in a different way, through a woman's eyes, it's a good thing, right? After all, your mother is a woman. Your wife is a woman. Your daughter is a woman, if you have a daughter ... who still speaks to you."

He was quiet for, like, a millisecond. Then he started in again. This time with a pointed finger wagging. A pointed finger wagging is a real stretch for me.

I stood there thinking how you can always tell a professor. Retired or still at it, pedantic. It's just amazing how often they mistake professing for conversation. Trapped as I felt, I had one thought, and one thought only: *Who needs this?*

I turned around and walked outside, vowed to have coffee at home from then on. Then, for some reason, I looked back at the window where Mr. P sat.

He waved. He winked. He gave me the thumbs up. He smiled.

In his smile, I could see we'd both just had a bit of *fun*. Good old-fashioned newsroom fun. When you are expected to fight for your story as a kind of sport in the male-dominated ring, one of the many, small, safe wars that keep men's testosterone levels in check, I think. I had to learn the game the hard way. And now that I know how the game is played, I admit, I like to play. More, I like to win.

Mr. P had forgiven me.

Which made it a hundred times easier to forgive him.

Even so, next time I'm confronted with someone like Mr. P, I walk away; *this* is my survival tool. If nothing else, I won't have to live with mental chatter waking me at 3:00 a.m. to scold, "You shouldn't have said that, you went too far." I'll get more sleep, for starters. Instead of lying in bed, nearly falling off the edge of consciousness and then, nope, I can't quite manage it over and over and over again. Until morning.

I'm not sure if I'll ever live up to it completely. But I'm willing to try. Instead of giving in to a sudden need to call a good man by a bad name, whenever likely, whenever *possible*, I will use only the private place of my writing to get back at someone.

I'm still not going to let you dwell on that ex-friendship again. Not privately, not ever!

The point is I'm ready now.

Let the New Year begin.

Love Is All You Need

"So-oo? You and your husband are a love marriage?" my new friend, Amargit, asked. Amargit is from India where families still arrange most marriages.

I didn't know how to respond. She added, "Ye-es?" before I could.

She looked a little concerned. She *felt* a little concerned. I felt a little uncomfortable.

I think back to that look, how she viewed me with such wonder, how I paused, and in my hesitation I realize we were taking our first leap of faith, when, in an instant, we both knew we weren't registering reality in quite the same way and how, if we were to become friends, we'd need to leap in from two very different starting points.

Back when we were new to each other, these leaps were more challenging. We'd smile through the silence, make our way back cautiously, move into conversation that didn't ask too much of us. We were clumsier then, not even close to the clowning around we manage now. We learned how to let go of the fear that made us tamp ourselves down as we struggled to share the everyday in an everyday way.

But our first leap really stumped me. I had no clue how to answer her question, how to put romantic love into words for someone still grappling with the English language. The ways of the heart are too mysterious, I thought, so maybe I should say something funny instead?

No.

Serious, then? Along the lines of how many sides love has, how many limits?

No.

Elaboration wouldn't do. It was a simple, direct question, not entirely out of line with the others we'd begun to bat back and forth over the cultural divide that separates us even if we like to pretend otherwise.

"That's right," I said, finally. "A love marriage." I shifted my bag to the other shoulder. I started to sing, *All you need is love, love. Love is all you need.*

When I'm nervous, I make a little fun. (I'm trying to get over this.)

Thinking more about this nervous tendency of mine, I believe it may have been key to my becoming a writer, though I hardly knew it at the time. As a young girl, I started writing in a diary as a way to handle my nervousness. I wanted to talk to someone. I wanted to admit my secrets. I wanted to be heard. Of course, my diary was a secret in itself; no one else was reading it. This was a huge part of the freedom it gave me.

Tilting her head to the right, Amargit said, "Ye-es?" lengthening the sound into syllables again, making more of a question out of the word and, though not intentionally, a fool out of me. Funny, funny me. My stomach flip-flopped. Humor can be the most difficult divide between cultures, it really can. Mine often goes missing somewhere in the unspoken space between Amargit and me.

With no reluctance—none—Amargit moved us onto safer ground. "Sanelli," she said, "You have a beautiful voice, ye-es?"

Honestly, if tact could speak, it just had.

I first met Amargit at Macy's on Super Bowl Sunday. I'd dipped into the store to use the loo after taking a walk, and was shopping for nothing, really, just strolling through the aisles, something I like to do between deadlines, and I remember thinking, *where are all the other women? Frying up the chicken wings?*

And, well, you know how it is in the Macy's ladies room lately, the heartbreak as soon as you enter, the women who nap on the couches, or just sit, surveying their hands, hunkered down, trying to stay warm? It makes me feel guilty for carrying a shopping bag, for having to pee, and I can't get away soon enough. I think that's what Amargit saw on my face that day: relief. And sometimes it takes no more than an expression to make you more approachable.

"You don't like football?" I looked up at Amargit who was smiling. And when she pronounced her name, I repeated it, barely, pretending to grasp the sound, straining to remember.

We got to talking. We intrigued each other. Amargit needs to learn

more about the freedoms of American women now that she *is* one,
I like to remind her, and I'm always trying to make more of a family for myself. And slowly, over the past three years, we've chipped
away at the bulk of our differences, only to find that underneath we
are just two women who want to talk, laugh, share ourselves. As the
years build, the more I realize intimacy, for women anyway, is defined
this way: *Talk, laugh, share ourselves.* It's the meaning of intimacy in
four rich words.

Last Sunday was a big, big day. For the first time, Amargit and her
husband, Tito, invited my love marriage, Larry and me, for dinner at
their home on their one day off a week *if* they take it. Amargit and
Tito and two college-age sons (their education the reason they immi-
grated) live in an immaculate basement apartment north of the city.
And as soon as I entered, I thought, *this is why she hesitated inviting
me here. She needed time to be sure I'm not the kind of American woman
who'd snub a friend who lives in a basement apartment.*

The whole evening made me think about a column I'd read only
days before, written by a local columnist who said that Seattle's recent
trend of outdoor cafes is another way of appeasing yuppie tastes. I
wanted to call him that very instant. I wanted to say, "I need to tell
you something you apparently don't understand. Outdoor cafes are
born of the poor. They are a slice of outside-ness for those who live in
the belly of a city. How easy it is for you, born in Seattle with a backyard of your own, to forget this."

That night I was shocked to learn something else Amargit hadn't
disclosed before: How in India she didn't need to work. By Indian
standards, she had plenty of money. She employed several "servants"
(I admit, I gasped when she used the word) who slept on bedrolls in
a corner of her home, waiting on her family's every need. Which all
sounds very un-Seattle-PC, I know, but what better example of how
much she sacrificed to ensure an American education for her sons.
And now they, Amargit and Tito, husband and wife, work six, seven
days a week waiting on *us*.

It's the kind of sacrifice I need to be reminded of because, only one
generation removed from all that, I don't come across real sacrifice in

my immediate world all that often, a fact I brought up last night, sitting around with a few of my fashionable friends. "Each of us should be making more of a sacrifice," I said, "because how are these crazy wars in the Middle East affecting us, really?" I was a little inebriated, yes, but I wasn't putting them on. I was, in any case, sitting on a cushy couch with my heels up, drinking a twelve-buck cocktail after declining the well vodka.

There was a moment of silence as my question dove in. And then I listened to my dear ones come up with a list of sacrifices, obsessing about the crazy high cost of organic food, whether to drive all the way out to Ikea or pay through the teeth at Bed, Bath, & Beyond a few blocks south. Horrible things of this nature.

Sacrifice, like everything else, is relative. My friends just want to feel like they're in control of some small part of life. We react by trying to control what we can, our homes for one. Our food.

Speaking of, the feast Amargit spread out for us that evening remains the eating peak of my life (sorry, Mom). Satiated, we got on to the subject of marriage, how her husband's sister went to her father and asked for her hand. Which led to a story about Tito, how he removed his turban and cut his hair his very first day on American soil, a ponytail that, since boyhood, wound around his head several times underneath his headdress. How relieved he felt. "I was freed from religious and cultural law," he said, "and *much* cooler. Life is more fair in America."

Ah, yes it is.

And why I could have said how *un*fair it is that he still won't allow Amargit to go anywhere alone, other than to work. Nowhere with me, certainly, not without him or my husband tagging along. And what fun is that?

But I decided not to wave my American Woman Freedom Flag so soon.

Nonetheless, I detect a bit of mellowing on his part. His younger son's girlfriend joined us, a beautiful Hindu girl he met at school, a match for a Sikh that wouldn't be tolerated back in India, making obvious how, in a single generation, everything can totally change.

The girl told us how she, her parents, and six sisters left Afghanistan seven years ago.

"Did you have to flee?" I asked.

"Oh ye-es," she said. "We took an airplane."

"No, I mean from us, the Americans?"

"Oh ye-es. There were many bombs."

Another bomb, of course, was her saying so. Bless her. And later in the evening when I baptized Amargit's husband "old-fashioned," he laughed. "Ye-es," he said. "I am very ancient."

Funny, originally from a family of immigrants, I fought my whole life to get away from such old world stuff. And then the years went by, choices, choices, choices, and here I am in a new city facing all the same issues.

All the wiser, I hope.

Small Town

"I'm a little homesick, tell me something good," I say on the phone to an old friend in Port Townsend.

Technically, Port Townsend isn't my home anymore; Seattle is. But once you've lived in a small town, it's forever a part of you. I cling to my friends who live there. They remind there is another piece to me, an earlier self, a former young poet once upon a time.

"Certainly," and then, with a flair for drama, she proceeds to give me what she calls the Local Express, that is, who did what to whom and why. Or why if *we* ran the world. This is the magic of having a real friend. We can gossip with absolutely no shame attached to our mutual regression.

See, I've been away from the Northwest for a while, living with Mom for the entire holiday season, the kind of promise one makes to an elderly mother. I can no longer say *no* to her. I don't have the energy to refuse her. I figure all too soon it will be her spirit pushing my buttons, so I opt for the real thing while I still can.

"Oh, wait, I completely forgot!" my friend went on. "Our main post office might get sold."

I was stunned. This was supposed to cheer me up? "No!" I said. "No, no, *no*!"

I took action, immediately calling someone who has the inside scoop. If I'm stuck for a story, he can tell me anything I need to know from the latest census figure to who's sleeping with whom. Sure, I could Google the story, but that's not half as much fun.

"Oh, yeah," he said. "Since the substation closed, people in wheelchairs have been petitioning the main post office to modernize. They've been without a post office they can, you know, get *up* to. And you know how insecure some of us get when we can't get up anymore."

A grin sails across my face. The way he can emphasize a word and, just by doing so, let you in on his greatest fear, well, it's a skill I admire.

Not only is the main post office in Port Townsend a fortress of history that takes up an entire city block, it is, for all practical purposes, the town's social center. Problem is, the steps leading up to its door calls to mind the scene in which Rocky Balboa just might win the fight assuming he can make it to the top.

Still, the building defines a way of life for those who'd rather walk than drive, suburban style, to the outskirts of town to pick up their mail. And I'm reminded every time I leave Port Townsend that a central location to come together with neighbors is something too few in this country get to experience any longer.

When I overheard a woman say her only social interaction is going "to the mall," I understood why so many people feel isolated, disconnected. I never feel quite right in a mall. Maybe it's the unnatural lighting, I don't know. But here I am, living a relatively wonderful life I've worked my buns off to create, and one walk through a shopping mall, every flaw I've ever imagined about myself echoes back. I don't know why the whole experience is different when I walk through a downtown shopping district, but it is. Walking into a store from an outside street, I feel a part of a city or town, part of the human flow. In every way I feel connected, good enough, great.

But a mall? Even though people are everywhere, nothing about it feels connected to anything else, there's no authenticity, all appeal was plowed away with the topsoil. It's like walking through a huge lie.

Living in a small town is often referred to as "quaint" because you can walk to the post office, the grocery, downtown. I like to call it humanly "accessible." I can't put it into words any better.

But here's where it all gets tricky. "Accessible" is the same word people with disabilities need to be able say about their post office, any post office, anywhere. And no one can fault them for organizing a petition in order to make it possible for them to get up impossible stairs.

The problem is, if they don't reconsider and change tack, that is, petition for a new satellite post office downtown instead of trying to update the main branch, no one will be able to save an amazing building built in a time when architects were considered artists rather than developers, save it from the wrecking ball or, worse, from something more profitable. Federal standards for accessibility are simple in theory and tremendously expensive in practice. Too many theaters, dance studios, galleries, and cafes that are wonderful, that still serve real food made from scratch, close their doors because they can't afford to comply with federal standards for accessibility. One petition and they're forced to shut down.

Maybe this is the thing I'm not supposed to say, but accessibility expectation for *all* public buildings tips the give and take—give to the disabled, take from preservation—out of balance.

If Italy can teach us anything, other than how modest a proper pasta portion really is, it's the way it deals with disabilities, *pronto*. I think of my time there, when in a little café with steps leading downstairs, a woman in a wheelchair peered down into its tiny interior.

So what does accessibility mean in Italy?

Two men looked up from their table, saw the woman peeking down, and immediately got up to lift her wheelchair up and over the hump. A remedy that's not going to cost the owner a million bucks to overhaul. Now what is so wrong with this picture? It seems pretty easy to me, responsible, involved. I smile remembering it. I admired those kind men more than the scenery, sculpture, and ancient churches combined. As an American, i.e., used to not having to be personally involved in the public welfare of another, I didn't even think of finding someone to help me lift the wheelchair, or worse, that I'd be *allowed* to.

This is what happens when fear of retribution enters the equation, fear of liability, *the* fear that keeps us from doing the good things we'd do for others if no one could sue us for acting on our kindness, even if things go a little haywire. How much this fear has affected our psyches, I can only speculate, but I will go so far as to say that too many lawyers are a big extra kick in the pants toward public inertia, enough to turn Americans into even more isolated creatures. Give us one more reason to keep to ourselves and not get involved, and tragically, we won't.

Because the feds won't consider that the post office can work as the core of a community. That's not how it works. They *will* consider a cost analysis and a twenty-year growth plan. They will build a post office on the fringe of town where land is cheaper. No one seems to remember this part.

And what happens to the main branch that looks over the sea and lets us remember that we don't have to go all the way to Europe to experience the elegance of marble floors?

That's easy.

Repeat after me: Historic View Condos.

Tax (Gasp) Season

I am a tax obtuse.

And I use this adjective as a noun because to say I am capable of obtuseness is to underestimate. On the subject of taxes, I have a stone where my brain is supposed to be. I will end up in the Olympic Sculpture Park, carved. My plaque will read, "She wrote with a certain level of maturity, but her tax age? Three to five years."

I'm most aware of my obtuseness this month and frequently in between. As in each time I walk past Stephanie Gale's office where *her* plaque reads *Gale Investment Management.*

I get a slight constriction in my chest when I say the words *investment manager.* I've got no business calling myself an independent woman, really. I'm more of an independent fraud. This applies to my savings account as well as to my checking.

I wish I were more like Stephanie, truly at home in the world of finance, someone whose help really *helps.* I wish I could think in numbers, the bigger the better. For all I know there is something hugely tantalizing about tax loopholes.

But I am not at home in Stephanie's world. I live in constant fear of taxes. In an unmistakable way that you will have to take my word for, if I even say the word *taxes* too many times, I can no longer hear the wind in the trees or feel the sun on my face; gone is a version of life that is mine to enjoy.

Even so, I rather enjoy Stephanie.

Because there is the kind of investment adviser that can demean people like me with just one long, appraising gaze over the top of their eyeglasses. And there is Stephanie, hard on people like me in all the ways she should be. Harder by far on herself. Which she'd have to be in order to stay up with ... oh, well, I don't know, all the many things she has to stay up with that I can't fathom. Or name.

And that she has the conviction to name her business after the woman in charge pleases me deeply. Think about it. In the grand scheme of things, you want a money manager with serious belief in herself.

One afternoon, I called Stephanie.

Not to talk about money. Heavens.

The time we did talk about money, or tried to, I lost interest pretty quickly. My mind disappeared into the sunny escape behind her office windowpane. Five minutes in and I had to keep myself from asking, "Um, Steph? Mind if we talk about something else?"

I called Stephanie to ask about the other Stephanie, the Stephanie-more-like-me. Because, after attending Barnard, Stephanie studied writing and dance. Unfortunately, she also needed to make her rent in Manhattan. She'd let this slip out while trying to teach me about the importance of having not only work you enjoy, but work that pays the tab.

Now everyone knows how many writer/dancers in New York wind up waiting on tables, but not Stephanie. Stephanie went straight to Wall Street.

I don't recall ever being that confident.

"It's not so different from what you do," Stephanie said. "One foot in front of the other with enough applied technique so as not to cause a fall."

Even put like this, it is impossible for me to imagine myself choosing the shifting flow of capital gains over jazz class, but I saw what she meant.

No, not really.

All I knew about money after college was that every bone in my limber body knew if I wanted to dance, write, and *eat*, I could not stay anywhere near New York. Around the time Stephanie was rounding up her first financial client, I was on a Greyhound headed west.

"I manage people's deepest lives," Stephanie told me.

"You do?" Now *this* is useful, I thought. This is the language of which I speak, the inexplicable vastness of a woman's inner life.

But when she started throwing out phrases like management options, high-yield tax funds, advisory accounts, mutual funds, short-term risks vs. long-term gains, my smile strained.

I suppose she never stops thinking in these terms. They give her confidence and authority. I can see that, but *my* brain stopped clicking, I glazed over like a baked ham. I yawned. I pulled at the corner of my eyelash. And just like that, I shifted from able to mute. Mute obtuse.

The truth is I was just plain old bored out of my freaking mind.

Inside my head, I tried to marshal the kindest defense: *Of course you're bored. This is not your world. How many books has Stephanie published, huh?*

Reactions like mine wouldn't bother me so much if they weren't so predictable. Because no matter how hard I smile my agreeable, grateful smile and try to listen to what Stephanie has to say, her words won't dip past my epidermis. My finance fears crumble me, sneak out from some intimidated corner to remind me just how fragile my fiscal nerve really is, how much I detest enumerating my spending habits, the habits that I, naturally, do not detest.

I think the worst part is how incompetent tax talk makes me feel. And I don't like to feel incompetent. It contradicts my feeling capable.

When we finally stood, I thought about giving her a hug, something I had wanted to do since we first met, but she is *so* businesslike. I held back. Not only because emotions in an office are tricky, but because I've always found my money-obtuseness sort of normal for someone like me, writer-dancer, you know, *artiste*, and therefore okay. But no more. Now it strikes me as immature, the simplest kind of sniveling: *Stephanie, I don't get it! I can't, I can't! PLEASE! Don't waste your breath. Just do the work and send me the bill, okay?*

Better yet, send my husband the bill.

Because it's all his fault. It was his Dad who left us a portfolio to manage, just to complicate our lives.

"Who ever thought I'd need a Stephanie anyway?" I said to Larry. "Far as I know, my Dad blew my inheritance on a second wife, second family, second home in Florida; so, let's face it, 'portfolio' on my side of the family spreadsheet will always mean the folder of recipes under the sink."

It's only fair Larry deal with the taxes. For many reasons. Like, for example, how many times has he scrubbed the toilet, grocery shopped, cleaned out the car, the closets, the fridge, bought the blades for his razor, or even snipped away the tiny hairs growing on the rims of his ears? How many things can one woman be expected to remember in such a busy world?

No, I have a feeling I'll be clueless about all things investment as long as my husband is alive. As long as *I'm* alive.

"You act like it's a great big mystery. Investing is way simpler than what you do. I never found anything harder than trying to write," my friend, Jackie-from-the-Bronx, said when we were speeding on the freeway. She's a realtor, dealing in money all the time, always on her cell, making moolah even when she drives. "And dance? Hardest frickin' thing in the world."

Thank you, Jackie.

Did I mention I've never, not once, balanced my checkbook? I honestly can't think of one good reason to take time away from my full life to do such a crazy thing. I just deposit what we make and hope for the best and so far, other than two bounced checks in thirty years, it all works out.

Larry, practical and steady, sighed after I bragged about this.

Can a sigh have an edge? I'm just asking.

It's a good thing, a very good thing, he smiled, too. The kind of smile that usually follows his sensible side, that has learned the secret to his wife's heart (years of training, *years*), that exists on some level beyond verbal communication and loves me with total acceptance and humor, or you can forget about it.

Because there are *many* things to argue about when you've been a package deal for as long as we have, like when we've just come from Stephanie's office and I'm late for a dance class and Larry is late for a meeting which he implies is more important than a dance class so that, now, of course, I have to remind him to get real, and money is the least important of them.

So I say, thank goodness for Stephanie!

And then there's the other guy, Charlie something, the CPA whom Larry sees about our *other* taxes, whatever they are. It's all "Charlie needs this" and "Charlie needs that" at our home right about now.

I don't ever want to know Charlie. I figure, between him and

Stephanie, they've got it covered: how inheritance works, how money produces more money (now you're talking!) if we're smart about it, the angles we can count on, how to keep our future from slipping through our fingers ... and turning into a year spent in Europe, say, if I get my hands on it.

Greece. The island where no cars are allowed. Donkeys, the only means of travel.

I will make sure we go there, Stephanie. Bank on it.

Pain in the Neck

I look back and marvel at the fact that it's been, what, only a year since the Virginia Tech shootings, and already I can't remember where I was when I heard the news. Or what I was doing. Or what I did next.

Tragically, I don't even think I was all that shocked. Over the next week, I thought about what little shock I did feel, how it dissipated almost immediately, stressing how appalling it is when school shootings become common occurrences. I do remember feeling this way.

And, no, I'm not suffering from any over-forty memory slip by not remembering where I was when the news hit, as much as I'd like to pin my lapse on age. I read somewhere that my kind of forgetting is a result of repetition, that no matter how appalling frequent incidents are, the mind begins to brush them off like so many muffin crumbs as a coping mechanism that allows us to say, "Jeez, not again!" after the worst mass murder in our country occurs. And seconds later busy on with our lives.

But here is the most interesting part: the outrage we *don't* exhibit lodges in. We don't get off scot-free. Every image of crime and death we've ever seen is ingrained in our cells and muscles and inner workings of our minds and I'm afraid a lot of us are suffering from an overload. The rate at which these images come at us is faster and greater than ever and I don't think any of us are built with enough storage space. It's too much.

I also remember turning in early the night of the shootings with a weariness that exhausted me. And waking the next morning with a kink in my neck, a stiffness like I'd never experienced before. It seemed unbelievable that the pain could be so bad, that it could have come on so fast or persisted so long. But it did. It was tough. It hung on.

Something was terribly wrong, deep inside, and everything else was knocked off kilter. I should have cried. Crying is the perfect relief for me. But for whatever reason, I couldn't cry. Instead of shedding tears,

I was too busy trying to shed the pain. I demanded it to go away. Who has the time for a neck that doesn't turn side to side?

Apparently I'd stowed a lot of repression in my neck where it wound its way into my second cervical vertebra, according to my massage therapist.

She also explained that the neck is a conduit for the spinal cord, the channel between your stomach, heart, and brain. "Everything has to pass by the neck," she said. "The neck is the *man*."

This didn't sound good. I know from experience how hard it is to tweak the man, a man, any man. "So, can you fix it?" I said. And slowly, under the weight of her thumbs, what I feared was a permanent pain in my neck, eased. Somewhat. But it didn't go away completely. Even now, it's there. I can feel it under my fingers. I call the nodule Virginia. Ginny, for short. It's my body's way of dealing with our inflexible gun control laws.

Ginny may sound unbelievable to you, but I know she's real

Maybe all this would be different if I didn't live in Seattle, where, for the most part, one can, with enough means, live in denial. Things are good here, comparatively. The city reassures, gives a sense of less dangerous. It's a world away. Even if any notion of separating our schools and streets from gun violence is as fleeting as youth if a disturbed young man can still walk into a gun shop and buy an automatic pistol.

And there she is again: *Ginny.*

Dammit, if we can't rewrite our gun laws so that men can't relieve their aggressive fantasies with a semi-automatic, what, really, is the point of civilization?

And please, please do not interject here with any boring Americanism about our right to bare arms to defend ourselves, the patriotic rah-rahs invented to keep us from thinking for ourselves. Don't go there. Just don't. We are so past the Stone Age when these laws were written, when we lived out on the Great Plains, alone with our kids in a one-room cabin, warding off the bears and hyenas. Defend ourselves? Against what?

Honestly, if young men weren't packing guns in the waistbands of their skivvies, what would we need to defend ourselves *from*?

The other day on the bus, I heard a man say where he'd been when Kennedy was shot, back when massacres could still silence the stream of American life. He made me remember where I was that day: in the hallway of my grade school, outside of Mrs. Adam's room, late again and afraid to knock because I'd overslept and missed the school bus. Mrs. Adams was my favorite teacher, strict, but not mean, and I hated disappointing her. I rode my new black English Racer (three whole speeds!) all the way to school that day and before I reached my class-room door, our janitor—no one said *custodian* in the sixties—told me the news. He put his right hand on my shoulder. He held a broom in his other hand. His right shoe was untied. Both shoes were scuffed, which fascinated me because my own father polished his wingtips to a shiny black.

I had another memory lapse right after the Amish killings, when I sat stunned in front of the TV, glued to the images, knowing that viewing them once is enough, more than enough. Still, I couldn't pull myself away. But I can't remember where I was when I first heard the news. Or who told me.

I do remember writing that night. At the time I was just finish-ing my first collection of essays, about to turn the manuscript over to my editor and then holding on to it. I *had* to add one last piece about what happened at the Nickel Mines School in Lancaster County, Pennsylvania.

I think of that essay now, how to this day, even with years more writing behind me, as the purest work that has ever managed to pass through me. And it did, the floodgates opened. I crossed a line that night, personally, professionally, physically, intrinsically. It was as if I needed to wrestle the man who killed the Amish girls to the ground, bury his face in the floorboards myself, muffle his shots, silence the children's cries by whatever means I had. I wrote way into the night. As the sun came up, I wrote. In order to cope, in order to make sense of the world, I wrote. It was all the push and power anyone who writes could ever wish for. It drove me. I had to find a way to stop blaming the world, that's what it felt like, and whatever will rose inside of me refused to let go until I found a way to forgive.

Strange how our best work occurs. I'd never felt such unity between my writing voice and my conscious one. I have found it since, gratefully, but it doesn't come easily or often enough. It comes when I feel a heightened sense of emotion, when I don't compromise, when I blot out everything else. This is what it takes; I'm not exaggerating. At the risk of sounding hopelessly self-advertizing, I hope you read the essay. Its title, appropriately, "Forgiveness" (in *Falling Awake*). And that you'll think of me, a writer unable to pull herself away from a horror that consumed her completely.

Naturally, here is where I think how, right here in Seattle, I was walking on Third Avenue when the women who were shot inside the Jewish Federation building were carried out on stretchers, an image one never forgets. Unless you live in a war-zone, where, I suspect, first hand accounts of death become so commonplace that people close their eyes and forget even before the witnessing is complete.

The man who shot the women was "at loose ends," according to the *Seattle Times*, a bit of a loner, without a job. He'd been arrested in March at a shopping mall for "lewd conduct." He apparently told his landlady he was moving to Pakistan because life was better there.

Better? In Pakistan? Why? For whom? For men who want to degrade women?

He also liked to catcall. To undo his pants and flash. It's not the whole story, but you get the picture. Not particularly fond of women. The angriest kind of man, I think, because they resent how impotent their solitary world is in comparison to the social one women share, visibly, with each other. Maybe this deranged man could never get his own mother to pay attention to him, who knows, and now, because he still goes unseen, he pulls down his pants.

But if he's not seen even when he leaves his fly open, what next? I think most women would agree that a flasher, *any* flasher, should not be able to purchase a gun. But that's exactly what he did. It's madness!

The name of the woman who died at the Jewish Federation was Pamela Waechter. She was fifty-eight. She worked in outreach, that strikes me as the most bitter irony. Still, I'm certain, sure, *positive* that even if she had a gun hidden in her purse or desk drawer, she'd still be dead.

This last paragraph, I am sorry to say, kinks Ginny again.

My therapist is right. It all passes through the neck. And if my mind can't handle it, which it can't, it's fed up, it's going to sit and wait, tapping its feet on my second cervical vertebra.

There are so many sharp sensations, tightening on so many little nerve ends on every one of us; it's the price we pay when we try to ignore. I suppose I should be grateful my own spasm makes it hard to turn my head sometimes.

Mostly, it makes it impossible to forget.

⌒

Sadly, my first rewrite of this piece was only four days after the shooting of nineteen victims including Congresswoman Gabrielle Giffords. I thought it would take a political figure being gunned down to bring the gun control debate to its knees.

Then Newtown, Connecticut. The guns were assault weapons with high capacity clips, easily purchasable. Then ... etcetera. Etcetera. Etcetera.

Forgive us, children. Please forgive us.

Abandoning the Garden

Come May when the sky begins to shift from spring to summer, so that by night, much as I want to sleep, I can't, what with the stars in clear view, and, I swear, I can feel the bustling underground where seeds are impossibly busy right now there is just so much anticipation in the air! And, yet, the only thing getting me down is the thought of my garden.

Why?

Because I neglect it.

As last year's nasturtiums spill over with abandon, life has come down to two choices: writing my next book, or traveling to read from my last one.

It wasn't too long ago that my garden was what I loved most about my tiny plot of land. I'd stand over my beds, pride spreading through me like current. But with the years, certain desires move on, they just do, either by winding down the way lust abates or by snaring. Like Kleenex snagged on barbed wire. With so much to weed, I'd rather write. My body tells me to get out there and separate the dahlia bulbs and I think, *wait, I just need to finish this next paragraph.*

It didn't help when my friend, Jenn, a bona fide Master Gardener, walked through my lavender patch, or what's left of my lavender patch, with major head shaking going on before she bent over and started pulling up weeds. I used to visit her all the time, back before my first book was published, when my garden was tidy and bloomed with the best of them. In those years, I suppose there are those who'd say, and they'd be right, that my garden took the place of children.

Each morning, I'd walk through my beds, thoroughly studying my plants, wondering where I could plant more plants. What I felt I knew about my garden, what seemed to speak to me from the very soil, was that gardening was holy, or a holiness *I* could believe in; an earthy, feminine holiness. Once you've grown your plants from seedlings in a Dixie cup, it's hard not to mother them to death.

And what did my garden know about me?

She knew to teach me to nurture, to follow through, to finish what I begin. I was so impatient in those days. My garden taught me, or she tried to teach me, that I couldn't hurry growth. There were even days when I didn't write, when I'd let my garden have her way with me morning till sunset. Through the seasons, it became more and more difficult to tell where her borders ended and I began. Any mother can relate.

Now?

Well, there are those who'd say that my books took the place of my garden that took the place of children. And what they are really saying is that my books took the place of children. And they'd be right, too.

Still, I miss the time in my life when I spent hours gardening and writing about gardening, when my new awareness of annuals and perennials guided my work. It made me happy. Without a garden to look after, I may have floundered forever. I decided to write a collection of poems about gardening: *This is something I think I could do.* I called it *Women in the Garden.* When it was published, it was hard to imagine that the gardener or the poet could be any more satisfied.

Then there was another book. And another. There went the garden.

How quickly I learned that gardening is, in all the ways writing is *not*, accepting of benign neglect. But not total neglect. Total neglect moves a moist Northwest garden, quickly and thoroughly, into an overgrown weedy mess, everything shooting up crosswise, beyond, over, farther, floppier with "absentee owner" written all over it.

Today, when I read over my gardening poems, I realize I'm a little jealous of all the time I once had to work in the yard. These days I'm more apt to feel like a billow floating above my garden on my way out of town.

In the beginning, I had no idea what it would be like to have to choose between two things I loved equally. Only now am I able to imagine how my future will be, if I'm lucky (and smart), once I've had enough of the road, a vibrant mix of my two favorite things once again: writing and gardening. I don't think I can ever escape what makes me the happiest. I need to be happy.

No, that's not it, I need to be working. And gratified by my work.

But that first morning I walked outside and saw the weeds popping up in my picture-perfect garden, I thought, *I'm so sorry*. It was a send-off to a big part of me. I got in my car and drove to my reading. With no doubt about what I was doing, I'd begun the complex process of becoming not only a writer, but also a speaker. There was no going back. From that moment on, my garden became more a seed of memory than of ones saved in tiny paper packets.

It grew rather wild-looking. But it kept right on rooting. And roots remember.

The guilt is easing. Mostly because there are a few truths I understand better. One is that choice is partly about sacrifice. And, secondly, that time is too short to carry around *every*thing I ever wanted. At once.

But there's another thing, even if I wasn't consciously aware of it before: If it wasn't for my writing a book about a woman in her garden, I wouldn't be writing this one about a woman in her ... well, one might say "garden" if searching for the perfect metaphor, because it grows in direct proportion to my keeping after it, page by unruly page.

Then, of course, a gardener has to go back in and prune. Pruning is *the* best comparison of my two gardens, past and present.

And the worst comparison is this: I remember how all the joy I felt from my garden was nothing compared with the pain I felt when the Master Gardener told me I should study books written by *real* gardeners. The put-down could have come from someone who knew nothing about gardens, or even someone I couldn't stand, anyone, a passerby, and I would have taken it to heart. Because it's the hardest thing in the world to be able to hear someone critique your efforts, so that in case they know something truly helpful, you can use it to improve your work, yet, at the same time, have enough confidence to not let what they say eat away at you.

So, when the going gets rough, as it often does, I picture myself on my knees tackling the dandelions, an entirely different battlefield from the one I deal with now: programmers, producers, editors, agents, the competitive world of writing and publishing, the mean underworld of performing, audiences who can't turn off their cell phones. I figure if I can deal with the doggedness of dandelion roots, I can deal with *any*thing.

It helps me remember my books are the crop, the harvest, the yield, the cost of choosing both what I want and what I had to give up in order to find it.

And when all around me seems to be more complicated than I ever imagined it could be, there is the simplicity of pulling a weed, the thing I can do that makes the most sense, that calms me. Wherever I travel, I walk outside, bend over, and pull up a weed in someone else's garden.

Or maybe, I just stare, with awe, at a determined, persistent vine.

Like a sweet pea climber, the way it finds its bungling way up and out of the dark no matter what. It's a lesson every writer needs to remember.

Sweet pea, I decide, is the best teacher ever.

I Remember EVERYthing

There are three words my mother likes to use that always manage to fill me with regret,

"You remember *every*thing!"

It's no compliment.

It is, however, her way of asking me to stop writing about her. Unless I praise her. Praise she finds agreeable.

How can I stop? Capturing all the ways my mother works her way through me is the best material I have. Still, I doubt my mother, *any* mother, would choose a writer for a daughter if given half a choice in the matter, and that's what mine said, in a roundabout way, moments before our latest "time out" as I've taken to calling them, when we stop talking and stare at each other until the room grows still and we can hear, actually *hear*, steam hissing through the air.

Next, we don't stand in a corner with our backs to the room like a couple of kids or anything; we walk away from each other in a huff, maybe even slam a door, then wait to see, after a few days of silence, who gives in and calls first.

Which is what a couple of kids would do.

My mother also says, "The way you write about your life and everything, well, I know it's something you like to do and all, and it's fine (code for it bothers her), but I think you should write a novel so more people can buy it at Costco."

I didn't anticipate how much her saying this would hurt me. Which just goes to show you can write all you want but you can never really count on your work reaching others in the way you intend it to. Or that your mother will ever truly get your deepest desire: your book facing forward in a bookstore, not in a discounted stack next to cotton panties, twelve to a pack.

This is the kind of Mom/me conflict that, at first, challenges me to be more accepting and forgiving. And in the next breath, depresses me completely.

To top it off, what my mother said about more people buying my book, well, honestly, I'd like that. She is so right. I should tell her. But it's her turn to call.

I shake my head, tell myself to pick up the phone.

Here's why. After standing in line at Safeway this morning behind two women who were discussing, as far as I could tell, their kids' T-Ball schedule, a particular T-Ball memory wormed its way in.

Which is a good thing. Worming is good. For a writer, absolutely necessary.

But it can also take a toll. So, after I poked at the memory for a while and wrote it down in a rickety first draft, I wanted relief from it, which usually means pouring another cup of coffee and calling Mom, because she can instantly transform me into her world by sharing what she's doing at the moment, what she'll do next, what she'll eat, won't eat, what it will do to her stomach, or worse, her bowels, if she does eat it, but not about how she feels about any of it, initially anyway, just glissading over the facts, which, she feels, *is* conversation. And this is where we divide, like two cells, into a woman okay with skin-deep conversation vs. the daughter who wants to venture in deeper and make things (so my mother says) *embarrassing*.

For instance, even after all these years, I still have to prod my mother into saying *why* she cancelled her dentist appointment to book a massage:

"Because no one touches me anymore. And poking around at my gums doesn't count."

Wow. Probably not the most suitable word, even in italics, given how important her admission felt like: how much we all need touch, how lonely life can become without it, how much more she needs from me than she lets on, how heavy this feels and then, finally, how much more she'll need from me in the years to come. Her admission reminds me of all I can't imagine myself being able to manage, emotionally, plus all that I must.

It would not have occurred to her to say how in need of touch she is, but if I ask, just like that, her inner life becomes all that matters and the floodgate opens.

It's our pas de deux.

She needs to be asked.

Anyway, back to Safeway and the two women discussing T-Ball. On some impulse, I Googled the game when I got home, and, according to the official T-Ball website, "It's a great introduction to baseball, a program that serves children five to eight years old and is not intended to be competitive but fun for the kids."

My first thought was that, right after the word, "kids" they should have said "and the parents." I spent the rest of the day thinking about how irritated some fathers sound when I walk past a T-ball game. What are they so worried about? That in all the cute little uniforms a Scott Bankhead or Albert Pujols is in the making? *And, dammit, that's what I want for my son, for me, for my son, for me, for him, me, him, ME!*

And the moms? Umbilically tied on a whole other level.

Ah, you see, I owned a dance studio once. Where, more than anything, I wanted to teach young girls how to trust their own receptive minds and bodies. Consequently, I finally had to put my foot down: "Moms are allowed to watch only on the first class of the month," read the sign on my door. I would have liked to go a step further and say a few moms could *never* watch, but I knew it would never fly. For one thing, they were paying me not the other way around.

But a few of them you would not believe. No self-control. Absolutely none. Their own insecurities rose right up, landing like bricks on their daughter's self-esteem. Sometimes I could see how they really did struggle with it, knowing they were over the top, but it rarely stopped them for long; the next remark flew right out: *She said the right foot, not your left, the right!*

Negative mothering was a positive learning experience for me. It got so I could spot these mothers on registration day. And I began to pity them a little. Visually, they were more and more of a warning sign, a manifestation, what unrealized and/or un-attempted goals and dreams can become, how people can age, then age some more, without ever accomplishing something of their own to be proud of. Maybe these women woke up one morning and found they were no longer able to focus on their career and couldn't adjust to the reality. Or maybe they never attempted one in the first place and feel cheated somehow. So they create a new line of work: motherhood. I think this is what is really happening.

I also think they would stop interfering if they could just get past seeing their kids as a chance *they'd* been given. No kid wants to be his or her parent's way of reaching for more, of gaining something else. "If they don't quit it," I said to my husband after one particularly trying class, "they'll be lucky, when senior year ends, to see their daughter on a regular basis."

Though we never talked about it, I think some of the other mothers and I knew these outbursts were hungers that, on another level, weren't directed at their daughters so much as at life in general. Pent up, they had nowhere else to pop but in my studio.

Up went my handmade sign. Made with the thickest Sharpie ever made.

There were many easy-going moms, of course, who were encouraging in the most supportive, positive ways. But my signboard couldn't be selective or the heavyweights would have come down on me. I was pretty sure of that.

And the girls?

They rarely, if ever, had the courage, especially in a room full of peers, to stand up to their mothers. The bonds between a young girl and her mother can be such a bewildering mix of need and want and giving and reluctance and guilt. Add to it a parent's cravings and you've got a lot of baggage built up in a child's memory.

So watch out. She, too, may remember *every*thing.

And write about it one day.

YOUR DAUGHTER MAY BE LEARNING A FEW DANCE
STEPS HERE, BUT YOU ARE KEEPING HER FROM TAKING
A HUGE LEAP FORWARD IF YOU CHASTISE FROM THE
SIDELINES. WHAT DOES YOUR DAUGHTER WANT FROM

THIS CLASS? I'LL TELL YOU, GLADLY. THE OPPOSITE OF
EVERYTHING YOU WANT. JUST LIKE WHEN YOU GO
SHOPPING FOR CLOTHES TOGETHER.

This is the sign I should have hung. Never mind the objections.
Why didn't I?

Oh, what we'd do over if only we could go back.

In the grocery line, I knew one of the women from another life, years
ago, friend of a friend. She smiled at me, blinked an eye, inclusively,
and my only thought was *No, go away. I can't be bothered, it's one of the
perks of not having children, maybe the biggest, I don't have to talk about
the kids.* Which, seconds later, even though I thought I'd stuffed it
way back into the furthest crimps of my brain, triggered my one and
only for-real T-Ball memory. (*Hi, I'm still here, poking like a cramp.*)

Years back, I went to my first T-Ball game to be a supportive friend
because I love my friend, Max, and her two sons, without reserve. Still,
I didn't know from Adam what T-Ball *was.* I thought it was short for
Tether Ball, the game I dreaded as a kid because it felt like too much
pressure, and not only for my wrists. I would have rather stayed on
the swings alone, *observing* the game, possibly the earliest sign I was
to be a writer someday.

But there was a whole world of my peers living by T-Ball schedules
and maybe, I thought, it was high time I see that world for myself. For
years I had told myself I'd go *some*time.

But sometime never came.

Until it did.

How could I have known T-Ball would be terrifying? Which
sounds like a silly thing to say about a game, but it's true. I was terrified. Silly, needless terror, but terror all the same. My stomach can't
decipher. My stomach knots up regardless.

I never told anyone about my dread of showing up at T-Ball. There
was no one to tell. All my friends were moms and I, the only non-
mom, couldn't confide in them; they stick together. Tell one of them
something and the whole circle knows. Whom could I trust? I put off

showing up at a game through various friendships and invitations.

Vividly, I remember the shock that struck me soon as I looked around from out-of-bounds. I was completely outside the world before me. I'll never forget that feeling, how alone I felt. Maybe when I'm ninety and I can't remember my own name anymore, but until then, I'm stuck with knowing just how completely alone aloneness can feel.

There I was, the only woman-without-a-T-Ball-player in a swarm of young parents. It seemed like the whole normal, fruitful universe had completely passed me by and I was the odd duck. Again. Just like in high school. And I had two simultaneous feelings playing bumper car in my head: The first was that I'd made a terrible mistake by not reproducing, and secondly, that the whole mommy-daddy-T-Ball thing might be contagious if I stayed one second longer!

I wound up fleeing on my bicycle before my friend's son even got his turn at bat. Soon as I reached home, sniffling and breathless with tears, I collapsed on my bed. Later I tried to apologize in a phone message: "I loved the game, Max, but . . .," I lied. I don't even remember what lie I made up about my fast-flying exit. I didn't want to lie to my friend, but I wasn't sure telling the truth would improve the situation, that's for sure.

The whole time I was at the game I kept hearing *woman-without-offspring-meets-reproductive-world* in my head. I started to doubt my choices, turn my life decisions into opponents. My ability to enjoy the game for what is was, my friend's world, pulled quietly shut. I showed up, yes, but I couldn't *experience.*

The grown-up me knew better, but I don't need to tell you how present Ms. Questioning was just then. She was big at my side, gigantic, spreading her apron wide. I had to climb out of her folds and remind myself, over and over, how much I love *my* life, my quiet writer's life. And, no matter what lie the drug companies spin, not one of us can have it all all of the time.

This is just what life is like in your thirties. It's not only the maybe-baby decade, but ten years of second-guessing yourself. You question *every*thing.

Before you start remembering *every*thing. Just like my mother says.

Before you start forgetting everything like she does.

And today?

Let's see. I remember walking out of Safeway without looking back.

And right through my writing time, my afternoon walk, my dance class, dinner with Mom (I caved; I called), I've done everything, I mean everything, trying to imagine my life turning out any other way.

And you know what?

I can't.

Grace

One of the problems with living in a small town for two decades is that, no matter what part of town I walk through, most things feel so familiar I can forget just how much has changed over the years.

Then, suddenly, someone I knew once, and possibly loved, becomes emotionally possible again, reminding me just how much things *have* changed.

Lately, this occurs whenever I take a walk through Port Townsend, a town that lies at the tip of the Quimper Peninsula. It's where I spent most of my twenties and all of my thirties and where I return to whenever I make time to do nothing but write. My husband and I still own our tiny cottage there, our first home that has, in recent years, become my escape from city life.

I can't seem to give it up.

Maybe it's just an emotional fact of life that the house you cling to is the one where you became yourself. Even if becoming "yourself" means that slowly, but with certainty, you build a bridge away from the house.

And then you cross the bridge.

My husband likes to say our cottage is inexpensive enough to hang onto for now. "Cheap to keep," he says. And it's true; it costs so little.

But for me, it's more than a transaction that does or does not pencil out. The cottage is surrounded by a patch of earth that means more to me than something I can define. But the feeling is real. And, aside from the pride I feel whenever I return to it, I'm also swept up in a wave of appreciation for all that gave shape to my current life in Seattle where, and quite to the contrary, home is a 400-square-foot condo five flights over a downtown sidewalk.

My new surroundings are certainly not up to me to coax into bloom. Cut off from home owning-distraction is exactly what I need to focus solely on my work. I take physical pleasure in the simplicity of not having a yard now, equal (or nearly equal) to the pleasure I used to have while tending one.

I became a writer in Port Townsend, the City of Dreams, a nickname coined years ago by a writer quite new to it. Why? So much natural beauty can lead to the hope and belief that geography alone can guide one's creative work in a positive way.

Sometimes it does.

But sometimes a wave of another sort, a flush of sadness, overtakes me there. All of a sudden a certain house or blackberry bramble will remind me of an old friend calling *Mary Lou, hello!* Someone from my tribe, the few friends who really got my sense of humor. Mind you, there weren't a lot of them. But there were enough.

Jane, for instance, who forgave me my flaws as I fumbled my way into maturity; and Jeane, who didn't; or Laine who shared a good gossipy laugh. But death prevents my being able to thank her for always making time for me. Which is what happened today as I strolled past a gallery on Water Street.

The gallery once belonged to Laine, whom I could count on to be, if not my only mentor, then certainly my favorite. She could mix it up in a way that instantly made everything better for us both. Like schoolgirls, we felt it right to move in close to each other, to pick a little fun at our small town that, we agreed, sometimes suppressed us. It was the kind of laughter I lived for then. And still do.

And, other than my dearest artist-friend at the time, Lucy, who liked to paint me (thank goodness because I needed the money those long sessions of lying around naked brought in), Laine was the only woman honest enough to say, point blank, what life is like for artists, particularly women artists, in a small Northwest town.

"Be careful," she warned, "there are some doors that will always remain closed to you."

Really? I remember thinking, so young and idealistic was I. See, I was still trying to be so much. *And* I wanted everyone to like me.

That's how young I was.

"You're from the East Coast," she warned. "Some of the writers born here, or pretending to be, with their beards and xenophobia, will not accept you at their roundtable."

Oh?

And from Lucy, "Never pretend to be someone you're not so that someone you perceive as successful will take you more seriously. They won't."

I was afraid of their warnings, afraid what they said would undo me.

It's taken me years to realize no one can undo me other than myself. Still, for most of my thirties, whenever I ran into one of the writers I saw as successful (for me that meant *published*), I felt clumsy, insecure. I wound up saying foolish, impulsive things I regretted.

Finally, thanks to Laine, I understand why I acted so ridiculously. I'd fallen into the trap of believing these writers held the key to my future.

Laine used to call these insecure moments a name, but, for the life of me, I can't remember what the word she used was, even though I used to run home to write down just about everything she said. I remember the gist, though: that between writers and artists, there is too often a need to pull one down from level. I sensed she didn't feel comfortable enough saying what she really meant, that the inner circles of a small town can come into power by their own making. And they'll do just about anything to stay there.

Maybe she feared for me, for my future. Maybe she'd learned, as I was just beginning to, that inner circles like to drag each other through the mud. "You have to work really hard to overcome the gossip, Mary Lou, and if you keep dressing like *that*," forcing me to look down at my pointy new boots, "there *will* be gossip." We both laughed. I think Laine sensed I had only so much patience for living like that.

I sought out Laine's perspective on so many things. She was a bit of a guru in this way. I never felt the full joy of an accomplishment until I told her about it.

Another thing Lucy said was how I was too apologetic, tempted to turn seriousness into a laugh in order to be liked. It was like a bolt of lighting passing through my young, permeable mind.

Today, when I walk through Port Townsend's loveliest hidden park, another kind of jolt passes though me. I swear I can see my old friend Steve's backside bending over the mower. Steve was the park manager for decades.

The man I see is not Steve, of course, Steve died years ago, much too young. Still, the run-in with his spirit is as familiar and rooting as life ever becomes for a transplant like me.

Thinking of Steve also makes me think about the new piazza around Port Townsend's Haller Fountain (a.k.a. the "naked lady statue") built smack in the middle of town, recently *paved* to honor Steve. Which, and I can only surmise, Steve would have hated. Steve would have planted huge, floppy, tropical plants around the fountain. And made us muddy our feet to get through the green maze of fronds.

This makes me wonder about something else. And thanks to Laine and Lucy, I'm just going to come right out and say what it is: Who in a small town (city, county, or state) receives memorial status, a statue of their own? Are we remembered for the best thing we ever did, or, as I read somewhere, doomed to be remembered for the worst, especially if we were born female?

Will we be remembered at all? Do we care?

Years ago Laine said that ladies' organizations honor the women and municipalities honor the men. And she said it with such a huff of resentment in her voice that I felt mad about it, too, even though I'd never really thought about it before then.

But ever since, I've thought about it a lot.

I'm still thinking about it.

Let's see. In Port Townsend there is, as I said, Steve's Piazza; the Dan Harpole Cistern; the Larry Scott Bike Trail; the James Broughton Bench in front of the Rose Theatre; The Joseph Wheeler Theater on the grounds of Fort Worden. All beautiful, all worthy, all *deserved*.

But where is the Laine Johnson statue? The Lucy Vane memorial? Just one woman? Not all. Just not no one.

Yesterday, as I was getting out of my car after being away for weeks, I saw an old friend coming toward me. David. Together, he and his wife own the local hand-made ice cream parlor. The sight of his face was pure joy to me, my very tall, bike-riding friend. If he were to die, I swear, I'd create a statue of him myself. I'd call it *Big Guy on a Bicycle*.

Next to him, just as tall, even though she isn't, I'd build a statue of his wife, Julie, her smile full of grace.

Oh, wait! I want to change the name of my statue. I want to call it *Grace*.

"Never be afraid to change your mind," Laine said. "Or speak it."

I can't think of a better ending.

Except maybe this: Laine, Lucy: whatever honesty is present in my work today is all because of you.

Blue Moose

There are mornings I wake and, for no apparent reason, I just know the day ahead will be different somehow, revealing, better than the day before.

That's the kind of morning it was when I decided to visit the Blue Moose Café. I'd heard of the place for years. Anyone who has lived on the Olympic Peninsula has heard of it. I just never made the effort to find it before.

When I arrived, the hand-painted sign alone had enough color to get me in the door, but it was the women who run the place who made me grab a menu. They were laughing so hard from behind the counter, it was like stumbling into a juicy secret, the kind of laughter that pokes a little fun while, in the same breath, no one gets hurt. A far cry from mean laughter. Nothing new between women who trust each other, which obviously they did. Affection is always something special to see. It quiets me. I go silent with approval.

They were obviously laughing about something that happened on *my* side of the counter, something so embarrassing it made me think of something I heard Roseanne Barr say in an interview once: *Real humor is like this people: It doesn't know for nothin' about being nice.*

My first impulse was to whip out my tiny notepad and try to capture the laughter's effect on me. I found it reassuring and there is something so great about reassurance when it happens. I care more about it than I do about an earful of local politics, that's for sure, the grind I supposedly came for because my editor wants more local politics, and lunchtime cafés are *the* place to find a story. Any new rumor scything through town is sure to end up here by lunchtime.

But no matter what the scuttlebutt is, it's going to be dull in comparison to two women laughing this hard; my mind is made up. My mind will wander if I listen to the gossip anyway. I'll forget what issue they're talking about this time, which city official is pissing them off today, what city ordinance is making them so mad now.

But the women laughing: this is a real story.

You have to be wondering what was so funny.

Soon as I walked inside, I turned to face a rather large man who turned sideways to let me pass, and while trying to squeeze past him, he farted.

I've always thought the funniest things are involuntary.

So *what* that the fartee turned three shades of red as he waddled away. There are just too many things to feel guilty about these days. Cross my heart, I'm not adding laughter to the list.

One of the women still had tears in her eyes when she walked over in her patchwork denim sarong to take my order, cheerfully present in her skirt from the past.

I sensed a few other intimate details about her, too, like how at home she seemed in the café, for one thing, but also in her own body, every curve of it. Some people whiz through life without ever reaching the place where life and work come together like this. They may be sure of what they don't want and how to grumble about it endlessly, but they never seem to figure out what they do want.

She had a pot of coffee in her hand and I'd had enough caffeine, but I nodded at the pot anyway, in the same way she glanced at the door and nodded, welcoming yet another boat builder to lunch. I typically can hear a silent hum of recognition when someone puts my face and my column together. "Ah," she said, winking at my notepad. I told her what I liked most about her café, "It's the right size," I said. "It fits."

The café was causing all kinds of physical reactions by then. Muscle memory kicked in soon as I walked through the door. The Blue Moose reminds me of the Seattle I discovered years ago when, freshly freed from the East Coast, I found a slew of funky-charming cafés just like it on the streets of Ballard, with menus I could afford. Back before Market Street was hip, when I lived on a sailboat with my hippy husband, worked on a fishing boat, scavenged driftwood off the beach to build a fire in a tiny iron stove to keep warm. Back when I made my own muffins. Made *dinner.*

How scary and exciting it was to scull our tiny boat out of the locks, to sail north, how we—my man from the Bay Area, me from New England—sailed all the way to Southeast Alaska to become "fishermen."

And there we were on our own in a cold wet land, where one finds out pretty quickly that building a boat is all about the romance of the sea.

But working the sea is another story entirely.

We ended up in Ketchikan and drank coffee in the local café, the only sense of place we could find in a small Alaskan town.

Déjà vus are a little spooky sometimes and for good reason. They remind us who we were before we grew into our present lives, especially if we are foolish enough to think only the present defines us. It's a strange sensation to feel the past work its way in, sometimes brutally, to remind us how far we've come and whether we want to go back.

A lot like family reunions.

I learned a lot from my Alaska days, the least of it about fishing.

First, there was the language of the docks, a language that, even more than my sister living in Brooklyn, taught me about *freely* inserting a specific verb into a string of words, e.g., "Take your fucking sailboat and fucking tie it up somewhere else. We gotta move our whole fucking fleet out of here too fucking early in the morning to deal with your ... whatever the fuck piece of shit that fucking thing is you're trying to fish from."

Rough translation: "We belong here. You don't. Go back home. White people, you can't *choose* our way of life."

They were right of course. You don't just wake up one day and decide to become a fisherman. You grow up with it. Over generations it becomes who you are.

Showing up in Alaska on our tiny dory-as-sailboat fit to catch one salmon at a time from our stern, built by hand in a barn in Sequim, Washington, and tying up next to creaky, century-old hulls with Native American crews who'd been fishing ever since the breast was pulled from their mouths, toughened me up, showed me how naive a girl from my background really is, how idealistically I viewed the world.

Best example? One morning I waited until no one was in sight before beginning my ballet stretches on our tiny bow. A hung-over fisherman stumbled by, stopped, asked what I was doing. So I said, "Oh, I'm a dancer." Of course, I didn't know that when a fisherman in Ketchikan still drunk from the night before asks why your legs are V-shaped and reaching toward the western sky, he does not conjure the world of ballet. I was horrified when he asked, "What club?"

And once, I don't remember why, but it must have been something about our catching our very first King so large it seemed like we'd scored a floppy sea monster, the fishermen were actually nice to us. *Oh boy, we're finally accepted! We're good, good buddies with the natives now!*

In fact, we felt so accepted, we blew off fishing that day and walked up to a bar with a couple of T'Klinkits. Actually, it was a strip club (how could I not have guessed?) where one woman was gyrating on the bar, her skirt hiked around her waist; another swung naked from a trapeze while inhaling and exhaling a lit cigarette *not* from her mouth, her legs circling the air rapidly to keep the filter in place.

After an hour of trying to appear as if the strippers were *the* most interesting floorshow, the T'Klinkits *the* most riveting conversationalists, I got so drunk I ended up on my knees in the ladies' room.

Mid-barf, one of the strippers barged in to tell me to get out of her bar because she didn't like stripping for women. My mouth dropped open. I stared at her. I grabbed another handful of paper towels and promised I'd leave right away. She checked her reflection in the mirror and wiped the corner of her mouth with her pinky, as if the hidden secret to her work was all in the way her lipstick was applied. She turned away and was gone. Her dismissal made me cry, or, shall I say, loneliness made me cry. I was just so out of place in Alaska.

And here I thought "the last frontier" would move me away from insecurity, past peer pressure, not deeper into it. Instead of removing myself from the bar soon as I entered, I pretended I was happy to stay, afraid to sound too much like a girl if I said *I'm sorry, I didn't realize what this place was. Goodbye.*

How hard is it to say the truth of how you feel, really?

Nearly impossible at twenty-one, as I recall.

Especially when my whole life suddenly seemed too manly, too raw and bloody for my liking. Where, in order to prove myself, I was armed with a thick wooden knife with a very thin blade. I learned I could cut into a rich, dense, wiggling-with-life salmon, well away from the bone, slice off a few soft, fleshy steaks for dinner like a pro. No fish too big to be deconstructed by me. Something they completely forgot to teach me at my private Boston women's college.

I was such a daredevil back then.

Most of it was an act.

I took a long time to eat my lunch. I liked returning to a café located in the heart of a boatyard. A place full of men who've moved from other cities, all of them, from lives of upper-middle-class privilege, most of them, to repair, rebuild, and re-launch their dreams, literally. Perhaps after drawing the plans for a keel on a napkin right here at the Blue Moose.

The Port Townsend shipyard is nothing like a shipyard in, say, West Seattle, where local men work, and have worked as long as their high school classmates have worked at Boeing.

No, Port Townsend is more of a white-collar turned blue-collar setting: men who left partnerships, associations, and academia to work in paint-splattered overalls, to eat in a café where the specials are written on a chalk board in *calligraphy*, where the woman who nursed her baby in the booth beside me went to Sarah Lawrence, she was happy to say.

Just think of the number of tourists who flock to the Northwest looking for a small-town experience. I'd bet the farm the Blue Moose is what they're looking for.

"We're a family here," the other woman, Tana, walked up to say.

Yes, that's it. The café comes without pretense, a minus that always makes me want more.

"So," Tana said after a while, "I nearly died in a car wreck six years ago." This was after working as a chef in the early days of Seattle's gentrification, she said, when trendy restaurants were just beginning to word their menus with descriptions that make a potato sound like a spa package, and affect their waiters with wine recitations that, try as they may, never pass for knowledge.

But this is the part I like best: When Tana recovered from her accident, her first thought was, "I need more than trying to be noticed as a great chef. I don't need the boys' club to make me feel good about myself."

Everything about that sounded familiar. It all came rushing back to me: The writer's conference where, night after night, a man always reads last. The editor who told me that my kind of writing was too "women-y." The degrading phrase "Chick Lit" for some of the best writing by women out there today. I leaned back in my chair so far my knees touched the table and I could see my coffee dancing in its mug.

Some memories are just too much.

Here is where I go back to the beginning, when I was lying in bed, knowing something good would come of the day, something telling. And it dawns on me that after years of my own quest to be noticed by some big literary gun, it has finally occurred to me that this chase can only add up to one thing: dissatisfaction.

But, wait, there was something else underneath my desire to have my work noticed, even then, a need to make sure I kept at it.

I can't seem to get enough of these kinds of revelations right now. Maybe some of my own professional hopes for the future will fall away, too. I hope so. Because I want, or I want to want, less.

So my advice is anyone trying to jump through the next career hoop in order to achieve "happiness" needs to visit the Blue Moose and talk to Tana. She reminds us how life can be full of want one day, enough the next, doubts one year, certainty the next. And that all of it comes together eventually, if we stay with it, like a well-planned garden where all the plants seem separate in spring. But come summer, they're one continual layer. Because, I swear, without fully recognizing it before, I've been trying to balance myself between these two pulls, between want and enough, for so long.

I rub the back of my neck, tilt my head to the left, lean back, count my pages for the day, stand up, look out the window, think how the Blue Moose was like a slingshot for me today.

It *was* the real story.

It flung me past myself.

After a lot of old stuff flew by, I came back.

And, like Tana, I landed on my feet.

That's Life

That's life, that's life. That's what all the people say. I'm riding high in April, shot down in May....

When I was a kid, these were the words that rang out of my dad's shower, lyrics that tipped me off there would be some blows along the way.

And there have been.

At a certain point they even began to suggest that the business of writing would have more blows to it than I ever imagined. I've internalized the words in ways that continue to reveal themselves to me to this day. I can't remember when I was first struck with how relevant and moving the song really is, how much truth is condensed into three catchy minutes, how helpful the lyrics are when I need a little bolstering.

Such as, when I'm in the throes of a performance schedule that has me reading in a dozen venues back to back, knowing full well that some of the evenings are going to go well, really well, and a few will be a total flop causing me to drive out of the parking lot thinking *why on earth am I doing this? Why on earth?* I ease my doubt (or some of it, anyway) by singing my favorite bar, *many times I've thought of quittin' baby, but my heart won't buy it....*

Because if any work demonstrates both the best confidence and the worst uncertainty, it's writing.

More than anyone else, my father has showed me how to go about making my dreams into reality, how nothing but hard work will get me there, how many hurdles there will be along the way. His rigorous work ethic, persistence (especially his persistence), and need to rise after the knock-downs, became my own. And when I think about what he, an immigrant, had to face in order to secure the American Dream as he defined it—employment, wife, house, car, kids, and later, a summer house on Long Island Sound—I have to admit such enormous drive was an amazing thing to watch.

If a little tyrannizing at times.

All that lay ahead for him was work, a fact he never questioned. And just like most immigrants, he was grateful to have the work, any work. His hands were disfigured from a lifetime of work by the time he was thirty.

And sometimes, I can't help but compare my dad to my peers who so often whine about their work, the high cost of this and that, every facet of politics, their very lives, and I don't know what all, complaining as if victims, without ever considering doing one single thing, whatever it takes, to change things for the better, or to get involved even at a basic, grassroots level. I listen and wonder how any of us can be so thankless and powerless.

We live in a country that allows us to change, to work for change if change is what we want so badly. At what age, what stage, did we lose sight of the fact that change is possible if we are willing to work for it, willing to sacrifice some of the security we think we can't live without? When did we begin to think of ourselves as ineffective? Where is our commitment to finding work we enjoy, to finding ourselves? Where is our dedication?

Oh, I just caught my breath!

Because *dedication* is the word I've been after and I didn't even know it. I've been at a loss to describe how funny it seems to me lately that so many Americans have either been to Italy or say they want to visit. I think this is because they crave all things Italian, which, in a nutshell, is to crave all things dedicated. Because it's great, isn't it, to be charmed by the past? By custom, tradition, commitment, allegiance, preservation—you know, *history.* Trying to absorb all this dedication to history during a ten-day vacation is not only good for the Euro, it comforts those who lack any dedication to their own architectural past and personal history back home.

I try not to cringe when my foodie friends go on about slow food and wine pairings, the length of time people take not only to prepare food in Italy, but to eat it. I force a lot of smiles when they praise, as if it were divine, *polenta.* I say yes, I like polenta, too.

What I don't say is how polenta was considered roughly on par with eating dog food for most Italians before it became trendy. Or that Italians are far less enamored by the past than tourists like to idealize. For one thing, they seldom romanticize it the way we do. For another, most of my friends and family who have emigrated from Europe intensely dislike antiquity. Their homes are more like showrooms for Lucite.

My father will not, not on your life, enter a second-hand store.

And you should hear him condemn provincialism. Why? Because ever since the horrors of the last World War, he's had to work inexhaustibly hard to dig out from under it, to not look back, to live in the present. How else could he have moved so far forward in one generation?

Consequently, the present was all my father would talk about when I was a kid. Most of my Seattle friends, and, I suspect, most Americans, don't understand this is why Europeans like to linger over those five-course meals, savoring the ease, holding on to the present as if to a mane, not wanting to fall off the crest they've worked so hard to climb because they know, first-hand, how far civilization can sink once the descent begins.

Without realizing it, this live-in-the-present mind-set became my own. Every time I experience a loss, I try to shift my focus to the present until I can see nothing ahead but the future. It's invigorating.

And every so often it even works.

I also try to keep a lid on the fact that most Europeans are not addicted to the next new shiny whatever, unlike my iNext-obsessed friends who don't seem to recognize how keeping up with so much gadgetry distracts them, tires them, keeps them from doing the things in life that really matter. Because, I don't want to sound *preachy*.

This obsession with new toys is exactly what my friend, Amar (not to be confused with Amargit), from India, is banking on. "Americans are so gullible," he said. "Always wanting the next new thing we will make for you, yes? If you keep buying, and you will, all of my people will be able to leave Punjab!" He was making fun, sort of, but I felt my throat tighten. I closed my eyes and those images of people lining up in the cold to buy whatever tablet is new flitters to mind.

Anyway, Dad. Like the tides of immigrants before him, he sought, eagerly and aggressively, the upward mobility America promised in career, and later, in real estate; but here's where things get a little hazy: he firmly mistrusts mobility in relation to friendships. His alliances rarely, if ever, venture beyond family ties, the only bonds he trusts.

This was true even after we moved away from the inner city to a suburb in Connecticut where we were pretty much the only Italian family for miles, which makes me think a lot about another characteristic my dad and uncles used to probe around the poker table where they also discussed (argued) passionately (meaning with plenty of yelling and table pounding) family, politics, but unlike American men, never sports. Their profound sense of commitment was not only to work but to each other. And I've been sort of dwelling on this characteristic a lot lately. It reminds me how another trait helped form not only the kind of woman I am, but the kind of writer: loyalty.

I am loyal. In the Old World sense. I've remained loyal to my marriage for thirty years, to my mother as we age together, to friends willing to weather the storms together, to my writing always, even when my soul felt drained and as though a stroke of luck would never come my way.

Oh, God. *Luck.*

Luck makes me think of a conversation I had the other night after a reading. I was just leaving the podium when a woman rushed up to say, "You are so lucky!"

Sorry, I thought, I just can't agree with you. I wish I could.

"My daughter wants to be a writer. How does she get started?"

A reply sprang into mind, ten words I heard in a movie I was dying to try out, "If I told you, I'd have to kill you." I laughed.

She didn't.

How typical of Seattle, I thought, all "tell me, tell me, please" yet void of a sense of humor when I do. "I'm kidding," I said. And stalling, because nearly every time I'm confronted with this question, what's really being asked is how one gets published, and this question makes me queasy. So whenever the question pops up I just say, "Tell her to write."

"Yes, but how does she get *published*?"

See.

"Tell her to *keep* writing," I said, but no one wants to hear this.

In most people's view, writing is publishing; "success" is publishing. It's difficult to find the right tone to explain how failure *is* success if you keep writing anyway, to a mother who wants only good things for her daughter.

"If she's wants to publish, she has to learn how to write, and it takes awhile for most of us," I added, to keep my end up more than anything because I don't like to venture into too much honesty, which can come off as negative, directly after one of my readings. Especially if I'm feeling the whole evening came off well. I want to savor the overall satisfaction I get to feel for an hour or so, tops.

And not to be manipulative, but if I want people to buy a book, and I do, I need to leave them feeling good, hopeful, positive. No one buys a book when they're discouraged.

"Thank you!" she said. "I want my daughter to be as lucky as you've been!" And then she threw her arms around me.

I felt like a schmuck.

I should have stepped back, taken the time to say luck has nothing to do with writing for most of us. Maybe someday I'll be able to say that luck is my friend, freely, believably, but I'm not even close to being able to say that. I've met lucky writers who have bestsellers right out of the gate. I am nothing but jealous.

If it wasn't for trying to address the notion of loyalty in the first place, I wouldn't have added all this luck business in the middle of my thoughts. So let's back up here, so you get where I'm coming from.

Where am I coming from?

Hours seem to go by.

My first collection of poetry was rejected fifteen times. Fifteen.

Still, I never thought of giving up. I never felt like I had the option of giving up. *Each time I find myself flat on my face, I pick myself up and get back in the race ... that's life.* How grateful I am Sinatra dug in and made such an early impression on me. It takes a lot of stamina to push your first book into the world. And it can tear your heart out along the way.

Likely, it will.

Finally, my manuscript was accepted by a small literary press in Eastern Washington.

Writing that last line doesn't begin to do justice to the turn around that happened to my self esteem, a release of fears grown so heavy inside. I could smile like a kid again, laugh without holding back. Because no use of the word "small" has ever played such a huge role in my confidence.

I did wonder, at first, if it was the kind of press I thought I needed, whatever that means. Back then, even now, I can spend too much mental energy afraid of missing the Real Press, the one the Right People will think serious enough, established enough, with enough clout.

But I never allow myself to stay long wondering about any of that. There is no end to the ever-changing inner circle of rotating publishers and people who deem themselves most important in the literary world. No part of me can keep up with all the politicking and still find time to write.

I had to close my eyes and jump, believe in the press if, for no other reason, because the press believed in me. As it turned out, the publisher was well-respected in all the "right" literary orbits, the elliptical paths a young writer yearns to circle in. Once in, it felt like a big, muscle-y arm held me up.

Except it didn't hold me up for long. I couldn't lean into it and relax the way I thought I could. For one thing, my next book was pushy. It threw punches, instigated, demanded I *get back in the ring. . . that's life.* I woke dreading the next round. I still wake half excited about/half dreading the next round. And yet the dread only dissipates once I throw my first punch, which goes to show what a vicious cycle writing really is.

And why I encourage writers to take a long hard look at a few questions before embarking on a writing life: Can you see yourself spending most hours of every day alone? Can you take limitless uncertainty and heartbreak? Lots and lots of heartbreak?

I feel horrible for not taking more time with the eager mother of a young writer. "Writing," I should have said, "will do wonderful things for your daughter. And, if she is *lucky*, she'll survive the rest."

I hadn't really thought about loyalty in terms of my writing before. Not to this degree, anyway. One mention of the word and it feels as if all the little pieces of my writing past came together today. Pretty quickly, too. I love when this happens.

I say this because I do move quickly (I walk fast, I talk fast) compared to what's accepted-Seattle-speed, way too fast for my first publisher, as it turned out. To show him just how fast I could sell my book, I got started. Ready. Set. Go. I began to see everything as an opportunity, much as my dad must have seen the new world as soon as he stepped onto American soil. I began reading aloud from my work in front of all kinds of audiences. I would not take no for an answer. What better way to sell my first slim volume of poetry?

Right up until now, I remain loyal to my readings and to the work of booking them, both of which I'm really good at. I kept up my speed until each and every hand-stitched volume of my first collection of poetry was sold, at a pace only another East Coast Italian can relate to.

Thing is, my publisher was, as I said, from Eastern Washington. And I was selling faster than his press (one man, maybe an intern, a wife who controlled the capital) could keep up with. Or wanted to. More than once he asked me to slow down, take it easy, let the work find its way into the reader's hands naturally, to chill out.

Chill out? What does this mean exactly? I've wondered ever since moving to the West Coast. Are people slowing themselves deliberately? No sliver of me lives like this.

I suspect my first publisher, like many who came of age in the 1960s and 70s, had chosen to loosen up, lay back, turn his nose up at the privilege he'd come from. A choice I'd become pretty familiar with by then, what with all the ex-flower children flocking to the wide open, green, then affordable Northwest.

The fact that some of these same privileged men try to regain their status in the publishing world, well, this is another subject, one I figure I'll get to eventually. But not today.

Today I want to say that I don't think I can remember a time in my life when I wasn't working hard at one goal or another. Come to think of it, my first publisher's work ethic was nothing I knew of before moving to Seattle, especially nothing I knew of men. And I would never have crossed paths with the idea of *choosing* less if I hadn't left my family's expectations behind in order to move forward into needing less in terms of dollars for myself, my only choice if I was going to be a writer. (I almost didn't make it; I almost hitched myself to a pharmacist in New England whose dream was to own a big house in a small suburb. My mother adored him. And so did I. But I had an uneasy feeling in me that was growing. I didn't want a suburban life, or what I perceived as an ordinary life, period.)

Anyhow, the selling I was so good at was the first time I remember my enthusiasm totally backfiring on me. I worked with a speed that made me deliriously happy but made my publisher nervous. I shook him up.

It's impossible for me to admit all this without thinking of something I read when I was in college: "Henry Miller was disliked by other writers not so much for his success as for his exuberance and admitting that he was, indeed, a happy man to go it alone his own way."

His own way.

I have noticed that if I say how happy the writing/reading niche I've carved out for myself makes me, there is, more often than not, someone in my audience who immediately disapproves. I've gotten pretty good at both spotting the disapproval and ignoring it at the same time. When I'm expressing myself, say, with a lot of hand action, lustily in love with my story and then, in an instant, one person can squelch me with just a look.

Or worse, ignore me completely.

Maybe it's become socially acceptable to nitpick, to talk about what's wrong with everything rather than to appreciate. And maybe some people think we aren't supposed to express enthusiasm, openly, after a certain age; but I don't want to be like that. The coldness would crawl through me like a virus.

And other writers?

Sometimes they are the most disapproving. Somewhere writers aren't so insecure and support each other with sincere generosity, but I don't live in that world. Most writers I know are more competitive than friendly. They play a game I don't like to find myself in. I have no stomach for the ring any longer. Even if my favorite song says I have to lift myself up and get back *in* there, I generally cross the street now, rather than try and talk to another writer.

At the last writing conference I attended, I was giving a reading when I felt a particularly serious stare from one of the writers on my panel, a stare no different than frowning at someone on the receiving end, or a finger wagging. I don't think it was intentional really; it was more like I could feel a lot of academe-buildup in her that, like anything tightly contained, needed to pop. But she couldn't pop.

So she turned huffy.

And, just like that, my concentration, how I perform my work, can sort of fizzle out and flip-flop if I'm not careful. It's a strange sensation, to feel a peer's disapproval. Yet, some of the most liberal-minded people, or so they would have us believe, have judged this quality of mine, my very Italian-ness, the harshest.

Choosing Italian enthusiasm over Seattle curmudgeonliness (hard work, by the way, to inject a little fun into introspective, serious minds), expressing myself at a frequency higher than what is considered proper-Northwest, can still feel like a mistiming, a blip, something to apologize for this far west.

It is something I stopped doing, by the way, after my friend Rachel pointed out that the one thing about me she loved most, my enthusiasm, was the very thing I kept apologizing for.

This was so good of her to say, I haven't apologized for it ever since. Rachel allowed me to be who I am. She expected me to stay that way.

And I did. For the most part, anyway. All the while and into a second printing of my first book, what drove me was the promise I made to myself: I will sell every copy.

So that's what I did.

And I can still feel the profound sense of accomplishment selling all those books left me with, how full of triumph I was, but, darn it, an awkward emptiness began to loom soon after: *Who am I now that I no longer have a book to sell? Now what?*

And so it goes. And goes. With each new title. To this very day.

And why, over my desk there is a small, handwritten reminder of another message: *Just do the next thing. Stay focused on that.*

The pages have added up today.

On many levels, loyalty has not been an easy topic to tackle, even for me. I haven't talked to my dad in years about anything more than the weather. Long sad story short, some daughters have to find their way in life with or without the support of their dads. That the one man who taught me most in life about loyalty is the man I had to leave behind in order to remain loyal to my*self* is a huge paradox in my life, one I've found more peace with as of late.

But not total peace.

Finding myself in a new city, with a new lifestyle, has been terrifically liberating. It's why I left the fold of my family to move to the opposite coast in the first place.

And though I wasn't fully aware of something else, either, until I sat down to address all this, I can see how expecting an Old World level of loyalty in a developing, transient city like Seattle has tripped me up. In big and painfully idealistic ways. I tell you, it has cost me.

I've been guilty of expecting way too much from my work relationships, even my friendships, deeply attached was I to the idea of making them my new family. And it's why some of my disappointments have festered under my skin for so long.

But living in Seattle has toughened me up, too. Made me stand on my own.

After fifteen minutes of thinking, not writing, just thinking, I return to my father's sense of loyalty. And this comes to me (with a lot of baggage): My only wish is that while my father was setting a loyal, hardworking, straightforward example, he could have enjoyed life more. Enjoyed *me* more. But maybe this, too, is another story.

Or is it?

I think it's why—it *is* why—I married a man whose family goes back three Californian generations, and why Larry has had such an influence on me. I found a way to look at life through the eyes of a man who has always walked his own, if a little asymmetrical, path, in a place of his own choosing, with something other than getting ahead in mind.

I will always be the product of two worlds, trying to bridge the old and the new. Loyalty vs. freedom from its constraints will always be the contrast that will make me feel both rootless and grounded in so many ways. The other day, I found a rusty silver earring faded from time on the beach, washed up from who knows where, and my first thought was, this earring is so *me*.

Writing is such a mental back and forth and sideways. With twice as much surprise this time, I look up from my keyboard. And what do you know? My wish is clear as day.

Just as when I needed to thrust myself forward by publishing my first book, now in this stage of life, I'd like, with the same amount of relish, to move ahead into feeling less desperate to publish my next. I'd also like full self-acceptance and confidence, though I'd settle for more of each, because I know how easy it is to fake all that from behind a microphone without knowing how to do it once I'm back home, tired and under the covers.

So, whenever I don't know where my work is headed (like right now) or what I'm doing in this cold, gray city or where I'm supposed to live, singing "That's Life" centers me, lets me remember not only that spring will come again with a lushness that can't, even in my imagination, be any more beautiful than in Seattle, and reminds me who I am, brings me back to the daughter who can sing at the top of her lungs, *that's what all the people say. . . .*

Then, pushing her glasses up on the bridge of her nose, she remembers a few of her own lyrics, more serious than Sinatra's, maybe: *Right here, within, is your work. Stay loyal to it. It's alive as you make it and as much a home as anywhere. And it's a solid place.*

These lyrics are a godsend.

They are loyal.

They are my commitment.

They are my luck.

Big Dreams

I have only to lay my eyes on the sun creeping lower in the sky and it's as if I can feel myself deflating.

So many years looking up at the sky for proof, any proof whatsoever, that winter is *not* just around the corner—what in the world was I thinking?—has developed into a recurrent issue that, in turn, has developed into a recurrent dream.

In one scenario, I fly to Greece for the winter. In another, to Hawaii.

"Tell me," I say to Larry. "How long do you think I need to dream a dream before it becomes . . ." I look at the vase of Shasta Daisies on my desk ". . . perennial?"

Trying to get Larry to talk first thing in the morning is like pushing a boulder up a hill.

"And how long do you think I have to act on it once it *does*?"

He's watching the morning news. He clicks to mute. Meaning he looks up but says nothing. It's not that he isn't interested in what I have to say. He's just not all that good when it comes to his wife's wondering-about-where-she-should-live all the time. He's more literal, relates to what's real, right in front of him, *visible*, rather than all the hidden sensitivities.

And, poor dear, he's married to a woman who is all about the sensitivities. Which, to be perfectly honest, drives us both crazy sometimes.

Nevertheless, for the past three decades I've been cutting through his Scotch-Irish conversational paralysis. And I have no intention of letting up now.

Finally he says, "You mean like in plants?"

"Just like," I say. "Because isn't it interesting how the fading sun has such an effect on me? Do you think it's biological, in my blood? Or all in my head?"

Silence.

So I say, "But I'm completely done groaning about it."

He looks at me, lowers his chin.

"For today, anyway."

Plus, my Larry hasn't had coffee yet. His face is deadpan. No, not deadpan, incapable. Nothing is all that "interesting" before coffee.

"Well," he finally says, "I recommend you find us somewhere warm to move to then. And while you're at it, somewhere warm where *you* make most of the money."

"Ha. Ha. Ha. Ha. Ha."

I should be stung. But I'm not. He meant to make me laugh. This is how it usually goes when I bring up something my dearest is neither all that shaken by or able to resolve/repair/change. So why talk about it? Why not just push my button and call it a day.

I've acquired new insight as of late: When I think there is maybe one more thing I could say to my Larry after I've already said enough, pushed enough, expressed enough, I need to stop. And think again. And keep my mouth shut, bite back the mere-dozen other things I could say. Because the only thing *he* can possibly say now is, "I'll live wherever you want to live; just make up your mind where that place is."

And that is just so unfair at a time like this.

Because, damn, taking the reins is such a scary thing. Compromise is easier than taking the reins. Taking the reins is so scary, in fact, I've lived in the rain for years because it's where Larry lived when we fell in love. Staying has been easier than uprooting us both. But I'm older now. I like the idea of deciding our future based on what *I* need. Of being followed instead of the other way around.

With no guilt about it, now that's the trick.

I walk outside in my flimsy nightgown. And there, sitting on my tiny balcony over Vine Street, I drink a cup of coffee as if I'm perched on a sunny lanai. I spend the next twenty minutes letting my mind wander. I like to do this before beginning my writing day. It helps pry me open to the minutiae of the moment. For instance, while willing myself to appreciate every bit of warmth still emanating from an après-summer sky, my thoughts, instead, are of what my neighbor will see when he steps out onto his balcony to smoke his first cigarette of the day. And no part of me is still wrapped in some illusion that I look beautiful half naked first thing in the morning.

What a luxury a backyard used to be. Sometimes I miss the privacy of a backyard. And on the off day when my backyard-longing shares equal time with my house-longing, I think about a conversation I had with a friend who is building her first "dream house" out on the Quimper Peninsula. Naturally, the whole thing is costing three times what she thought it would, which can turn a dream into a nightmare pretty quickly.

I took her hands in mine. I listened. I smiled. I wanted to say that, in my experience, dreams come from within, not from a house; that nothing made of sheet rock gets us to where we need to be. Maybe a little closer, but not *there*. How accumulating dream house debt is a slow death if ever there was one. Especially when it comes to being able to choose the kind of creative work she says she wants to do after her "sentence" (her word) at Bank of America is over, the kind of work that will satisfy her soul once the guestroom is painted and the deck is stained red.

But I kept still. I knew she was feeling pretty insecure about the house, that she'd bitten off way more than she could afford, working way too many hours to pay for her dream, so that I wonder just when she'll be able to enjoy the greenhouse and craft room she just had to have.

But it's all part of the grand, big-dream experience, along with paying off the loan to fund it, and sometimes we just have to go through it to get over it.

Not long after that conversation, my husband and I moved out of our house and into a condo close to Seattle's newest big dream: The Olympic Sculpture Park, my new backyard. I like to walk there if only to hear people's reaction to ... well, even if a lot of us can't bring ourselves to call some of the sculptures "art," there's plenty of grass and trees and rules about what we can and can't do which makes me feel right at home, plunked down in my dad's dream yard, the consummate New England lawn where we weren't allowed to play for fear we'd fall into his cherished rose bed.

But isn't there something totally unsatisfying about public art most of the time? All that money given to art-by-committee while working artists are priced right out of the neighborhood.

But who am I to say?

Because the whole dream of a worldly sculpture park is a positive one, better than more condos, that's for sure. I also think, yin-yang, that any attempt to improve our neighborhood or our*selves* by fulfilling a dream is still a good effort. Even if the word "improve" means something distinctly different to everyone I talk to.

There's a man, for instance, new to our building, who, quite candidly, shared his new dream with me. I can't recount his every word, only that he said, quite memorably, how tired he was of the suburbs and dreamed of being part of our "close-knit Belltown community."

I nearly laughed out loud.

I didn't say how we mostly keep to ourselves this side of Denny rather than mingle. How living in such close proximity makes us live even further apart. I thought of saying that real friends, in my experience, take a lifetime to build and community is only what we make it. But I didn't let on. Not a peep.

Because I know how dreams can take our loose ends and tie them off for a while. Besides, people don't want to be afraid of what others will say about their dreams.

All I have to do is think back to know how true this really is.

There was a time when my new dream was to live in a tiny shack in Sequim, Washington, forever, before most of its soft green fields were sold and subdivided. There I was, right out of college, a haughty little East Coast escapee, living my fantasy in the woods with no electricity, no running water, blissfully wallpapering the outhouse, hating when my friends put their reality checks all over my back-to-nature-dream by saying things like, sooner or later, I'd tire of the whole *au naturel* charade.

Hated reality even more when the neighbor guy in overalls tried to warn me that my wooden privy nailed together with carpet tacks would buckle in the rain, that its shit hole wasn't deep enough, that its flimsy cedar sides would shift in places in the heat of summer, tear the wallpaper to shreds, exposing me, my privates; that I'd have to start from scratch, build a new crapper come spring, dig a hole deeper than my height.

But I was much too much in love with my dream to complicate things with *experience*.

And if anyone had told me that I'd be living in a condo some-day—a condo!—had let that little genie slip out of the bottle, well, I likely would have said, "YUK!"

And not a funny "yuk!"

An unbelieving, indignant you-don't-know-a-*thing*-about-me yuk. Incensed.

And I do mean *incensed*.

Guess what? I did it. I took hold of the reins. Now, we live in both Seattle *and* Hawaii. Larry followed. I knew he would. And, it's just like he said, I just had to *decide*.

Still, there is no way not to address what you are thinking.

So, okay, yes, he still makes most of the money.

Empty Nest

It seems that I'm in a period of loss right now.

No one close to me has died or anything, but for the last year, I've spent nearly every waking moment rewriting the last draft of my first memoir.

Memoir. Now there's a word.

It's as if I've been writing about some other woman, a younger woman, who lived not so long ago on one hand. Eons ago on the other.

Then I sent her away.

That's it. Years of work zipped through cyberspace to my editor.

In my head I got up, ran outside and twirled with my arms like Julie Andrews in *The Sound of Music.* In reality, I just sat there not knowing what to do. Or how to feel. *How should I feel?*

I suddenly couldn't believe how empty I felt, how light of head, how much I wanted to call the pages back. There was nothing to do now but wait.

Waiting is the worst part.

I straightened up my desk, brushed off the keyboard, swabbed between the keys with a Q-tip; that's how lost I felt. I remember feeling that if I were a color, I'd be a streak of lipstick smeared past the lips, out of sorts, out of place.

This is the period of time that slices me in half, when I'm not only in between writings, I'm in between selves. Nowhere near my best self, either, when I'm fired up, when a book is in its infancy, when I'm scared, absolutely, but all that fades soon as I begin.

Half of me feels like I need all the focus and discipline in order to survive.

The other half is quite happy to live without that kind of pressure. She fears the only place she knows herself well anymore is cloistered in her office. She needs a break from all that, to disconnect for a while, to kiss her work good-bye.

I can't even fathom how the book pulled off writing itself in the first place. Every writer says the same thing, "I have no memory of writing the book whatsoever." It's as if the harder we work, the less memory we have of working at all. Where our minds go in the long hours each morning is anyone's guess.

And now?

I get a couple of weeks, three if I'm lucky, to add a little spaciousness to my days, partly because I won't feel the weight of a deadline hanging over my head, and partly because I won't be living an intense performer's life and an intense writing life at the same time. It's been great, but I need to separate my writing time from performance commitments.

I will remind myself of this every few days.

And then the email I both await and dread pops up. The subject line reads, if a little indifferently: CORRECTIONS. I lean forward. There is a crucial decision to be made: Open it? Don't?

You would think that because I've been through this process many times, I'd know how to handle the stress better.

Unfortunately, no. Fear is not a feeling you ever get used to.

I stand. Walk away from my desk. Stare outside. To let off steam, I shout at the man with the leaf-blower. (Does anyone but me miss the soothing, swishing sound of a rake and broom?) My relationship with the leaf-blower (both man and machine) is a horrible one.

I clomp back to my office, sit, tap my fingers, inhale, exhale, clear my throat, before finally, resignedly, clicking onto the attachment, every page filled with red lines, dots, arrows that will rip me open, as necessary, first with glaring RED-ness, then with expertise, which may explain why I am, and will always be, in awe of good editors.

But before all this, before I can even get this far, I will think, *No, sorry, I can't do this.*

I will shout "I can't do this!" so loudly it will travel through my office wall and scare my husband, causing him to come running before he sits to listen as I go into overdrive, explaining why I'm convinced whatever I wrote is crap and that coming too close to it all over again will cause me to crumble inside, that I don't deserve to be a writer, that I'm not worthy, that I can't do it, I can't do battle again. It will kill me.

Until I, taker of risks, walk back to the front and go over the text again.

From the top. Page by page.

I read somewhere that courage is like a starfish. It regrows.

Well, it's true for me.

Most of my writing life has been spent waiting for my nerve to regenerate.

This gives me plenty of time to perfect the way I will myself not to overreact when someone asks me what I do and when I say, "I'm a writer," they tell me how much *fun* it must be to be a writer. Before they say something like, "Actually, I have a little book I work on now and again. I'm somewhat of a writer myself."

A *little* book? *Somewhat* of a writer? I don't understand.

"Really?" I'll say, "good for you." But what I'm thinking is how much I envy Joanne, my dentist. No one says to Joanne, "You know, I do a little dentistry on the side. I'm somewhat of a dentist myself."

Would you listen to me? Obviously, I'm in a bit of a mood.

Here is where I'm going to change tack and "count my blessings," as my mother likes to say. Because my work really is going "great guns" (another Mom-ism). In fact, if I stop to think about it, the email from my editor threw me into rewrites so challenged, I felt as though I could write forever. And when the process works like this, there is no better feeling in the world.

I should end here, on a "positive vibe" as my friend Diane would say, but I just have to tell you that other times it feels as if there is no way out of the rewrites, that I'll be lost in them forever, that I'm incapable of finding my way back to real conversation with real people, and, worse, unable to separate my writing life from my real one. Because both keep asking the same questions: Am I grateful that writing is my life? Or is it a curse, all this reflecting? If I'd known when I began what I know now, exactly what being a writer demands, how poorly it pays, the stresses and burdens, the isolation, self-esteem nearing and departing (and so willingly), would I have become a writer at all? Should I continue working on the Next Book that is already trying to sweet-talk me, or move on to things in life that are lighter, that don't demand so much of me?

This has got to be what it feels like to leave your youngest at the bus stop for the first time or your oldest at college for the last.

Any way you slice it, it's an empty nest.

I carry on. I sweep. I dust. I wipe down the kitchen counters again. (Here is where my husband would add that I'm finding him all kinds of extra chores to do.) I sit on my balcony bundled in a blanket, watch the sun slide onto the cedar tops in the orangey way it does this time of year.

It's been a crazy year. I've never been so up and down.

Thank goodness my subconscious took over to remind me that lousy things are going to happen in life, in my career, in general. And my job as a woman, a writer, a wife, a daughter, a friend, is to enjoy the ride anyway. "It's all about the ride," she will say.

Then—noticing, I'm sure, the neediness in my eyes, because moving another book into the world will not include much of the thing I deserve: money—she will add, I know she will: *Remember, you write for another reason, a reason that stays with you long after you've blown your wad, so, please, don't torment yourself about money; it will crush you. And it bores me to tears. And while you're at it, think about what the cost of having work you love is worth. Who could afford to pay you such an exorbitant price anyway?*

And, gratefully, I won't have a comeback to that.

Anna

It was an early evening on a clear September night, the moon rising over a crystal blue lake. Nothing could be more beautiful or expressive of why, the first time I visited Lake Crescent, when I was twenty, I stayed for three months, living about as far west as one can travel in this country without quite leaving it. I swam in the lake, drank from the lake, bathed in it, fell in love with my husband in a tiny cabin on its northeast shore. I came to know, or thought I did, why the first recorded interpretation of the Holy Spirit was not of a man-like nature at all, but "spirit" as the word applies to a body of water, the liquid giver of life. I remember reading this and feeling that at *last* I'd found a faith that made sense to me: We begin in water; we are saved by water. Water is holy.

I'm a believer.

But the lake is not my only story here.

So on with the reason I baptized my toes in my favorite lake again, before I wake tonight and think, *Wait! I forgot to write about Anna!*

And I want to write about Anna.

I also want to write about Womenfest: an annual celebration where women from all over the state of Washington gather in a place called Camp David (I wish they'd rename it), an outdoor recreation camp on Lake Crescent's north shore.

And what is so completely true about this gathering is that the women who attend have lived through careers and kids and marriages and divorces. In other words, we've learned how hard we can make life when we don't trust ourselves more. And we are generous, or generous in the way a lot of us are, that is to say aiming for it but sometimes failing, with an occasional greedy nature, and inclinations toward too much giving so that, from time to time, we are taken full advantage of.

I was invited to give a reading. *I'm so lucky to be here,* I remember thinking. *It's so good!*

Then something bad happened.

I wanted to write about it at the time but somehow I couldn't. I thought I needed to let my steam cool, even as I sit here thinking *why?* Why tamp myself down?

For a minute, a brief one, I even tried to shake it off, the anger that was growing, feeling myself divide in two as a speaker so often does in order to do the work we do, half of me turning into a more suppressed version of candid, the candid that comes with years of experience in how to stand in front of an audience totally exposed without letting the spotlight overwhelm.

And the other half into totally honest no-matter-what.

In this case, there was no brave face to put on. Honest me won out.

I began by telling the audience what I always tell people, that a writer doesn't write in order to convince anyone of anything. We don't put our thoughts down so that others will agree, but to figure out how *we* feel. Writing is like being given soil to grow in. Then, if we become good at what we do, good in terms of knowing our craft, maybe, just maybe, someone will publish our work. We certainly don't do it for the money (that's a good one). "So fasten your seatbelts," I say, "because, like writing, a reading tends to drive me instead of the other way around. It takes the wheel and heads me off where it thinks I should go."

After my first piece, the room went still, a good still, full of nods. I shared the last lines of an op-ed I wrote back in April, 2003 (2003! How long we've been at these wars now!): "My new faith has become this: If a woman suffers because her brother, husband, or son might come home prone in a plastic bag, I support her and politics be damned. That's enough certainty to keep me sane through all this."

Then, like an arrow, a woman shot from the room.

Do you know the feeling when your confidence completely

flip-flops, when you know you've just said the wrong thing, pushed a little too far? *I'm such an idiot; what have I done?*

Even if I've gotten better over the years at not taking things personally, I'd still be lying if I said the speed of the woman's exit didn't hurt my feelings a little. Not only did everyone look in her direction as she flew from the room, but this kind of interruption means I have to work doubly hard to win my audience back. And the dynamic can make you lose your courage if you're not careful. And if your courage fails, believe me, it shows.

On the spot, a speaker has to decide, while facing an audience, whether she's going to say things she needs to say, is paid to say, but some people don't like to hear; tell her listeners exactly how she feels without crossing the line (and lines, I've found, are not clearly marked until it's too late), or wimp out and deal with her topic more gingerly, coat it with sugar, add humor to a serious issue, or remove it, figure out whether the former or latter is the one her audience will respond to seeing as how they are mature women already, about as knowledgeable as they can stand to be, thank you very much.

But pandering makes me nuts; it just does. So most of the time I just deliver my work my way and let the chips fall. And once I make my decision, I can't apologize for my choice. I won't. Not an easy thing, in my experience, especially if one is born female. It's taken me years to get over the assumption that it's my job to try and please everyone, personally, professionally. It's my job to do the best I can do under the existing circumstances, and that's about it. That's all I can do. When I'm finished, it's another success or failure (I've had plenty of both) added to the heap.

As you might have guessed, the woman who ran from the room was Anna.

Anna lives in Port Angeles, a mostly working-class town near the northern end of the Olympic Peninsula, isolated in many ways, where a lot of boys grow up to view the military as a shot at something more, a life adventure, better than signing up at the local paper mill for the next thirty years.

Fast forward past Anna's running out of the room to an hour later when Anna and I sat on either side of a wooden picnic table, our hands around mugs of tea as she shared the reason that she ran out of the room. "I lost a nephew in Iraq. My son came home disabled. I hardly know him now he's so medicated. My other son is about to ship out."

I went still inside. And a part of me, not a small part, wanted to apologize right then for what I'd read aloud.

You can't do that, another part of me protested, *a writer has to be honest or what's the point?*

It wasn't just unsettling sitting across from Anna, I was nervous. And why I would say something as stupid as this, and especially to Anna, is beyond me. But this is what I said: "This war is so fucking crazy! Why aren't we, every single one of us, taking to the streets in numbers too big to ignore?" *Oh my god,* I thought, *you are quoting Helen Reddy!*

I did wonder for a split second, before rattling on, if there is a rule of etiquette I wasn't aware of when speaking to a mother of a veteran. Was there something I was supposed to say? Not say?

In the end, the way I enter the surf is to dive in. Those swimmers who walk into the sea slowly, wincing? I want to push them from behind.

At first, I tried to write an account of the evening as if no one would read it. That way, I'd be sure and say just how angry I was, get to the center of it, write so quickly it wouldn't occur to me to censor.

But who am I kidding? I *wanted* people to read it. I want people to read pretty much everything I write. This is as true an admission as I've ever written.

And there's more.

I not only want people (someone, *any*one) to read my work, I want them to *get* it, to get *me*, to place me on their bedside table in order to read another paragraph when they sit up in the middle of the night because they can't sleep.

Eventually, I had to walk away from Anna.

Before I did, we laughed about something or other, because some-times the only healthy thing to do is to laugh, and then we hugged each other goodbye. I got my coat, checked the time, circled my scarf around my neck, found my keys, thanked the coordinators and started for home. And, yes, I could still feel my anger rising, but I had to drive to Seattle, pack, take a cab to the airport in order to fly out in the morning to San Francisco. And it's hard to focus on logistics when you want to throw the furniture out the window.

Or cry. Because tears overwhelm me; I don't bounce back as quickly as I used to. I am not talking about whiny tears, but when every hope deserts me, as it does whenever I think about how we've done it again—we've marched into war, expecting our kids to kill people again—now wait just a minute, how on earth, I'd really like to know, can anyone think it's okay to do this?

They say there are stages we go through when something shocks us. First, a wave of fear shoots up our spine. The second is also a wave, but fear supposedly squares off with anger at this point. Then anger takes center stage, becomes a solo act, totally fired up. I've forgotten what happens next, but something akin to fire happened inside me that night.

I couldn't stop thinking how many men in the world seem to desire war. That's right, *desire*. Because I know men well enough to say one true thing about them: If they don't desire to do something, it's pretty dang hard to get them to do it.

But I couldn't let my fire burn me up completely. I had too many audiences to face. I couldn't afford to go limp with anger. I'm paid to be *up*.

Yet, I couldn't move past it, either. Anger kept sweeping me back.

I couldn't stop thinking about Anna. It's one thing to witness war from the safety of our office or living room couch, but when you meet a mother of a soldier, well, Anna made me face these wars again until I could *feel* how, before our kids enlist, they are our sons and daughters, intact, with next-door lives. They are rolling down the sidewalk on a skateboard, goalkeepers of the soccer team, with moms like Anna.

Which is why I can finally say in my normal voice, *Thank you, Anna, for waking me up.*

And that I am such a fool. I've grown too used to these wars like everyone else, numb. Now I'm angry again.

And that's good!

True, I may never know how hard it is to be the mother of a disabled or deceased son or daughter, but I do know the remorse of too much apathy. It only took me thirty years to forgive myself for being too cowardly to march against Vietnam with my peers. I was afraid. Afraid of what my father would do if he found out. (I feared my father. Do you remember the scene in *The Godfather* when the man takes a belt to his wife? Think belt-to-daughter whenever words failed him. Add to it the fact that English was his second language while, even as a young girl, I'd already begun to rely on words as offense. Words were *my* weapons. My tongue struck back.)

That night, oh man, the drive out of Port Angeles was eerie. I didn't think I believed in such things, but I have to tell you, everything I saw felt like a manifestation.

A wisp of smoke rose over town and hovered.

It was only mill smoke, but I imagined the cloud as a young soldier returning home to say something like: *Hey, there's Civic Field where we used to play baseball! Remember? Remember? And Gordy's, where we went for pizza after the game. And there's the elementary school; it hasn't changed a bit. And there's my bicycle in front of the basketball court. And my skateboard overturned on Mom's front lawn.*

I forgot to put it away again, sorry.

Faith

What is it my husband is always saying, especially after some catastrophe happens and I want to know why life is so unfair?

"There's no answer to why some things happen."

Even after all our years together, he can still underestimate my determination, how far I will delve to find an answer, even in the worst scenarios, no matter how long it takes. And it's taken me until now to realize my stubborn determination is really nothing but faith.

Good old faith.

Even if an Italian girl suspects, from a very young age, that faith in God the Father, is no more than faith in another male authority, there are still some things about being raised Roman Catholic that will stick, regardless.

True, I look back and see a long, narrow guilt trip.

But the more I mull over the teachings of the church, the more I see how I was left with self-reliance of the simplest nature: Down deep, I still believe things will eventually work out. It's the one thing the church gave me for keeps, and I try, to the best of my indwelling nature, not to over-think it. Other than that, I've stopped trying to reconcile the constructive and destructive parts of Roman Catholicism, having been saddled with plenty of both.

Besides, by the end of this writing, I'll likely be right back to the beginning of my fundamental thought about all religion anyway, that it has less to do with the search for a spiritual path than with man's quest for a scapegoat, one with no actual presence, no way for the human eye to see if anyone is really there or not. An invisible fall guy is the *perfect* fall guy. Anyone more real wouldn't do. Anyone more real would expect, and possibly force, us to behave ourselves.

And yet whenever I'm feeling totally comfortless, it's back to the House of Faith for me, as in my mother's newest interpretation of it. Technically still a Catholic, even she, after years of living in California, then in Hawaii, has absorbed a more cosmic definition, along with her Chinese herbs and fruit smoothies, and now prefers to think of herself as "spiritually whole."

Still, without a doubt, and no matter what depiction she uses, she is the most faith-devoted woman I know. Even so, when she takes my question, wonder, or curiosity and places it "in God's hands," I still cringe. Every time.

Simultaneously, I'm relieved. *Whew! Take my problems, holy man; you're welcome to them.*

Besides, in my mother's presence, no good will ever come from doubting the size of God's hands. Even I, the eternal skeptic, can see how in her advancing years, they are just about all that holds her to earth now. I might still be surprisingly clueless about many aspects of mother/daughter, but I know my mother's limit when it comes to questioning her faith. It's a boundary line clear as the nose on her face.

Even so, when I told her about the column I was writing about the untimely death of Kristine Fairbanks, and she said, "God takes the good ones first," I was stunned. Trying to wrap a faithful cliché around such a tragedy made me mad, and I told her so. I don't like pat answers and I don't generally like to spend time with people who rely on them. This has been something of a problem since my mother relies on them all the time.

Funny, though. To this day, whenever I think of Kristine's murder, my mother's words are the only ones that prove helpful. Especially when I look at the tiny photo of Kristine I cut out of the newspaper to add to my woman-hero collage. Her face is there, along with Mother Teresa, Madeline Albright, Benazir Bhutto, Malala Yousafzai, and my Aunt Connie who sent me a check to cover the cost of a much-needed root-canal.

Not enough of us, even in the state of Washington, know the story of Officer Kristine Fairbanks, how she worked alone in the woods, patrolling—what did I read?—300,000 acres of public lands with her K-9 partner? How for more than twenty years she tracked down thieves and poachers, the lone K-9 officer in the state before being shot and killed by an unhinged man at the Dungeness Forks Campground in the Olympic National Forest.

But I want to share another story about Kristine mostly because I need you to know there are real heroes in the twilight woods of western Washington, not just the creepy phony vampires Hollywood is cashing in on.

First, Kristine was courageous, courageous in ways I will never be. The first time *I* hiked alone into the Olympic wilderness was the last. I stopped to pick a handful of blackberries. I heard someone *else* picking berries. *What the. . . ?* When I peered around the bush, I saw a bear. And, holy Christ, the bear saw *me*. Both of us jumped back, inhaled a gasp, and ran, terrorized, in opposite directions.

This was moments before I met Kristine. Way down trail, she asked me why I was running. I told her. Actually, I couldn't *stop* telling her. I was overflowing with adrenaline in my snappy new hiking boots. She smiled and said the bear was likely more afraid of me, making obvious the fact that bears were everything she knew as real. And smart.

As was I, another tourist. Minus the smart.

This is why, after I stared at her newspaper photo, I thought about the whole bear story for the first time in years. And the only words that have helped me wrap my mind around what happened to Kristine are: *God takes the good ones first.*

The implication that Kristine is needed elsewhere helps calm the tightness in my chest. Skepticism is one thing, but when someone remarkable is killed, I need to believe in *some* kind of higher power: *The problems, the endless problems, Kristine! We need your help from above.*

It's a lifelong process, letting faith in.

Writing about Kristine, I feel something warm and revealing working its way down.

Slowly.

Faithfully.

Election Night

Last night I went to my first election night party, a celebration on Upper Queen Anne—as opposed to Lower Queen Anne, a distinction anyone who lives, or aspires to live, on the highest peak of inner Seattle will remind you of if you presume to forget and want to think of the entire Queen as only one zip code. It's not a mistake you want to make.

I think you get what I'm trying to say. The room was filled with well-off people. Well-off white people. Although I'm not trying to prove anything by saying so.

Well, maybe a little. Queen Anne is the kind of neighborhood most people, black or white, could easily fall for. But more white people can afford it, so they do.

I distinctly remember the day I fell for Queen Anne myself. It was the day I had to bag the idea that living in the trenches of downtown was any fun anymore. It took only one stroll through Queen Anne's storybook streets. That did it for me. Between the early hour when commuters flee down the hill to work at Google or Microsoft or Amazon, and fly up it again eight to ten hours later, a crow's caw is the only sound in the air. Not easy to find anywhere, let alone in a city, and perfect for a writer in search of quiet.

Unfortunately, a small town neighborhood within the perimeters of a huge city comes at a huge price. If only I could afford it.

Still, that particular leisurely walk was full of the kind of awareness a neighborhood can dole out in any season, in any number of ways until, all at once, it feels as if you know where you belong next.

Because I yearn for quieter streets. I yearn for a proper neighborhood and a privately owned video store with an owner who knows my likes and dislikes (no horror, no special effects). I yearn for a local bookstore, a grocery store with a checker who remembers my name. This is the kind of connection that is important to me.

What I don't miss is a small town in isolated form, where too much power is held in too few hands, like corporate America, which is weird because the small town I lived in worked pretty hard to keep all things corporate at bay. I had my romantic illusions of what small-town living is really like. And some of it matched my fantasies. But as the years went by, more and more of it didn't. I gave it my best shot, but it started to feel as if there was not enough space for me to grow. I can't blame the locale or the people or even myself. The dissatisfaction was my own failed root system. My roots wouldn't *take*. It was the strongest self-acknowledgment I'd ever known, and I still feel completely sure of my decision to move back to an urban environment. I guess some of us are better off in cities, that's all.

Still, a dose of small-town romanticism is not a bad thing for anyone. And that's what Queen Anne felt like to me that first hopeful day, like an updated version of my small-town fantasy, more to my liking. Surrounded by a larger, glorious, horrendous city, full of glowing features and dark, dark failings.

I can't afford to move up there yet, dammit, but I can dream.

Maybe I should have taken you inside the party straight away, but I needed to get my thoughts together about where the party was held, not evade them, which would only make them more obvious in the long run.

First of all, the house was grand. E*nor*mous. Front porch, back deck, garage, dormers, skylights, a widow's walk, two huge terra-cotta pots on either side of the front door, posed with pampa grass shooting up and ivy spilling down.

I heard people laughing inside. I watched through the window for a minute, trying to picture the host in his skivvies, an ancient remedy that still works for me when I have to address powerful men of a certain age. One look at two veiny legs and a belly pouch can pretty much raze the playing field to a level I can handle. I imagined his wife who'd offer me a cocktail in a beautiful dress. Then I'd hightail it to the buffet table.

I took another deep breath, peered through the bay window

into the living room where CNN blared from one huge flat screen, MSNBC from another. The room was painstakingly made festive with bouquets of flowers, hors d'oeuvres on trays, fine wines and chocolates. I searched for the hostess who, after one short conversation we had while shopping at Anthropology, invited me to what she enthusiastically called her Obama Party. I wore my best, body-hugging, all-silk, just below the knee dress that has, more than once, transformed me into an absolutely confident woman. And this may be taking my thoughts a bit far, and not a Seattle-kind thing to say, or even true for all I know, but as far as I could gather after a few introductions, no one at the party (old friends, a loose set of new friends like me, friends of friends, and family) has ever lived next door to, or quite possibly ever *befriended*, a black person.

Or, for that matter, an Italian.

But none of that mattered, and that's what made the night so exciting. Everyone was cheering, *sincerely*; you can tell the difference. We watched the countdown with ears tuned, feet planted. The weight of the last eight years had collapsed our insides, we said. No shortage of anxiety, we griped.

Forty-four years after the Civil Rights Bill was signed, we'd gathered to pour champagne for a man who felt like the best leader the world could deliver us (after Hillary, I thought to myself, but I was determined not to be a spoilsport). Half black, half white, a mysterious mix of ethnicity, definitely the best kind of politician, we agreed, and all our glasses clicked again.

"Not to mention," I whispered to the ballet-slender woman beside me, "what a well sculptured handsome he *is*, tight all over, his pants look like they could slide right off his hips."

"I've had a few thoughts myself," she said.

Did I mention the stars were out, the skyline unusually twinkly? All this made it particularly easy to say how much we love the guy. "When he speaks, I listen," I said, "I trust."

Well part of me trusts, anyway, but I kept a lid on the other part. The part that knew he'd eventually have to lie about something. Things are too out of whack for total honesty. But the man doesn't make the world seem any less sane, so you could say when I cast my vote I was desperate for any sign of credibility. Which reminds me of something I heard an actor say once, how a huge part of life is figuring out which liars we should cast aside and which are worth loving. It validated everything I believe, how some lies, told by others as well as by me, have affected my life in ways unexpectedly good and bad.

But the weirdest thing is, seeing as how we'd all gathered to cheer on a black man—though every time I hear the press call him "black" I think *why leave his mother out of the picture?*—the difference from how I thought about prejudice before that night, versus now, has grown rather than receded.

For instance, I'm more conscious of what lies ahead in terms of confronting, say, my own mother's narrow-mindedness, or this question: Is it just as intolerant to walk away from a friend because she adamantly said to me, "Mary Lou, this *country* is not ready for a black president!" And, because I know her so well, I knew that by emphasizing the word "country" she was, in fact, talking about herself. But more than that, and harder for me, is how closed she is generally, how unwilling she is to confront the prejudice I know she feels. So here's one for you, do I remember that she has stood by me through a decade of thick and thin, and accept her, prejudice and all, which is the only way a friendship has a chance of enduring?

Or take another tack?

Like the tack I took at the party.

This is what happened: I was standing next to an elderly woman obviously thrilled to see the electoral votes tally up. But I could hardly believe what she yelled next, "I can't believe we just elected a colored man!"

A gasp filled the room. *Colored? Did she just say colored?*

Oh, how I wish I'd let it go, taken into account her age and the heft of so many world changes stacked on her mid-eighties shoulders, and kept a socially correct silence like everyone else. But I took it upon myself to "help" her. For whatever reason, I spoke up. I also embarrassed her. Which is a far cry from helping.

As soon as the words came out, "Um, excuse me, we don't say

colored anymore, we say *black* or we say *African American,*" I tried to apologize. (Even though my friend Elaine, *my* only black friend, truth told, other than Charles who is my best black friend, tells me all the time she hates the term African American. "I ain't never been to Africa, I ain't never going to Africa. I'm black. Call me black. Ain't nothin' wrong with black!") I've regretted my actions ever since. It's one of those things I'll always feel especially crummy about.

Time to wrap this up. Because I want to get to the best part of last night.

The most interesting part of the evening was not watching a new man become president, but meeting the Pakistani cab driver who drove me home after. I watched in awe as he hustled over while yelling at another driver who also wanted my fare, a Sikh whose white turban suddenly paled compared to the ferocious red of his face as he verbally fought back, reminding me how business is done in most of the world.

"Hold on guys," I said, not wanting to return home guilt-ridden times *two* because I was forced to choose one driver over another, both reminding me how living in Seattle has buffered me from such open fighting for turf, made me more sensitive to it, while they handle fighting just fine by throwing up their arms, cursing, moving on, and to hell with excuses.

The next part was even better.

While underway my driver, very calm and well-mannered now, laughed when I complained about the last eight years of American politics. Then, after inhaling a rather large breath, he wagged his finger at his rearview mirror and scolded, "Life has no room for self-pity! You must be grateful! Here in this great country of yours, you elect a bad president, you admit you have done so, and then you elect a good man, all in eight short years. This is wonderful!" And then he said it again, "This is wonderful! In my country things have been bad for centuries!"

His outcry caused me to reach for my tiny notebook, jot down in a hurry: *Is this what happens when we have too much of too much too much of the time? Do we turn on ourselves out of guilt? Why do we take ourselves, our petty problems, so seriously? Why do we forget to thank our good fortune openly and often? Don't we get that our advantages are amazing to people from all over the world who would do just about anything to have a shot at them?* I don't think I exhaled while writing these words.

"You're right!" I yelled back. "No more sniveling about the past."

"It would be a start," he said, politely.

Thy Neighbor: Round I

Helplessness

NOVEMBER

This morning, in the elevator, things with my neighbor suddenly turned uncomfortable.

To be honest, resentment had already begun to build.

Like dried out grass next to the freeway, once a cigarette gets tossed the smoldering may go on for hours, but eventually the fire erupts.

Let's go back a little. Where the spark fanned into flames.

Understand, I've always had a soft spot for guitars. I remember vividly how many hours it took me to get the hang of a single chord. Still, I welcomed the challenge, loved playing, couldn't imagine giving it up.

But that's exactly what I did and here's why: Around the time I was learning to play, I was also learning how to be married, the most difficult dance for two. The long practice sessions when my fingertips burned from pressing into strings, I was equally distracted by marriage's rhythm which, I soon came to find, needs a lot of practice time as well. Because it is work, good work, the best, but it is still work. And there are only so many hours in a day.

A certain confidence comes from paring down, of finding a way to hold on to what's most important while letting go of the rest, and I was just beginning to learn the importance of this concept in my early married days.

It was only a year or so later that the reason I stopped playing music became even clearer to me. Whenever I'd see a guitar, I saw how my decision to stop playing music stood for leaving behind one life, a single one, to move into another, coupled. Selling my guitar was not so much a line drawn, but a line drawn in warm white sand after I hitchhiked to Mexico with my new husband right after the ceremony.

So young, so broke, so in love.

On one side was my evening practice time, an hour minimum after dinner *even on my honeymoon.* This, after an hour of writing, an hour of dancing.

On the other stood my husband waiting to take my hand and walk with me on the beach outside our flimsy, roach-infested casita.

I may have been young, barely twenty-one, knowing nothing at all about what life would throw at me, but I suddenly carried a knowledge of music vs. marriage in my head. I just did. My husband thought I was joking when I told him I was going to stop playing my guitar, but I *wasn't* joking. He would never ask me to give up something I loved; that's not the kind of partner he is and why I agreed to marry him in the first place. It's just that I knew if I wanted marriage to be first in my life, or anywhere close, I would have to make sure I made that happen myself.

Turns out it wasn't that easy to walk away from my guitar. I went back to it twice before leaving it behind for good, like people return to lovers before they're finally able to jilt. Change is slow. Cold turkey is not the way it happens for most of us. We have to wiggle it back and forth gently, patiently, before it gives. Like moving a huge ceramic urn after years of rain has welded it to the sun deck. If you try and force it, god, what a mess.

Finally, it does budge, and I see how letting go of my guitar marked a beginning of my paring down on a whole new level, how we sometimes have to let go of one thing we love in order to embrace something we love even more, a deeper understanding of the need to hone as we grow if we want to master something, which I did.

Ending my music was the true beginning of my deeper commitment to writing, yes, but I remember it most as the day I married my husband, Larry, more than the day I actually did. I began to see the real truth of transitions, how they shift on their own time and stake nothing on a wedding date, how you have to toss the notion that a silly ceremony can show you the way.

Today we live in a small, rather sparingly built, condo beneath a novice guitar player who likes to practice at midnight. And even after sharing my own guitar dependency, the sound of someone practicing at midnight is still something that, upon first hearing it, made me foresee a big problem. I live in fear of not getting enough sleep and having to face writing my pages blurry eyed and feeble headed. "Call me the sound police," I said huffily to my sleeping Larry, "but when someone plays his guitar this late on a *week* night what we have is a situation."

"Sorry," he answered flatly, "your call cannot go through at the moment. Please try again later."

Night after sleepless night, I've had to remind myself that a city dweller needs to preserve her protests for the truly intolerable noises and conditions of urban life. Like, say, when a tribe of frat boys, in from the suburbs on a Saturday night, goes ballistic under our window sill or uses our building entry as a urinal in the interminable hour after last call.

But the late-night plucking was too much. Self-pity gave way. I surrendered to the urge to do something. There is a fantastic thrill when you give in to the idea that any action is better than letting rage collect. I'm a petite woman, five foot two, a hundred and five pounds give or take, but there are certain times when my need to act is enormous. It gets the best of me.

Don't give in; it's only a guitar; you'll be okay, I heard myself warn.

But I wasn't okay.

All the way up the flight of stairs I remained relatively calm. I didn't pound on his door and wave my hands around while he followed my gesticulations with his eyes, anger making me say terrible things. No, I strove for an easier confrontation, relying on my pink Post-it pad for support.

Beginning with a polite apology—*I'm sorry to have to ask but*—I asked him to consider practicing earlier in the day and stuck it to his door after peering out both sides of the stairwell to be sure no one saw me.

One of the worst things that can happen between neighbors, just ask anyone who has tried, is to point out what annoys you, even in fun, about their noise, their pet, their habits. Whether your neighbor's dog is dropping its business in your yard, or you live in an apartment and noise is the trouble, as it mostly is, once the complaint is vocalized the relationship is forever doomed. Even if things are civil and considerate at first, even if you leave each other laughing about how no-big-deal these things are, neighbors hold grudges in ways I never would have imagined. I've been observing this for years in my old neighborhood as well as in my new one, and I'm not sure I understand it, but I've come to accept that where there is possession, there *is* war.

Oh God!

He knew the note came from me. But how? He has three other sets of neighbors, each right next door.

In the awkward proximity of our elevator, a pair of thick eyebrows faced me to ask, point blank, if the note came from me.

My face, I remember, went very still. I'm almost positive I let out a squeak. "Oh ... yes, it was me," I said, somehow finding my voice, abashed to learn I had no clue how to handle such a confrontation, how to stand my ground. I could think of no other words than what I was thinking: "I think it's selfish to practice your guitar so late at night when most of us have to work in the morning."

He promised, in more of a patronizing than conciliatory tone, not to play in the "wee hours of the morn, ma'am," (ma'am? nice one) and I thanked him (through clenched teeth). Because what I fear he meant, as far as I could tell, is something more along the lines of, *You sound like my mother.*

Anyway, it's amazing how long it takes certain messages to sink in, but once they do, they go in deep. After that, change is pretty quick. (Like when suddenly, after wearing thigh-high leather boots outside of my jeans, I realize in an instant, while passing a windowpane, that I'm ten years too old to carry off the look.)

Maybe ill-will between a musician and a writer is simply the inevitable high-rise consequence. My truest pleasure is in silence and I have no business living in a city in the first place, other than the fact that I can't handle small towns or find any meaning whatsoever in a suburb.

Why not just invest in good earplugs, then? What's really going on?

I think I know.

I've been turning my focus on my inner world again. Essential for a writer, true, but I need to get a grip on it every once in a while or it gets out of hand. Getting upset with my neighbor is easier than thinking about the worldly issues that are making me crazy, to blame some guy with a tin ear rather than mankind's daftness; it could well be that simple. Helplessness is an emotion, too, strong as every other one. How can there ever be peace on earth if I can't even get along with my neighbor?

Besides, I'm not the perfect neighbor that's for sure. I fully expect one of my actions to annoy the hell out of the man below me. For example, when I run my washer at midnight knowing the spin cycle vibrates the floor causing, I bet, his nerves to chafe with disbelief. Or when a really good Motown song comes on Pandora and I turn up the volume and dance like there's no tomorrow? Well, eventually I'm going to hear about it.

As well I should.

Stay tuned.

Thy Neighbor: Round II

Mercy

Midnight.

I stare out my bedroom window through a shield of snowflakes, counting how many times the Space Needle elevators rise and descend. I've been longing for a winter storm just like the one we're having, the lull that comes in a white hush of snow, the city silenced.

Except for *him*.

I don't think I can take much more of this.

I've never once been late paying my condo dues. I stopped running my dishwasher and washer/dryer after eight o'clock and, as of late, I only dance on the carpeted part of the living room floor, even when my feet yearn to break bigger steps. Doesn't this give me the right to a little quiet on a weeknight from the night owl who shares my four hundred square feet of flooring (his) and ceiling (mine)?

But I don't want to complain. Again. I fear being labeled a complainer, a *New Yorker*. It's happened before. People talk. People love to talk. People talk all the time, especially about the newcomers. Especially a newcomer who, in a fit of passion, forgot to voice her grievance at the monthly board meeting in a polite manner: *So, um, do you think maybe it would be okay to talk to the man who keeps playing his guitar at midnight, please?* Which, under pressure, clashes with my instincts in a big way. The real me sounds more like, *Christ! What is your problem? Do something about this guy, already! I've asked you a frickin' million times.*

I'll never be beyond talking like this. I have to curb myself living in Seattle.

I have to curb myself a lot.

I throw back the covers and sit up. I fret this is going to happen every night until my neighbor learns his seven basic chords. And then what?

I feel it rising: Dread of the Next New Noise, the one that will happen every morning, every day, every night from now on. Anyone who lives in a city knows of the dread of which I speak. Noise is the largest downside to city life. According to the EPA, the intensity of urban noise approximately doubles every six years.

Every six years.

But, the thing is, there is so much to worry about already. I'm pretty sure there has always been a lot to worry about, but this is my time on earth. And when I'm this upset, I have a habit of not being able to imagine the worries that came before mine; my worries are by far the worst worries ever. "This time of night!" I yell at Larry who can sleep through anything ... except my yelling at him. "He can't possibly be practicing his guitar!"

"Says who?"

The trick is, if I want him on my side when I complain, is to rub his back. I scoot over to rub his back.

"I don't even hear it. Just close your eyes and try to sleep. I have a deposition in the morning."

An aside: On every level, I get that marriage is a good thing for people, even if I can't exactly feel it right at the moment. Even if I lie here letting my thoughts of younger days come back to me when my bed was my own. But it'll pass. It always passes. A little blip is all, a short, like electricity flickering off for a second. Because he's amazing, really, right here beside me thirty years later, still taking up most of my bed.

I close my eyes tight.

Open them again.

The strumming is still there.

It is still annoying.

Now I'm up, writing this column instead of sleeping and I'm thinking two things simultaneously: One is that I want to thank *City Living* for asking me to write a monthly column. When I was new at column-writing, I had no idea, none, how long it can take to make it seem as if it takes half an hour, tops, to collect one's thoughts into a focused, relaxed editorial.

Secondly, and on the positive side of city living, I want to add that, in general, condo-hood is a satisfying way to live. For one thing, we don't have to mow or weed anything. And there's always some neighbor making noise, so it's never lonesome.

Still, all in all, most of us don't want to be at odds with our neighbors. So I'm marching upstairs this very instant to talk ever so nicely to mine. Face to face. No email. No text. No Post-It. No elevator disadvantage. I'll move this forward. I will make this right, I will fuse the two halves of our misunderstanding. They will meet. They will connect.

I nearly talk myself out of going up there.

But the strumming this late at night when people need to be up early?

Go! Before you change your mind. Just go!

I wish I could relax about this. I really do. But there is this insistence, this need that longs for quiet, that doesn't want to accept this modern world it finds itself in, that refuses to grasp the magnitude of sound, couldn't care less about any more technology (enough already!), ties itself in knots, tells me I must hoof it upstairs to keep it from going gaga. It wants what it wants: air without noise. *What's that noise? Who's making that noise?*

Okay, dumb-ass, you can't practice your Mick Jagger at midnight!

I scold him all the way up the stairwell, back down again, all the way up.

Three firm knocks at his door. I don't sound like the police or anything, but I give a serious enough pound. I mean business.

Oh, for Pete's sake. My hands and knees start to shake. I'm paralyzed. I turn to run, but he opens the door. Seeing me, he shakes his head. There is mutual disgruntle. We share a *humph*. And then he says, "Please come in."

And I think, *why not?*

⌒

Life lessons are subtle. Even when complex.

Turns out, my good neighbor is not rude or discourteous. It is not his intention to drive me crazy. *Why would you even think such a thing?*

My neighbor is a veteran. And, as a result, nearly deaf.

And, as soon as he said so, my shame lowered its eyelids and sighed, tried to forget the half-crazed woman climbing the stairwell in a huff, in a *bathrobe*, the wild woman she just was.

He went on to tell me he's been an insomniac since his first tour of duty and that the only thing that calms him is playing his guitar. Having come so close to death, lived through so much death, he needs more of what makes him feel most alive, *music*.

Which is exactly how I feel about writing and dancing, but I didn't say so because, suddenly, everything about my life seemed so naïve and small.

I watched his face, the way he glanced down at his feet when he spoke, which I found terribly sweet since I do the same thing when I'm uncomfortable. I kept looking for the kind of guy who says what you want to hear, the guy I remembered in the elevator, for any deception beneath his expression and I couldn't find any.

Because there was none.

And just like that, a few womanish tears arrive because it's emotionally impossible for me not to cry at times like this. I cried because the whole escapade had gone on for months and I was startled to learn it's all been ... a gift.

That's right, a gift.

To practice forgiveness.

And mercy. If you are blessed by the company of a young man who has been sent off to war and made it back alive, you surrender.

We talked, an hour at least, because once you begin a midnight conversation about war's evils and petty politics it's hard to stop, long enough for him to tell me something I'm sure a lot of you already know, but I didn't, not the exact figures anyway: that the 9/11 hijackers spent half a million bucks to attack the towers, whereas all our attempts to prevent another attack has cost our country billions. Bil-lions! And we are still spending. "Attacks cost nothing compared to the price of defense," he said. "Part of the price turned out to be my ability to sleep."

I hugged him goodbye.

"I'll practice earlier," he said, my exemplary neighbor, squeezing my arm a little. Then he opened the door and I went back to bed, exhausted.

I could sleep through anything.

For instance, let's just say there was a guitar strumming softly above me, although I hope not, but, honestly, I can't even hear it.

The Waiter

Anyone who has chosen to spend the holidays by taking a glorious, stress-free getaway with their spouse instead of visiting either set of in-laws or, for that matter, any family whatsoever, knows how hard it is to inform your mother/mother-in-law of your decision, how the call can play heavy on your conscience for days before you make it, as well as for days after (afraid going in, shamefaced coming out).

It weighs on you.

That is, right up until the moment you receive the sense of relief that comes from knowing you've just done something really good for yourself.

Oh, and your partner, of course.

For some of us, the choice gets easier. For others it would be an unspeakable alternative.

As it was for our waiter in Santa Fe last Christmas. For days I've been walking around with him in my head, his wide red cummerbund over a white dress shirt, his Latin accent and manner, a gold cross around his clean-shaven neck, hair so black and luminous it shone in the candlelight; it was easy to look into the mirror of him.

Larry and I flew off to the desert to spend the holiday under a pocket of blue sky in a hacienda I read about in a travel magazine, a desert world far from our rainy one. It was hard, with the rain pouring down and the heat turned up, to imagine flying from our weather to the opposite in only a couple of hours.

No internet access. No phones. The definition of holiday has become this for us. Warm sun/no work/no plans/no itinerary.

I respect the kind of care our mothers doted on the holidays, am in absolute and total admiration of all the work and time they put in. But it's not me. Nothing on God's green earth could make me do it. Running away from all of it lets me remember how joyful celebration is supposed to feel: free, spontaneous.

To remember the waiter's exact words would be a stretch. It's more like I remember his attitude: *It seems impossible that you are here in this restaurant on Christmas Eve, instead of at your family's home with your mother and father who sacrificed so much for you.*

"Just the two of you?" he asked with a thick, professionally cheerful, accent.

Beneath his smile, the word "just" was there, implying. At least that's how it felt to me. Probably because a sliver of guilt was still poking at me between my shoulder blades, a feeling I wanted to keep under wraps because even a trace of it can curdle a celebratory mood quicker than when my father used to tell my mother she was too fat just as she was about to reach for another pizzelle after she'd spent the last week making stacks of them by hand.

Or maybe I've constructed a wall of defense against the word after so many years of traveling alone and, when the stress of performing is over, treating myself to a wonderful meal. But nothing makes the fun of entering a new restaurant collapse faster than the question, "*Just* you?" When, clearly, anyone with half a brain can see that, yes, I'm alone. And why? Because I've just came from revealing myself to a room full of strangers so that my aloneness feels like the greatest luxury in the world, *so bring me the wine list. And don't you dare clear the other table setting. Just leave it.*

But I had never experienced the "just" question when dining with my husband. I suppose to a lot of people, dining as a couple is as close to dining alone on Christmas Eve. And yet, I didn't find the waiter's eyes judging. In fact, the reverse was true. I know he didn't mean to embarrass us. But for a second I did imagine he was about to cross himself and I'd spend the rest of the week thinking, *Forgive me, Mom.*

And it should be noted that I had just completed my first nonfiction book, a memoir about the friendships in my life, sitting down morning after morning for the past two years to reveal my own shortcomings, so I felt *in my bones* that I didn't want to look too far inside myself for a long, long while.

So, even though I didn't want to, mentally, I started to object to our waiter.

Especially after his next question. "Your family is at home?"

Dammit. Words are swords. They stab. I shook my head. I cleared my throat. "We *are* our family," I said. It was something I'd gotten used to saying, was comfortable saying by then, but it was clearly awkward for him. Just as it is for most anyone from the third world—gasp, no children?!

He stared.

So I made a face, crinkled my nose, and scrunched my shoulders.

He stared.

Do not ask me another question other than what I'll be drinking.

He paused for another moment and then, after snapping my napkin and placing it on my lap, said, "I had to leave my family behind. To come to this country."

Now here it is, years later, and I'm still thinking about what he said next. I'm paraphrasing a little but his message was clear, even though I know he was struggling to be kind, and that it was just as awkward a conversation for him as it was for me: "My people leave family behind to find work."

Oh, man. I pretended not to care.

But, shoot, I did care. Especially every time I looked over at the Christmas tree with its lovely ornaments, a reminder of everything I love about the holiday. What I don't love is the endless cycle of searching for the perfect gift for my mother and falling short and trying harder the next year and falling short again. Or feeling like it, anyway. And the fatigue that overwhelms me whenever I watch her trying to make everything perfect for everyone else.

For courage, I took my husband's hand. And to my own eternal appreciation, I remember the highly ridiculous words I finally found: "And some of us leave home to find our*selves*."

"Ay," he said. "My parents will come. That's why I'm working two jobs. So my parents will come." The air inside the restaurant felt too hot all of a sudden.

Okay, so unfair to play the two-jobs-so-parents-will-come card. Especially when my truth runs in the opposite direction. "You know what?" I said. "I *don't* want my parents to come."

True. But I shouldn't have said it.

And maybe that's *why* I said it. I wanted to be free of the one person in the room who kept reminding me of the Christmas happening elsewhere. So my husband and I could be alone together, privately.

To this day I don't know if the waiter, or my husband for that matter, sensed as I did, how much I needed to wipe the whole other reality of Christmas from my thoughts in order to go with the one right in front of us about to be served on hand-painted plates from Mexico. If the waiter said one more word, I feared my every thought would wander to the table we were missing from. So I had to say something dismissive, anything, to get the waiter to leave us alone.

In a mirror, I watched my eyes watching the waiter as he strode across the dining room. He was nodding his head, I noticed that, and then he filled his cheeks with air and released it soon after. I don't think I've ever watched a waiter for so long. It was as if I couldn't stop, so I purposely turned my head away and picked up my fork.

We'd traveled to a high desert instead of flying home to feast on the seven fishes my mom will serve, has always served, alongside the pasta with homemade tomato sauce. "I can almost hear my mother saying it's our loss," I said.

We laughed. Laughter was what we needed to get back to.

We dipped our fingers into green pepper salsa: *pepitoria.* "It's unlike anything I've ever tasted," Larry said.

"And why we are here," I said, "with green instead of red all over our chins."

Larry reached across the table to take my hand.

"And *this*," I said, grabbing hold of thanksgiving—of all that we are, and all that we mean to each other—at last.

Part Two

"Life is what happens between drafts."

— DENNIS R. MILLER
(who spent 23 years completing his novel)

Inauguration

On Inauguration Day, in a burst of column-writing confidence, I gave Port Townsend's mayor a call and she called me right back. "Mary Lou," she said, "we have a long way to go, but we now have a leader who, I believe, will be a good beginning."

Now *that* was thrilling. No politician had ever called me by my first name before. Other than a certain charming womanizer, who used to be the mayor of somewhere, who said my name in a voice that stirred my insides in a way that made me imagine him dropping his penchant for city management, not to mention his wife and kids, and running off with me. So help me, that was a long time ago. Ages. I was in college. I was a kid.

I thought about contacting the mayor before, but something always stopped me. For one thing, I figured, with a fair amount of certainty, that I could infer what side of an issue she stood on by simply remembering the open-sided electric golf cart she drives.

For another, she's been in the political spotlight for decades. So, naturally, there are a few rumors floating around. Which is why I thought it high time to contact her directly, a good place to start with my New Year's practice: If I think I know someone because I've heard the gossip, I want to think again. It's one of the small changes I want to make, to be sure my relationship to any person I've heard about but have never talked to is my own.

Because, seriously, if the earful I've heard about me were true?

Well, let's see.

First of all, I'd have an eating disorder (inferred by a roly-poly who thinks thin + dancer has to = anorexic); I'm unhappily married (I travel alone and, yep, I guess you know what *that* means); and by far the most loaded assumption: I don't have children because I couldn't have children. A friend heard this rumor from her hairdresser who heard it from a client. This, in a small town, means everyone's heard it. (Wait,

I've heard about this hairdresser. Oh, the rumors *I* could spread. *Quite the little drinking problem.*)

Still, I am, right this instant, having a good laugh at myself. Because now you can go ahead and bury everything I just said about gossip and assumptions and judgments and presume, rightly so, how *I* felt on Inauguration Day. And I don't even drive a golf cart.

My goose bumps popped, I noticed that right away. And when Aretha, goddess-of-soul, sang the national anthem, I felt flushed.

After Bush was sworn in, I took a breath and somehow, I'm not even sure how, I got on with my life. But the resentment I felt never went away and I hated living like that for eight long years. I had some pretty brutal dreams, too, especially after he was reelected. I dreamt a huge, unmanned scythe was taking us down, thinning us out, those who'd voted against him.

Feeling politically reassured is wonderful stuff for a writer, but I couldn't write about the feeling right away, not in a way that felt my own. For days, I was glued to the tube. (Is there still a tube in a television? I don't think so.) But I didn't want to sit in my office trying to put words to everything I felt. I wanted to savor that politics was finally a two-way street. Polite. Respectful. Diplomatic. Statesmanlike.

Imagine.

After the swearing in, I could hardly contain myself. I wanted to give in to the wonderful new feeling of actually liking my president, to have me one huge cookie with macadamia nuts and M&M's baked right into it!

The woman behind me at the bakery said, "The world already feels like a better place," and I, without so much as a pause, turned to give her a hug in the giddy way that comes over me sometimes when I've spent too much time in my office, in my head, and then, when I finally go out, I talk to strangers as if they are intimates. It's like I've just been let out of jail.

But the most incredible thing happened. She hugged me back. And then we both got teary-eyed. We wiped underneath our eyes with the crook of our index fingers, a gesture all mascara-wearing women perfect by the age of sixteen, and then she said something I will never forget: "No matter what happens next, I'm sort of storybook-positive again."

I've been around the block. But no election, local or national, has ever made me hug a total stranger. In any event, we were no longer apathetic. And this is as clear in my mind as if I had spent all of last Tuesday trying to write it.

And because sometimes politicians get it just right, I agree, this *is* a good beginning, Ms. Mayor. Thank you for calling me back, and not only because I needed a story.

The Straddle

If ever there was a time to go back and take a closer look at a few of my reader's comments—one that sort of bugged me, another that really bugged me, and, since I'm highly susceptible to the power of gratitude, one I really liked—this is it. Because ... because the last made me remember why I love writing a column. Hearing from readers the same day my words are published is a rush. So immediate, this genre.

Though every now and again there's an email with such a mean presence that it snatches the heart right out of me until I am certain that no writer, certainly not this one, could ever live up to playing it cool and ignoring such a callous, cruel comment.

Once I regain my confidence, I typically write back, as I did this time, partly out of pride, plus, who the hell does this guy think he is anyway?

It's not that I wish I hadn't responded. What troubles me is that criticism can still bother me, that my mind will suffer the same old insecurities I seem to always be dealing with in one way or another, that I had such a primal reaction to it, that I wanted to run from the man who said it, that I felt like such a sissy.

It's a given that writers are an easy target for angry people, and after I went through my own little hissy fit, there was sort of a mental switcheroo on my part. I figured any comment, positive or negative, for better or worse, proves people are still reading the newspaper, which is always good news to a columnist.

Still, it hasn't gotten a great deal easier, opening an email that I know, I just know, is going to berate me. I'd rather keep my mind on my work, not fuzzy it with interpersonal relations. I could just delete it, but somehow I never do.

The good part is, even if one reader is ornery with a deep-seated need to take all women down a notch (though he'd never admit it), there is the next reader, the kind and generous reader, the reader who *gets* me, like Sheila, who said, "There is so much about you that is me!"

It wasn't vanity I felt reading her words, well, maybe a little, but mostly it was satisfaction. I mean, come on, everyone loves a bit of praise, and I'm no exception. I answered eagerly, more to prolong the compliment than anything. There aren't enough compliments in this line of work. Most people want to chew me out.

There is a paragraph in Ann Patchett's book, *Truth & Beauty*, that comes to mind here. When Ann tries to tell her friend Lucy that the point isn't to hear what a bully has to say and then to reject it. The point is to cross to the other side of the street when you see the bully coming. I suppose deleting an email before opening it would be the equivalent of crossing the street, but for whatever reason, I did open it. Even though the subject line was screaming with five exclamation points, "You're ALWAYS … !!!!!"

What gets me the most about this kind of punctuation-in-overdrive is not only that the sender is already yelling at me; the sender is aching for a fight!!!!!

After opening it (oh, why did I?), the rest charged at me, "… writing about your own stupid life, Sanelli, who cares?!!!!!"

Strange to hear reverberation over the Internet, but that's what I heard, I swear. To console myself, I had to stop and call my friend David, also a writer. Of *code*, but, still.

"We need to find the bastard and beat him 'til he bleeds," David said.

See, that's why I love David.

"Don't you think it's a little weird that this person who hates my column so much even bothers to *read* it?"

"No one ever writes to me."

I empathized.

But there was a pea under my mattress now. On the one hand, I knew time would erase the comment from my mind; it always does eventually.

On the other, a little payback would do me some good.

It's complicated, this writing thing.

And so, for fun, I imagined my reader's stringy hair; his beard like a shrub; his inferiority complex because he didn't go to college or because he can't get it up; or, worse, can't get *published;* his selfish notion that my inbox is a vat for him to pour all his bitter disappointment into. Mean. Mean. Mean.

I could have answered him straightaway, shot back a dose of my own venom; but, truthfully, as crummy as he made me feel, I didn't feel like it. Yelling back through email is a losing battle if ever there was one.

But for days his email grated on me. Time seemed to stretch uncomfortably long. Still, I needed a clear sense of what I wanted say.

What did I want to say?

God, I hate email. Why is all this immediate access a good thing again?

Like most writers, I'm more comfortable gathering my thoughts rather than snapping back. Plus, did I mention this reader *kept* sending emails, each nastier than the next. In my experience, bullies hate to be ignored. To be noticed is why they bully in the first place.

"Be nice," I heard my professional voice warn. "Wait, no. Cut the professional crap and tell that jerk-off you don't have time for his time-sucking drama!"

Turns out, I didn't need to go that far. Once my fingers hit the keys, there was no need to defend myself. My answer wrote itself. My response, totally professional, had only a hint of superiority, which seemed only fair at the time.

> Dear Reader:
>
> I think what you are really trying to say is how you've noticed that I am both the story and the storyteller. I am. But hear me on this: I have no interest in trying to teach you anything.

I thought about ending there. But sometimes you have to get to the end to realize you just aren't finished at all.

> And, of course, you have the choice not to read my column. That might work for you.

Even now, my reply is like witnessing my own evolution. Pride pours over me. I glow with a radiance no lotion can bring to my face, the feeling every woman I know lives for: *This is what it's like to be true to myself.*

I received another email right before Obama was elected, when the Sarah Palin punches were in full swing: I BET YOU'RE HAPPY NOW, SANELLI!! read the ALL-CAPS.

Oh, no, I thought, here we go.

I opened the email: NOW THAT A WOOOMAAAN WILL BE VICE PRESIDENT!!

And the man (I have to assume it was a man) didn't add all those extra Os and As, I did. It was as if I could hear him draw out the sound of my sex and I was fed up. I was sure some patience still existed for the whole Palin-shenanigan, but I didn't have any. Even now, when I hear her name, my whole body yawns.

My reply was eager to be let out, like a dog with a floppy tail.

Dear Reader:

How right you are. (It's always good to tell a bully, up-front, how right he is, to lie this way; it helps.) True, I would like to see more women in office. But Sarah? Sorry, no. I was hoping for a woman who grasps how much we need to protect our planet in the same way she needs to protect her home from the cold. I was hoping for a woman who wants to put an end to the wars we've started, not prolong them. I was hoping for a woman in favor of all the so-called "liberal, feminist" issues you accuse me of. (His email was three pages long.) Not just a woman, but a woman who can articulate how she intends to better things. If my own life has taught me a thing, it's that if I can't say what it is I want, I'm pretty sure I won't be able to make it happen. So, no, Sarah is not a candidate I'm all that happy about. We deserve better.

But suddenly I was not about to let anything get in the way of the emergency the rest of my answer felt like. I could not imagine

finishing without addressing the inequity of some of the cracks reporters made about Palin's clothes, her hair, her measurements for God's
sake.

So I continued.

> Having said this, I don't like how the media plays up
> Sarah's lack of experience as if it's some huge offense, a
> danger to mankind, when in actuality, Obama has even
> less. It's really beginning to grate on me. So, go ahead, call
> me a feminist again. No offense taken.

> By the way, how do you find the time to write such
> detailed descriptions about how you view me? Does it not,
> in fact, deflect from what I can only imagine must be a
> very full and gratifying life of your own?

"Happy now?" my conscience said.

"Very."

"Did you hold back *any*thing?"

"Actually, I restrained myself."

I started to say I wouldn't have said more, wouldn't have gone too
far, but she stopped me.

"You get your nerve from me, you know."

"Absolutely."

A more recent reader's question was easier to answer. Actually for a
good part of this morning, I am right up to my elbows trying to. I
would have done so face-to-face, but the other reality of my work
intervened at the time: sales.

Her question did make me think a lot about what's been circling
in mind anyway, ever since a fan of my work (thank God almighty!)
took me aside to ask why I ever chose to live in both a small town
and a huge city, simultaneously. She wondered if I ever felt confused
about where I belong.

Only every day of my entire life.

Just as I was about to make a stab at an answer, I was pulled away to sign a book for my friend Laura. I don't get to see Laura all that often, hardly ever, so when we do meet our eyes seem to say, *You live in your world, I live in mine, but we are together.* Then we nod and go our separate ways.

When I looked up, the woman was gone. I didn't get her name. Only that she enjoys my column because, graciously, she took the time to say so. I hope she reads this.

As far back as I can remember, I've always wanted more than one life, more than one way of living. So, after giving a lot of thought to her question, I've come up with this: My cottage in the country is so lovely it distracts. I can putter away my writing time, snipping away at weeds for hours and be happy to do so. Nature moves me in so many ways. But the cottage is old, drafty, and downright freezing in winter. If I were fiscally responsible, I'd spend more on upkeep.

Emotionally speaking, there is even a better answer. Each time I return to my writer's cottage, get closer to it, I also realize I've moved farther and farther away.

In contrast, our tiny condo in the sky is new, tight, warm and snugly. It's not a writer's cottage, far from it; but a writer's nest all the same. With no upkeep to speak of, little distracts me. And in this productive part of my life, this is all I desire in a home: no mental confusion about how to spend my time. Focus. In this way, it's more like an office. No part of me gets too emotional about any of it. It doesn't disrupt my work.

But the main motivation to live in the city is this: It's where people are willing to pay me for the work I do. I am paid to write, to speak, to teach dance, to perform. Somewhere along the artistic line, this became important to me. For whatever reason, Port Townsend — a supposedly artist community — still expects an artist to give away time and talent. The reason hasn't been clearly defined for me as yet. I'm still working on it. I think it has a lot to do with the fact there are so many artists living there. And a division in people's minds exists, one that separates "local" from "worth paying for."

Or maybe an artist has to leave the place he or she is known, or perceived as known, to be taken seriously.

So, no, I haven't turned into two people; my two lives don't collide. They balance out.

And I straddle the divide best I can.

Oh. One last: To the woman who sent me a scary little card saying that man/woman equality runs against the nature and word of God, I would like to ask you one question:

Tell me, please, in your *own* words, what are you so afraid of?

The Rotten Economy, A Love Story

It's so heavy right now, problematically heavy, money-wise. A lot of anxiety has slipped into the lives of nearly everyone I know.

One way I deal with anxiety is to ask a lot of questions. So that's what I did. I began asking my friends whether they are looking ahead to a better future or scared silly about the economy getting worse. Maybe if I write about their worries, I thought, I'll think less about ours, as in: what our assets are worth compared to what we thought they'd be worth.

Which is hardly enough to fund my winter wanderlust this year, Larry reminds me, not disagreeably but *frequently*.

And so I begin my questioning with him, since he's the one who thought stocks were such a great idea. "Things are a little slow, but honestly I don't want to work as much," he said. "Time is getting away. I want to slow it down."

"I don't think we can slow time down," I turned from my screen to say. "Can we?"

"I sat in on a City Council meeting once, that worked." We laughed. "But, I'm not going to worry about what we lost. I'm going to think about what we do have and manage the best I can with that."

I felt so tender toward him right then. I hadn't seen him quite so sure of things in a while. His humor had been shrinking right on par with our investments. One thing I've always admired about Larry is his resolve.

But, still, can we choose *not* to be anxious? Can we pooh-pooh it, really? I wondered. I felt my forehead wrinkle. Comparably, I can slide into worry over the least little thing. When things aren't going well with my work, to hell with things like dwindling returns. If, say, one of my columns is cancelled, book sales are down, or my thoughts are sticking to the keys, this is when the world is a real mess. And worry is such a crushing thing, far beyond anything rational most of the time.

Still, I've never really given much thought to it as a choice.

Maybe we can choose how to *deal* with it, but that's about it. Worry comes, like it or not. All we can do is wait it out while trying not to let it get the best of us.

But things are looking up. If I compare how long it takes for worry to work its way through me to how long the process used to take, well, it's a wonder I made it through my thirties, that the slow, sinuous writhing didn't kill me. Now, two days of stress, tops, and I can thumb my nose at the thing I imagined was going to beat me, that as usually presents itself by day three, is really no big deal.

And yet, Larry, like *that*, can find the pivotal thing within himself that re-shuffles his worry, as well as my own. This is the real definition of a good marriage I think, being so well wired together.

But my own worry is like bamboo: it shoots up everywhere.

Take the novel I'm working on. Should I think about mass appeal and titillating love scenes, a real page-turner that could help pay the bills? Pages and pages of best girlfriend, cheating husband, lover on the side, walks on the beach, mean mother-in-law, gay sidekick, crazy drunken neighbor, standard novel stuff. Even though the word "novel" means "different" or, "new."

Or zoom in on the inner workings of the mind, who my character is on another level?

Crazy worry, isn't it?

But this is the world I live in, where leaving one genre doesn't guarantee I will know how to live in the next. For instance: I seriously doubt my ability to write a contemporary steamy scene, the kind of sex that could make a woman sitting on the beach come in her spandex; but I'm giving it my best shot. My own expectations for sex have been adjusted along with my bra straps, but I'm good at writing from memory. And while the vision of a more humbled sex life may sound scary, pathetic, and hopelessly dull to you, sweetie, let me tell you something: love that stays by your side when your breasts slide down is the love of your life.

Because here's what I *don't* worry about: Larry.

If I let myself, I could go on about Larry all over again.

But I am going to take an about-face and stick to the other people in this story—friends, acquaintances, mentors—because they took time from their busy lives to answer my question when they may have very well wanted to delete my email. I asked them to get right into the gist of a nerve-wracking subject most of us would rather ignore.

And they did.

Margery, for instance, an eighty-four-year-old artist, one of the busiest women I know, always preparing for one show or another. Her response came back the very same day, which, in itself, blew me away. I have friends twenty, thirty years her junior who take days to respond to an email.

Another friend still has a rotary phone and no computer, bless her heart. I'm thinking of her now, in her late seventies, she splits her own firewood, which is way harder than learning to email. The last time we spoke, I was sitting in her kitchen, waiting for homemade (homemade!) croissants to come out of the oven. The jam and butter sat in front of me in tiny bone china teacups. The pink-and-yellow floral cups you see at estate sales and think warm little tea-time thoughts, then pass them up for a laser print cartridge still in the box.

To loosely paraphrase her latest conspiracy theory, "They are spying on you, reading everything you say in those emails so they can use it against you. It doesn't look good."

I remember those four words distinctly, "It doesn't look good."

For a second, I thought about saying something to ease her Internet paranoia, even though I harbor a fair share of my own skepticism lately. But, as I said, homemade croissants. With chocolate centers. She could have said anything.

Back to Margery: "This country has faced many serious challenges through the years; we'll get through this." Margery reminds how people in their late years are more forgiving of major flubs. They've lived through a myriad of ways the world has struggled and turned around again. Their perspective appeals to my sense of balance. I used to fear crow's feet, flabby knees, and grey hair. Now, if I want *not* to be bored by a conversation, I seek out crow's feet, flabby knees, and grey hair, especially if they belong to someone like Margery, a woman still passionate about her work.

Julie owns an ice cream parlor. Before I called her, I did wonder if people stop eating ice cream when things get bad.

Nah.

To quote Julie, "I believe we have to participate in the changes that will make the world a better place. This is the foundation of my optimism."

What could I add to that? I thought about the cardamom ice cream she makes by hand. A daily scoop of it would make me more of an optimist, too. What I'd give.

My friend Charlie drives a delivery truck. "Investments? My marriage is my greatest asset. You know what I mean."

Charlie, I do.

And Laura.

Laura, Laura, Laura. You pop up in so many of my thoughts. You take up good space.

Laura is a professional debt counselor who understands how overbuying can botch up lives, but the real secret of her success is her vibrancy. She has such raw, generous energy that helps people relax, listen to her advice, and get back on their feet. "I want to focus on relationships now," she said, "who cares if I can buy more?"

Laura already knows important work from the trivial. She does nothing with half a heart.

"Obama was left with a horrible mess; I don't want people to forget this." This from Bonnie. I've had friends who, for one reason or another, fell away. But not Bonnie.

This last thought stops me in my tracks. I allow myself to stop for a minute and miss a few of them. Because I do. I miss them so much. I thought I'd grow old with some of these people.

Bonnie is also the mother of one of my best friends, which is not really connected to my story here, but it's connected to what I love most about telling one: friend, mother, daughter, continuum.

⁓

"Hope was *the* media slogan for a while, but I knew they'd have a heyday telling us how Obama fails at it now," says Joyce. Joyce is a woman with a bullshit-receptor as a third eye. Not only that, I can say with a fair degree of certainty that she's right most of the time. I, too, detected the Obama-shift right away. Only weeks after the election I looked away from the news and shouted, "Shut up! He's not even been sworn in yet!"

"I did lose a buttload of retirement savings." This from Gale, my accountant/actress friend. Leave it to her to use a word like *buttload*. I love it. Almost as much as I love Gale.

One last. Marilyn. Elegantly coiffed, owner of an upscale kitchen boutique a lot of us rely on for that special gadget when Christmas rolls round. "My husband informed me we may have to die a few years earlier than expected." The world is so unfair sometimes. Somehow I can't see Marilyn shopping discount like the rest of us. It's sad, really.

This is just a handful of my people in our part of the world filled with high ideals and views of the sea.

"I've been thinking," Larry again, hours later, back in my office, saying something I think he's been trying to avoid saying all day. "I *prefer* a slow simmer, actually."

I know he's referring to how many years he's been working in the pressure cooker, running his own business; how much he'd like to cut back; how hard he's been at it. But "slow simmer?" This makes me laugh and not just because I'm up for a good laugh; it makes me laugh because I know Larry has been watching Rachael Ray again.

"Rachael?" I ask. He smiles.

"You have a crush on her." He hesitates. He shakes his head.

"Do you know how red your face gets when you lie?"

I'm surprised by how fast he leaves the room. Rachael would let him eat more meat, for one thing. And butter. Lots of it. Like when we first met. Butter on his mayonnaised bread. Butter on his peanut butter sandwiches. Back when he tried a push-up on one arm to impress me, the two of us flirting, so in love.

Love. It's February. Little sugary hearts are everywhere. So screw the economy. Because there are times, like right now, when I try to be all serious-writer and swish money matters back and forth, but all I manage to do is learn, all over again, what's important: the man who can say he refuses to worry about what he *doesn't* have is the man for me. He saves me from dwelling, if not completely, then long enough to write, if a little indirectly, this tribute to him, long overdue, and leave the economy up to someone who can fix it.

Not hopeful; too many wars!

Because have I ever had a friend, or even a family member, as deeply generous as my Larry? Honestly? Almost. But not quite. So why am I teary?

Because, as our savings shrivel and the value of our home has been slashed in half and keeps dropping from there, I know how rich I am.

Rosewind

I'm reluctant to drive all the way out to *RoseWind*. For one thing, the Olympic Peninsula is a long drive out of the city. For another, it's too cold in February to do anything fun once I get there.

But I need to turn something in to my editor. So it's time to head to the commune.

"Not a commune," I remind myself. "Co-housing *community*. Don't be sarcastic before you even get there."

See, what happens is, each month when it's deadline time, I wake convinced I won't be able to come up with a story. Same old self-doubt. It never wins, is good for nothing; I've never missed a deadline. Yet, it returns with a vengeance. The only way to shake it off is to plow in until I can't tell self-doubt from self-confidence, from any of it, because I'm swept up.

When I was newer at it, the dread was even worse. I would dream about missing my deadline, or meeting it but my file was corrupted; no one could open it. I dreamt about losing my ability to write, losing my columns that aren't much, really, but they mean a lot to me. I dreamt one of my editors fired me in a text message I had to pay to receive.

All right, let's go see what co-housing is all about.

The first thing I see when I pull up to the grounds of *RoseWind* is a huge wild rosebush. I lean against the steering wheel, look up at the bush glowing in front of me like a scene from my past when I would pinch an entire bush of buds in no time in order to turn out the heart-shaped wreaths I sold in a shop on Madison Avenue.

The Madison Avenue.

I read about the shop in a magazine, how it sold homemade crafts from all over the country. I sent a photo of one of my wreaths (back when you still put a photo in an envelope and kissed it for luck before dropping it into the bin), never dreaming the shop would make an order.

They made an order. Then they made another. And another.

It got so I could strip a bush clean in seconds. I started going out at night so I could creep further into people's yards. The wreaths were selling like mad and, after another season of thieving, I had to decide, then and there, whether wreaths were my future.

I gave up stealing rosebuds and never looked back.

Somehow I grasped that this was a life-altering decision: manufacturing product or stories? Wreaths or books? (Wreaths pay better, sad fact.) But wreath-maker seemed an embarrassing way to describe myself after a while. I don't know why.

The idea of doing both did occur to me. But at the time, I owned a dance studio, was artistic director of a dance company, and I was desperately trying to publish my poetry, in the way all poets are desperate for a little, even the tiniest, morsel of acknowledgment. I was tired of sustaining it all. I was no longer up to my every dream and aspiration. I had to lay off doing so much and find a refuge in one dream and one dream only.

Two at the most.

After that, I closed my studio. I say "I," but *I* locked the door one last time and walked away, leaving the actual tear down to my incisive Larry. I couldn't face disassembling my world. In the next two years I took a writing residency in Spain, one in France, another in France, one in Costa Rica.

I can see now how I was succumbing to a transition from dancing to writing, or of giving writing more weight than dancing, something I hadn't done before. For twenty years, I tried to weigh them out equally, but dancing was heavier most of the time, requiring more from me because dance involves dealing with a multitude of egos on a daily basis.

After letting go, of making it through the passage, I kept dancing. I will always dance, but more for fun. Honestly, who knew it could be fun? Little about dancing professionally is fun. It's a lot of other amazing, incredible, competitive, challenging things, and no part of me regrets any of it, but fun is not how I'd describe that kind of pressure. Fun is not the point of having fun on stage. Any real fun while performing is too great a luxury. The focus is too intense. It's not like my work as a speaker, the words in front of me if I forget. The fun you perceive from your seat is an act. Dancers are great actors, the best. Add strength, style, technique, and muscle memory to undivided focus and acute stage awareness, and competence is what you are viewing. Most of the time we are scared shitless.

The rosebush in front of my car was so big that when I tried to open my door against the southerly, I had to push with my shoulder, then with all of my weight. I may not distinguish, off the top of my head, a southerly from other prevailing winds, but wind that feels as if it could lift me from the ground, I pay attention to.

And then it hit me, *rosebush* plus *wind* equals *RoseWind*. There is no shortage of housing tracts named after the trees mowed down in order to build them. I liked how closely the name *RoseWind* matched the present experience.

I first heard of *RoseWind* in the early 90s but paid it no mind. I like to think I'm the kind of woman who could live in co-housing, but I don't fool myself. I didn't last a week in a college dorm. The only "co" I'm committed to is marriage, and most days I still see how I could do better at it, do more, say less, say more, try again.

All I have to do is imagine "co-housing" and all I can see is a lack of privacy, too many social obligations, internal politics, and who *are* those people traipsing through my yard?

All of which makes me doubly intrigued as to why both my parents recently moved into "co-housing" situations of another kind: retirement communities, the kind sprouting up all over our country because no one wants to live with their parents.

Wait! I want to update that last sentence. I have personal experience of another kind; i.e., I overheard my mother (she has no idea how loud she talks now that her hearing is failing) tell a friend that she could *never* live under the same roof with me: "My daughter, I've just about *had* it with the way she mothers me." So, there you have it, parents don't necessarily want to live with the kids, either. It was an answer to my prayers.

I wonder, though, other than the age requirement of retirement communities, if the idea is much the same. Both retirement and co-housing communities revolve around a common theme, be it age or political leanings, as well as a common room where residents meet for activities, meals, socializing. And both think of themselves as separate from whatever town or city they skirt for whatever reason they define themselves by.

Naturally, I'm not talking legal differences. I'm more interested in the expectation of the word "community" from its residents. The idea of co-housing may be firm in their minds, but for me the interpretation of the word is just beginning.

Feeling very journalese, I call Doug, one of the original co-housing advocates at *RoseWind*.

"We're a tribe," he says.

"A tribe, really?"

Excellent, I thought. Usually it takes more time to extract such honesty. As far as interviews go, I find that if I ask people direct questions too soon, they get nervous and pull back. If I let them meander, eventually they'll tell me everything I want to know. But Doug jumped right in, gave me what I needed right off the bat. Because, to me, the word "tribe" more than "co-housing" explains what he was looking for when he set out to form a community: an extended, chosen family because his real family isn't in the picture. Or maybe they are in the picture. But he'd rather they were not.

The word "tribe" also makes me think of the word "chief" which, I believe, Doug likes to think of himself as. Five minutes in his company, this much is clear. One never gets so close to the chiefs of this world as when one mentions they are writing a "story." Chiefs like to go on record. Chiefs enjoy the spotlight. Center stage is no problem for a chief.

Incidentally, there are a lot of chiefs living out on the Peninsula. We used to call them "spooners." A spooner is not only born with a silver spoon; he/she likes to pretend no one knows how much money they have.

Everyone knows.

Spooners like to see themselves as egalitarians, I think, it gives them something to struggle with. But if you try and treat them as such, their stance shifts as they suddenly remember just how much they prefer being deferred to.

Anyway, humans are tribal by nature; I've always thought so. We look to find our own. And once we find them, and they happen to be as well-off as Doug is, it can make tribal living look like another choice among all the many, many choices out there, which makes decisions even harder sometimes; but the upside is that it also makes them possible.

And the possibility of working out everything from "what to raise in our community garden" to "how to share a lawnmower" gives Doug something to do. "Figuring it all out is my life goal and why," he says, "I want to live in co-housing."

Which immediately makes me think of two other things, no three: that sharing hardly feels like too high a price to pay for a community. How there is room for as many interpretations of the word "community" as there is for, say, the word "art" (those horrible debates). And that Doug might as well come right out and say *independently wealthy, time on my hands*. Because who else, in early middle age, has time to dig all day in a garden? And, frankly, who has the energy for working out every little thing mutually? *What do you think? I don't know, what do you think? It doesn't matter to me, really. Me either, so you decide. Oh, I'd rather you decide.*

And so on.

The other day I ran into an old acquaintance who moved to Port Townsend twenty years ago, around the same time I did, before I realized, a decade or so later, that the town I'd chosen was smaller and drizzlier than I'd bargained for. It took a friend from a far away, sunny city to say, "I think that rainy little town is making you crazy," for me to admit she was right. "You gotta swear you'll move; your attitude stinks."

I may die before ever being able to thank her enough.

Anyway, I was sort of mulling over my Doug conversation with this person. "I hate the word *tribe*," she said. There was a lot of hostility in her voice, too, which is so unlike the woman this woman wants other people to believe she is and so like the woman she really is, which is why she has to work so hard at the facade. Facade is a part of life for a lot of people who migrate west, I think. People who tell themselves they are mellow, who want so badly to be mellow, who *practice* mellow. Even though they are certifiably type A.

Then she said something that startled me even more, that she rarely shops at the little uptown, privately owned, Aldrich's grocery anymore since "out-of-towners" bought it and "changed its feel."

What? As if she and I aren't out-of-towners. She is from New Jersey, for Pete's sake. What she was really saying is the new owners were Chinese, i.e., not part of her assumed tribe, her Nia-dancing, vegan, divorced (or on the verge), Volvo-driving, pot-smoking Caucasian tribe that even after years of living mellow, still judge one another faster than the speed of sound. Though she'd never say so. And hates that I *did*.

But nothing I've ever said is truer.

Carol Shields, one of my favorite writers, described herself as "boisterously honest." I think maybe my honesty is more a matter of the Italian thing then the writer thing. The problem is, in some of us there's the combination of the two.

My conversation with Doug struck another chord, too: Where's my tribe? I thrive here in the Northwest; I'm a hardy transplant, but like the cedars, my roots don't go all that deep.

"You wrote a story once," Doug says, "about your elderly neighbor, how you watched her tend her garden year after year. Think how well you could have known her if you'd sat down to dinner several nights a week in a co-housing experience."

My first thought? *Doug you're lonely; that's what you are.* (Why do we, any of us, have such a hard time admitting we're lonely? What will we do with all the loneliness that can develop in our lifetime? Because it does. Even when we are surrounded by people we love. Even when we are surrounded by people we *choose*.)

"Are you kidding? I didn't want to know her any better. She was a nutcase."

Thank god Doug laughed. Because, in my experience, spooners can have a difficult time with teasing. It stuns. You can see it in their eyes. They don't know how to react, how to drop their guard, how to ease up. So they don't.

Because even if I don't completely trust the forced neighborliness Doug is proposing, I like that he has a sense of humor about it. Humor is the grandest gesture, it really is.

Where's my tribe?

Well ... the only definition for me right now is that I find my tribe wherever I can. It's the best I can do. My tightest friends live hundreds of miles away. When I think of "community," it's Diane and Lena in San Francisco or Sheila in New York or Shanta in Ireland or David or Vicki or Max in Seattle or Richard in Palm Springs or Jane in Port Townsend or Yvonne in Hawaii or Amargit, in India for a stay.

And even if my way is just more of an idea of community, whose isn't? I don't think it's ever wise to confuse proximity with intimacy (think airplanes). And, so far, I've not found intimacy with any of my closest neighbors. Honest to god, a few of them I avoid at any cost.

I can't even begin to pretend I am anyone different than a woman who wants a lot of privacy, who would do just about anything to guarantee it. There's no confusion about this in my mind. To live commonly would feel untrue, wrong for me. To live around so many like-minded people would feel isolating, another community with walls, the concentrated sameness of the people around you.

It's blissful, privacy is. Like tonight. Larry out of town on business, the whole warm bed to myself.

But as a steady diet?

No.

I'd have to make him come home.

Calvin

Ladies, close your eyes and imagine the kind of man you notice no matter what else you are doing.

Calvin is that kind of man.

And it's not only that I want to write about him; I revel in his story, so my work today will be easy. Easy is key right now. I was out last night dancing until the wee hours of the morning. I need a painless topic to tackle.

The frequency of fuzzy hangovers has decreased with age, so that's good. The bad thing is that recovery time takes twice as long. It's pricklier than I remember. And pitifully unattractive. If you were to take a good look at me, you'd gasp. So the way in has to be easy, especially easy: simple. My view has to be clear.

Imagine, too, this man saying: "Hey, Sunshine, how ya doin' this morning?" His smile radiating like a child's, a stack of *Real Change* newspapers in the crook of his arm, "Do ya want to help me out today?"

I say yes I do.

I like Calvin. I get his need to smile even when the weather scowls. He gets mine. It's how we cope. For a man living on the street, Calvin has the remarkable ability to give me the most positive sense of my neighborhood, of belonging here. Way more than I can say about most of my neighbors.

Sure, he likely calls every woman on the block the same sunny nickname. Still, I'm a sucker for compliments. It works. I blush. I buy his paper.

A year later, I'm still buying it.

A week ago, even as a hard wind blew into his eyes and a plastic bag blew past his feet, Calvin smiled, From that point on we crossed a line, shifting from an awkward exchange of a couple of bucks to matters of the heart.

"My mother's in the hospital," I told him.

"Yeah? Mine is passed now. Love yours, Sunshine, whiles you can."

The thing about the homeless is that they're there, tugging at your heartstrings. And you have to find a way to let them in that goes deeper than sympathy or guilt. On any given day, if you walk from the Space Needle to Pioneer Square, you'll see homelessness spread out in all directions. It's become a living, begging, competitive world of its own, involving not only joblessness, but mental illness and all despairs in between. And their numbers are going to increase; this is a given.

But I'm not going down that road. Not with this hangover.

Still, I've had to work pretty hard at viewing some of the street folks as less of an "other," familiar enough to think of as acquaintances, neighbors, people I need to respect, if not always welcome—especially the addicts; their desperation scares me to death. There really is no other choice, other than completely ignoring them, which I admit, I do sometimes, not because I'm a cruel, cold person, even if anyone watching might think so, but because there are days when I'm just trying to hold it together myself, when I'm sort of unraveling like a ball of yarn already, so I can't let myself cross the threshold, emotionally. On these more-fragile days, I have to concentrate on my life, the one in front of me, the one I need to keep afloat. So I insulate, seal off, just so I can move on without caving, and I think this is what a lot of us are doing, whether we realize it or not. Because it's not only likely that I am going to get hit up for money if I take even the shortest walk through my neighborhood, it can be depended upon. Until, by the time I reach my destination, I feel completely awful for cutting so many people off and I think, *I need this like a hole in the head.*

But the *Real Change* vendors, people like Calvin, offer a fair exchange—a couple of bucks for a well-organized paper and the seller's time to pitch it. I assume some of you know the history of the *Real Change* newspapers. If not, here's a short summary from their website: "It's a hand up, not a handout." Still, as I'm discovering a little more every day, I can't give money to all the paper vendors, surely. So I pick Calvin.

Calvin stands out. Along with his smile, he pays genuine attention to passers-by. Add this to his good nature and narrow, but not hauntingly thin, body, and the word that comes to mind about his personality is an old-fashioned one: *winning*. Even when he asks, "How ya doin'?" the question isn't disconnected from any real interest. He looks you straight in the eyes and listens to your reply. Ladies, how many men do you know who do the same?

Once I remember Calvin saying, "Sunshine, how ya doin' today?" in a way that caused me to forget my troubles and utter what I knew to be a stinking lie, "I'm great!"

A better man, where is he?

Back in October, Calvin was on Fourth and Virginia dressed in a suit jacket and white sneakers that looked almost brand-new. "Calvin, you look dashing," I said.

"It's my graduation day from *Real Change*!" he beamed. His eyes were lit up circles of pride.

"Calvin's respectable," another vendor of *Real Change* turned to me to say, "not a bellyacher like the rest of us poor slobs, but a real gentleman." I wanted to hug this guy for giving me a perfect word for Calvin. Sometimes I can be lulled into the illusion that my words are *the* words. Not this time. "Respectable" is the adjective I've been after. *Calvin is a respectable gentleman.*

A little over a year after I bought my first paper, Calvin told me he had a job at the Goodwill store in Ballard. "But I gotta keep selling my papers, comin' back to my roots." He was more reserved with me, though, as if purposely containing himself to make sure he didn't say or do anything too "street." Realizing how hard this was for him, and yet how necessary, made me respect him even more.

"It took courage to do what you've done, Calvin. I'm so proud of you!"

"Can you believe, Sunshine, that I'd be someone some day? It's a choice, a real choice, every single day, yes it is."

"Yes it is," I repeated.

And now? Calvin works in sales at Macy's. "They seem to like me just fine," he said. "I just hope I can keep at it, keep myself up."

I hope so, too, Calvin. So much that I can't write any more just now.

It is the rare person who can inspire me beyond words.

Holy Park

I had given myself the morning to read in bed, to think quietly, reasoning that once spring arrived, I wouldn't allow myself to miss much of it. When sun drenches the sky, I literally jump out of bed. When it's gray or blowing a gale, "late" is too early a word for the hour I can read to.

I read another page and then, to my everlasting gratitude, there was something bright I noticed about the morning. I sat up and threw back the covers.

Tech-y as it is, this city is also a lesson in sensuousness. Just when you allow yourself the full lazy pleasure of rain, sunlight cuts through your window, everything from your wrinkly sheets to your faded wallpaper suddenly ablaze with golden light that could soften even the dingiest room, reminding you of motion, of energy, of the way you felt as a kid when you were running rather than walking to get outside, all of you fired up.

It wasn't full on springtime yet, but it was enough.

There's an adage that says humor is the best way to make the unbearable bearable. This line hangs in the air ... I need to think about it for a moment.

Okay, true. People who make me laugh are rare and wonderful. But if I close my eyes and think what it is that makes the most intolerable tolerable for me, it's sunlight. Sunlight. Sunlight. Sunlight. It pulls everything good to the forefront. I am lifted. Anything else is a runner-up.

The lack of sunlight in the winter months has been good for the writer in me. But the moist and leafy green that comes in spring distracts. It's the greenest green you will ever walk through. I've often wondered if the aim behind such miraculous shades of green is to sweet-talk me into believing the past winter was like any other, that all the icy snow wasn't so bad. Frigid, icy snow in a city without any real history of frigid, icy snow or any budget for snow removal? Piece of cake. Forget about it.

Because this is how it is for some of us, sunlight can make even a lie more convincing. It's a cryptic trick, I think, some sort of deliberate intervention. Nature does such things; it's amazing how it finagles. If you forget the manipulative nature of nature, well, you're in for trouble.

I'm suddenly struck by how, no matter where I am, the very mention of nature always brings me back to a certain park, Chetzemoka Park, a park you may not have heard of but, trust me, it's the kind of park that is so full of green that any other version of "green space" is just plain incomparable to me.

Through six poetry collections and on to my first book of essays, the park saved me from the anxious sense of isolation that sweeps over me when I spend too much time indoors. All I need is to take a walk through its green wedge of land that slopes down to the sea, and, just like that, my mind projects into all the good grateful stuff. The natural world never fails to cut my worry down to a manageable size. If Mother Nature can wait patiently for each and every storm to pass, I can surely do the same.

I think we can forget what this feels like if we don't make time for it, if we don't cut off from distraction in a quiet place still intact. It's Chetzemoka that keeps me from selling my writing cottage and moving to a warmer clime for good.

Not that one park can be more beautiful than another, my park any quieter or more beautiful than your favorite park; it's an impossible comparison, like comparing the innocence of toddlers. Still, it's difficult to explain how I feel when I walk through Chetzemoka and breathe it in. Overcome?

Maybe "overcome" is a little over the top.

Yet, it's more than appreciation, certainly. Trust, then? As in, I trust Chetzemoka Park in a way I can't trust a more formal public property?

God, yes.

It's a refuge. In a time in my life when I need a refuge more than ever. For one thing, the rest of the world isn't visible over the heights of its cedars; this is the first sensation I feel looking up into the sweeping canopy of branches instead of out to sea, because sometimes looking out over the sea anywhere near Seattle can leave me feeling a little lost. It's not the kind of ocean you rush into laughing and splashing before you swim a clumsy lap and turn over to drift on your back with a great big smile on your face. You'd last twenty minutes, tops.

Even so, Chetzemoka is where I return to when I want to know why people, once they visit, want to stay, want to chuck their old lives and call a realtor. One day of sunshine in such a sparkling green place and you're confronted with the rawest meaning of beauty, which, I decide, is what I'm always searching for in one way or another.

Even if I have to put right out of my mind the truth of my favorite park's past, a fact my friend, Cindy, reminded me of after I told her I wanted to write this tribute.

"I hope you don't write something totally naïve," she said (I call her Surly Cindy). "Because every time *I* enter the park, I'm reminded of the indigenous people we took this place from, how we had the gall to name the land after the chief who was our friend. Chetzemoka Park reflects the worst of white man's ignorance and now, the best of our community: weddings in the gazebo, Shakespeare in the Park. The irony is sad."

Oh, I cringed, *that*, the other truth, the past I can't put right, the guilt-ridden stuff. *Cindy, could I maybe have my stardust back?*

I had to work really hard to stay in the present after talking to Cindy. It's not that I want to scrape off the surface and repaint to my liking, I'm deeply disturbed by the harmful human impact on nearly every issue regarding history. But I try not to take it out on my friends. I wasn't prepared for deserving blame, for my appreciation to slither to the ground. Knowing too much about the world at all times, without being able to undo past mistakes, is pure craziness for the modern human mind, a guilt-guarantee if ever there was one.

Enough! I'm done with the guilt.

I'm doing the best I can. I recycle. Unless I'm leaving the city, I ride my bike or walk. I'm ready with a foldaway bag at the grocery, I care for my elderly mom, manage her responsibilities so that she can play bingo and poker and golf and not have to worry about ending up alone.

So thank goodness tributes are, as they say, in the hands of the one who writes them. I'm grateful for Chetzemoka as it is *today*. I'm sticking with present tense, present day.

Oh, and along with dropping the guilt, I want to make more of an effort to say "thank you" whenever it applies. So thank you to the men and women who keep my holy park in bloom, cropped, maintained and accessible, but not too much. It's still rustic enough. With paths that weave rather than shoot me in one direction.

How I like to follow most paths in life.

Free Zone

It happened again, third time this month.

Actually, I've been dealing with it for as long as I can remember.

I don't fully understand what goes on. It remains one of the great mysteries of writing. My thoughts are clear, I'm dancing over the keys with a smile on my face, and then, out of nowhere, another story rear-ends me, jarring and forceful.

And not to minimize my hold on subject matter, but nothing makes my first idea crumple faster than another idea, a *better* idea, scrambling for attention. Even if I started with a good idea, or was fairly certain it was a good idea, after a paragraph or too, I can hear the crash.

It's hard to believe, but writing has become a collision course, thumbs down on anything I try and handle the long way around. It's as if the road to what I want to say runs north, but for whatever stubborn reason, I keep driving south. That is, until the road buckles, heaves, and buckles again. Until one side swears it has a point, but the other sees something looser, more relaxed, its only point is not to have one. Yet.

The only explanation I can think of for resisting at all is that I must, on some level, still believe I have some sort of say over what I write. And this is the part with my foot on the gas. Until I spin out. Until I leave words that try to be more than skid marks, but, as I can see in her rearview mirror, are not.

And if it sounds like my new idea is maybe a little too pushy, it is. More so for having been in check at all. So, with no will to fight it, I pour another cup of coffee, print out this morning's page and try again. By now there's no time to over think it; there's a deadline to meet. And nothing can make me feel more pent up than when an idea is trying to break me open and I can't relax enough to let it, how resistance can make the whole thing drag out way too long with no pay-off in the end.

I take a deep breath and realize, not for the first time, mind you, that writing about writing can be so much like writing about sexual tension I can hardly believe it.

Just as, sometimes, pay-off comes twice, maybe three times, without delay.

This, I like.

For instance, this morning I started to write about my first true Obama-letdown, his stand on the death penalty. No more than a hundred words in, I see the only person who let me down, of course, is me. Because I only just now bothered to look up his position on whether any man has the right to take the life of another. How uninformed does this make me, the voter?

Very.

In my defense, I bet a lot of women understand how, when looking for a little class in a man, we can fall under charisma's spell, how we want to believe a man who looks so healthy, must share her fundamental beliefs about things like whether we should ever consider murder justifiable. Until the day she wakes up and feels not the bed of roses she imagined lying in, soft and pink, but a shrub with few hundred thorns of its own.

Then I thought, *Hello. Two daughters, dedicated to his wife and mother. A lifetime of protecting women dies hard.* So, of course the man is in favor of offing the child rapists.

Nothing more to say, really.

Have you heard of the cyclists on the Burke Gilman Bicycle Trail who yell like staff sergeants, "ON YOUR LEFT!" as if I don't *know* that's the side they are going to take me on, seeing as how I'm already riding on the grass in fear, pedaling away from those who ride like the wind instead of like a woman (me) peddling along on a beach cruiser at a genteel pace that allows her to peer into the windows of all the lovely homes and imagine herself eating canapés in a living room nice as theirs?

Well, I don't care for those cyclists much.

The likely explanation is that they are Microsoft worker bees, while I'm the freelance butterfly! I have flexibility. I have color. I move from flower to flower. While they, poor babies, have to beeline from A to B or get fired.

The next idea put an end to all that bicycle nonsense, shoved its way in and yelled, "DRUG RING BUSTED!" It was the headline in the *Seattle Times* a few weeks back, a story about a Honduran drug ring busted in Belltown. I knew the story was important to me but for the first time I understood *why*. It made me remember my last editor at said newspaper, now retired, Lee Moriwaki, who used to like my stories, compliment my stories, once in awhile even publish my stories, a gesture that always made my day. "Why not write more about the street violence downtown?" Mr. Moriwaki asked me once.

Like I know about it?

I was too embarrassed to say I knew more about the boutiques on First Avenue, the Happy Hours on Second. But the brawls and gunfights? Not my world, really.

Though on any given Saturday when the bars empty out, I can hear the sidewalk free-for-alls like everyone else in my neighborhood, during which time I usually pick up my book and read a few chapters. No part of me, not a single cell, was willing to go down there to chat up the drunks, bullies, and dealers just to get a better story for Mr. Moriwaki who'd pay me, what, a hundred bucks? Two hundred if I embarrass him into it.

Second, the headline made me remember meeting one of the Honduran crack dealers arrested in the sweep. I talked to him once, shook his hand. And as soon as I saw him in handcuffs in the newspaper, I recognized him as the man, a boy really, who stood outside the Belltown Dance Studio, peering in as if his life depended on it.

I think it did. It was a look no dancer could miss.

Let me establish why I shook his hand before you run off thinking I contribute to one of our nation's few growing industries. The dance studio amplifies Latin music onto the sidewalk to attract students. And because these dealers, these dirt-poor boys who are rounded up in their villages, persuaded to deal as if it will make *them* money, who won't inform on their bosses because they fear for the safety of their families, well, they aren't at home on the streets of Seattle; so, the way I see it, the boy was trying to get back home through the music streaming overhead. And I, naive one, thought he'd stopped to inquire about dance classes, so I opened the door and handed him a schedule.

What I saw was a boy swept back to a time when he likely Salsa danced on a Saturday night instead of hustling the streets for buyers. Rather than living in a harsh, high-rise world behind a dumpster in an American city with tiny plastic bags hidden in his body. I can't find the exact words to describe how happy he looked standing there, swaying slightly, but his smile was oblivious to everything but the sound. I fell in love with how he fell in love with the music because I know how music can liven up the dark like a lit fuse.

And that's what we shared, the drug dealer and me. The pleasure of air filled with beautiful music, where it's easier to feel yourself free.

Afterward, I began to think of the sidewalk outside our dance studio as a free zone where the boy and I are not unconnected people from different worlds, but two dancers, together, who find certain sounds and rhythms impossible to resist.

Among Friends

April makes me want to fling open the closets, clean them out, go through the cupboards, clean them out, vacuum under the bed, maybe throw a dinner party.

And I was all set to sink my teeth into describing the dinner party I'll talk myself out of (fun and breezy on the magazine page, but *I'd* have to do the work). I was ready to enjoy myself too, admit to peeling off my socks and booking a pedicure before my guests arrive, add a few luscious details . . . like the heavenly leg massage the Thai women give while my head falls back in pleasure before walking my pretty toes downtown to find the perfect dress to wear, say how thrifty this makes me because, thanks to the refusal of so many women around here to wear anything but jeans, sneakers, and fleece, they are practically giving the dresses away.

But when I held the last paragraph up to the looking glass, my reflection bore an unmistakably questioning expression: *None of it makes up for the dishes you'll have to wash, the wine stains on the carpet, your friends arguing about health care reform and refusing to dance even though they know I feel more at home on the dance floor than in the kitchen.*

It was right about then that a friend called.

We took a while to catch up.

I liked listening to her go into detail about raising guinea hens because ever since her only son left for college she's been trying to refill her nest, first with the dogs, then a goat (for lawn maintenance, she said), now the hens; but I was also thinking how, when I indulge in conversation first thing in the morning, I have to work late to get my pages written. Or I won't be able to write at all because it's hard to get back into the flow.

But I tried not to let on.

When she started in on the major difference between guinea hens and chickens, I was also thinking, *Is this why her clothing is so . . . so . . . what is the word? Dated.*

Oh, in case you are thinking I am completely insensitive, my friend has no financial difficulties. In fact, the opposite is true. Two exes—long story—plenty of money.

But none of this is the point. The point is, the way she dresses bothers me. And I'm curious why it matters. It's not *my* wardrobe.

I should also say, right away before you hate me, that my friend is in her early forties, has a dancer's body, and rarely misses a workout. She's gorgeous. Too young to give up, fashion-wise; too fit to go to seed. On the rare occasion when we meet for dinner, I take in her clothes and I think, if she only *knew.* These are the clothes of someone older, with no imagination, no confidence. And she has both. Maybe she just doesn't *know.*

Maybe I should have stuck to describing the dinner party . . . played it safe.

But if you only knew how tricky the writer inside my head is. I'm pretty sure the writer needed to devise a way to bring this issue up because last night at the Intiman Theater a man in front of me wore sweat pants and a baseball cap he refused to take off which made the hat a far more pressing issue than it needed to be. And, because I am still upset about that boorish guy, I need to find a way to say, in print before your very eyes, how clothes *matter.*

Maybe not crucially. But significantly.

"Exactly," I say to myself.

"I read that clothes say a lot about where someone has settled inside."

"I couldn't agree more."

I have to work to keep my face from falling when my friend walks through the door. The thing is, five minutes into our conversation, our laughing, I don't give my friend's clothes another thought. Why? Because she is my friend. I love her, of course.

Besides, she is not faultless. She is always saying something about how I should do this, how I could do better at that, so I can't help but want to throw in a few tidbits about keeping up with a personal style versus a look that tries too hard. Nothing out of malice. I can do that. Absolutely.

So far, not a peep out of me. I know telling a truth someone doesn't wish to hear is a boat-rocker if ever there was one, no matter how inevitable a little boat-rocking is now and again between too close friends. I fear, after the wave settles, we'll drift apart, so I hold my tongue. I can't even remember how long I've been holding it.

Consequently, I've been working through my conflicting feelings to get at the underlying truth of why my friend's clothes annoy me the way they do. I knew there was more going on than the fact that I have two opposing personalities in regards to this. One is that I was a creative director for a dance company for nearly twenty years. I can't help but think of all the tiny details that can make any presentation work better. It's involuntary for me, the creative directing.

The other is that I'm abashed to say just how involuntary it is. To not start directing in mind would be like holding in a sneeze.

So I did a little research.

Only to find what I believe is the underlying reason my friend's Dacron bugs me the way it does. And, as it turns out, it has little to do with her clothes and everything to do with my background, my history, my people, *me*.

The truth is always close to the bone.

I tell myself I'm not nostalgic about my friend, that I know the difference between her life and my own.

I tell myself this, but it's not true. She is the first Italian friend I've made since leaving the East Coast. After a recent trip Back East, I came to see myself in relation to my family more clearly. Maybe too clearly. When I was younger I was so mentally busy telling myself I was not going to be anything *like* my family that I couldn't see how much like them I already was. And when I catch myself gauging my friend's appearance, I wonder if I am any better than all the old world, squinty-eyed, fault-finding, black-wearing Italian aunts I couldn't wait to leave behind.

My family. Poor when they came to this country. My father used to say that the only thing he left Italy with was his pride. I've seen pictures of how he looked back then. His stance says it all. And ever since the war that changed everything for him, for humanity, he, like most Europeans, believes in the illusion that a refined appearance will grant him the confidence he needs to compete in the world. And the world, to most immigrants, still means America.

In contrast to American-casual-always, most cultures—perhaps not England, but there is absolutely nothing to learn from grown men who wear knee socks and shorts—see life beyond the four walls of home as more of a formal affair. And this way of seeing the world is as ingrained in me as my fingerprints and it pretty much defines my take on reality. Absurd to think I could revise all this ingraining in one generation.

Still you'd think, given I'm always inside my head reaching for some new way to grasp what I don't understand, that this realization would not have felt as startling as it did.

But it did.

It also made it easier to acknowledge that clothes really do arouse in me many qualities, perhaps my favorite qualities, of being Italian.

Even so, admitting this is causing the back of my neck to prickle. But what is beginning to really frighten me is that my readers will throw this book down, calling me a heartless snob; that this admission is going to annoy some of my friends right out of their Crocs.

But all the women in my family are a little delusional about something. Aunt Connie with her rosary beads, her fifteen sets of Hail Mary's; my mother's collection of Hummels (factor in the shelves to house them); me with my treasured heart-shaped shells I won't give up because somewhere deep inside I believe without them I will lose my way, forget how to write, go unwritten, grow positively desperate.

And, dammit, I've worked so hard at leaving parts of my past behind. I thought I'd drowned most of them out for good.

Yet, like it or no, these submerged parts rise to the surface whenever I see my friend. So, this is what bothers me: How can my friend betray our very Italian-ness?

And I know how far-fetched this sounds. Even if it makes sense to me. But, either way, this was a complete and utter catharsis for me. And once I got through it, I shared my revelation with my friend. Boy did we have a laugh.

So how could I be so honest and cross such a dangerous line?

Sometimes admission is the only way. Unless it totally flops. (Life is a risk!) Besides, I suspected she's known all along how I feel.

I also told her that when we are old, she'll be the one whose bank account shines. "Me? I'll be the woman pushing a prized mound of shoes in a rusty grocery cart."

"I'll take you in," she said, "but don't worry, I'll vacuum first."

And that's when it occurred to me that maybe my friend had chosen me for the same reason I'd chosen her, to rise above. She thinks my clothes are a ridiculous waste of money, my fastidiousness a total waste of time.

I remember feeling such a deep sense of appreciation for her, for us, feelings far more basic and key to my well-being than anything about what she wears.

Like shoulder pads.

In this day and age.

Defending Rachel

On Saturday Night Live, there's a skit where two women play NPR hosts, and it's so funny I could die of laughter every time I see it. Usually after watching TV, I want the hour of my life back, but *SNL* still lets raw talent do original material, not easy to find these days when most programming, even comedy, is an imitation of something else.

The result is not always hilarious and sometimes it's a little clumsy, but it's tough work to find the distinct balance comedy requires. To watch comics get better at it as the years progress, that we get to witness, live, what it takes to move from youthful confidence to the level of comedic skill a long-standing career demands, well, it feels like a gift.

But my own National Public Radio experience?

No laughing matter.

Although I find retelling it sort of funny.

Sometimes I look back at that period in my life and I think it's the first time I understood what people mean when they say they are weighed down by a memory. I certainly am by this one, a good indication that's it's high time to let it go rather than keep it inside. My worst fear, health-wise, is to keep things inside.

It might seem a little naive of someone who writes for the media to say this, but I remember the exact moment I first sensed that NPR has an agenda just like any news program. It may not sound like it, but don't kid yourself, it does. It may be unlike Fox News, but only because there are so many people who prefer listening to the "take me back to a non-existent time" tone of Garrison Keillor to programming where scuffle is the whole show. And once I realized what this agenda would mean for me, because I don't think of myself as a funny writer, per se, my insides felt like a late-night-panic-attack getting straight with me. Fast.

⟶

"Everything I mistrust about people is all over the network news," I said recently at a reading I gave about women and friendship. "One minute the delivery is all sparkly fun; next they go for the jugular." And suddenly, without intending to, which happens a lot when I speak in front of a group, I knew precisely how I felt about the particular person I was thinking of, but I also knew exactly how I felt about too much of the news media in general lately, how it plays to the basic dual-nature of human beings, our seemingly limitless need to learn and relearn the same old lessons, our capacity for blunders and cheating and screw-ups which, somehow, doesn't stop us from blundering and cheating and screwing up all over again.

The *All Things Considered* (*ATC*) producer who called me said, "You live in Seattle. Write me something Seattle."

"Something Seattle," I repeated with a fluttery feeling in my throat. I always get this weird sensation when I talk to editors, agents, producers. It's as if we speak across some great big borderline that divides everything. I've learned to suppress it until the conversation is over, but it never goes away.

A moment passed before she said anything else. Then another, each more silent than the last.

Up until then, there had been a part of me that fantasized my commentaries would continue to air no matter what, that I'd make the transition from *Weekend Edition* to the more entertaining *All Things Considered* with no problem whatsoever.

Even if, in the way a person just does, I sensed from that silence, right off the bat, that my new producer didn't take to me all that well. (Or me to her, frankly.) Sometimes it takes no more than a few words: "Where is it those fishermen throw the fish back and forth like a baseball? Pike's Market?" she asked.

Oh, no, please. Not the salmon tossing. And, by the way, they aren't fishermen; they just dress the part. And it's not Pike's Market. It's Pike Place Market. *Pike.* With no mark of the possessive.

My flinch at her mispronunciation was just a reflex, that's all, nothing that need get in the way, I thought, a roll-my-eyes reaction to hearing my everyday market mispronounced, even by people who live in Seattle.

Like when someone calls me *I*-talian. Long *I*. Really, there is no polite way to correct this misuse of sound light years from appropriate. *Soften the vowel.*

Same with Iraq. It's not *I*-raq like "I see you." It's Ear-ak. *Soften the vowel.*

Really, if we spend our retirement savings to visit a country, or invade one, maybe we should learn how to pronounce it. Flawlessly. It's the least we can do.

I said none of this, of course. I just nodded my head and told myself, *I can't write about salmon tossing; everyone writes about salmon tossing . . . BUT I WILL!* And so I agreed the way any writer consents to any number of requests if they want something bad enough. Because we do. Even those who pretend otherwise. It's demeaning, I know. I can't explain why we do it, how far we'll go, how much we'll compromise to get our work out there.

"And make it funny," she added, just before she hung up. "Light. That's what we're looking for at *ATC* these days."

Funny? Light? These days? See what I mean? Agenda.

And as soon as she said it, I knew we'd be sending more troops to the Middle East. I'm the last writer in the world anyone would call a news writer, but I remembered something I learned about Hollywood the last time I worked as a journalist. My story was about humor as a media influence, how throughout the 1940s and early 50s, when America was either gearing up for, fighting in, or recuperating from World War II, movie-goers wanted relief from the horrors of war. Happy musicals and unquestioning praise for "American values" took precedence in radio, television, and theater. *Anything but the truth, honey.*

That said, I was extremely relieved she didn't ask me to drive out to the Olympic Peninsula to write about vampires, the hot topic in pop-everything. Where even the Chamber of Commerce in Forks now refers to their city as the "Home of *Twilight*," cashing in on the vampire theme, lock, stock and barrel. So much for its logging motif; crosscut saw is *out*.

Vampires are even sinking their incisors into my world. I recently emailed a proprietor of a certain classy Italian restaurant out in Port Angeles (the largest town you pass through on your way to Forks) to ask, "What's up?"

See, he used to prop one of my titles on his wine bar, a book I wrote about *being* Italian and *eating* Italian. Now my book is somewhere in the way back, stored with the cannellini beans. *Twilight* took its place. There is just no competing with vampires in the marketplace right now.

At any rate, it made more sense to go with the flow and write something funny/light Seattle. Even if I couldn't see myself exaggerating the fish tossing, or making it the whole story, I could add a touch, no problem, like adding salt to soup, a pinch rather than a handful. Fair enough. I know how to salt. It goes with the job title: writer.

Like, for instance, salting our wounds, as in checking our email every ten minutes, scared of rejection; pretending we are fine to our spouse, our friends; acting very matter-of-fact cool, when we are just sizzling inside. *Is my writing good enough? Is it? Is it?* The erupting crater that continually bubbles over and can ruin just about everything good about writing if we let it.

Then what? What's the next NPR insult? *I'm sorry, this commentary is not for* ATC *at this time.* Come again? This cold, bitter trench of non-personal after a phone call *from* the producer, access to her cell? *This wildly busy producer made time for me, and three rewrites. Aren't I lucky?* Is this what I'm supposed to think? Producers. I think they could get writers to do anything. They wield power. Play a mean game. It's not fair.

Now that I think about it, there isn't all that much I like about writing for NPR anyway (this is not salt; *this* is sour grapes) other than the opportunity to show off a little because nothing makes an audience sit up at attention on comfortless folding chairs more than the mere mention of these three left-leaning upper-case consonants strung together.

Several hours later, I am still thinking about all the editing and rewriting that went into those 400 words of commentary.

My last Weekend Edition piece came in at 418 words and right up until the end, when I was already in the booth gargling with vinegar, the producer was asking me to shave a few words. I cringed. "Sure!" *Why don't you just ask me to shoot myself?*

There I was, trying to find an effective, immediate way to say something without writing it down or, for that matter, saying it at all. I consented. I was so nervous. *Please let me do this right without diminishing everything I've ever loved about writing even though the sentences are already pushed to the brink and if I throw one word off, one pause, the whole thing will go haywire.*

Writing for radio is so compressed, and so exact, like adding ingredients to a cake made from scratch. It's amazing how little tampering it takes for one of those hopeful combinations to look like a bubbling sump through your oven window.

Anyway, I secretly knew my brief, short-circuited, smack-of-funny-on-purpose version would be rejected because Significant Other said "Truth?" after reading it. And only someone who's been married to him for as long as I have could interpret how hard he was struggling to say the best thing while fearing he'd already said the worst.

"No, honey, lie to me."

"Okay, it's funny," he said in neutral-WASP-tone, and that's when I made it clear that my commentary, *my* commentary, was no longer any of his damn business.

All this to say that there is clarity that comes, eventually, when we hold on to our work, and to ourselves, our way. It's a focus that allows us to see all kinds of other, better, funny/light ways to describe what it's like to write for a commentary producer. It's like ... well, it's like when I see beautifully sculptured shoes, rows and rows of leather before me in a shop in Rome. I see the next pair and fly to them, like a bee to a bloom, to run my fingers over the fineness. And so it goes all the way down the aisles. I won't allow myself to over-think the joy I feel. I won't let any carbon neutral vegan guilt thump my happiness. I don't want to buy each pair; well maybe I do, but I won't. I just want to be near them, try them on, turn them over, feel quality in my hands.

That is, until my husband comes along and says how many shoes I already have. And I am instantly reminded that shopping, just like writing, with another person looking over your shoulder, rarely, if ever, works.

From my desk to your eyes, ta da, my *ATC*-funny:

(Oh, I've decided to include the book-length, freed-up version, with all the twists and turns I love, rather than the abbreviated, 400-word, NPR rewrite. It's the only version that doesn't embarrass me at this point.)

Well beyond the mix of crafts, food, and flowers in Seattle's beloved Pike Place Market, there is a Senior Center, a food bank, a daycare and preschool, and a health clinic most tourists never see.

And then there is Rachel. Rachel the Pig. The Rachel *every*one sees. The commissioned, life-size, bronze piggy bank that stands under the famous red Public Market sign in front of the fish-flying vendors, men who like to toss all that delectable drama into the air.

Quick update: In 1986, Seattle's Market Foundation held a contest. Local artists submitted drawings of piggy banks. Rachel was chosen. Ever since, Rachel's been collecting donations for the Market's charities. People from all over the world rub Rachel's snout for good luck. When Rachel gives, she gives big.

Normally, I need the right level of excitement to straddle my legs around another. Today, I don't have that level. But the little girl climbing up on Rachel does. What's even better is her dad's smile. It's wide. Very wide. Arsenio Hall wide. No one needs to know anything more about this man to see how much he loves his daughter. I stop to watch. And that's when Rachel gives off a sort of audible giggling sound. I swear to God.

I wish I could ride Rachel. But I don't have the guts. How can I explain this? About trying new things lately, it's as if I'm a keel caught in sand. On the success side of life, I'm doing okay. Really good, best ever. But, on the have-more-fun side, I'm sort of stuck. And one has a tendency to take stock at junctions like this.

My next thought, considering the girl astride Rachel looked incredibly happy: *The price of embarrassment? Who gives a flying fish? Someday I'll straddle Rachel, too. I will!*

But not today. And I was just about to get on with my shopping when something unspeakable happened: A man kicked Rachel's behind. It felt like he kicked me. I yelled, "You've got some nerve, buster!" It was one of those fantastic lines right out of a Betty Davis movie that comes to you, if you're lucky, at just the right moment.

"This pig made of gold or what?" he asked.

"Bronze," I huffed.

He shrugged defensively, as though bronze is close enough to gold to make no difference.

The nerve of this guy.

I don't know why it felt so important to make him respect Rachel, to know how cherished she is, how charitable; how her practice is always to give of herself, her curvaceous body a bright spot in the Market even on the shortest, wettest, darkest days of the year.

Are you thinking I kicked him back?

I didn't. I did, however, feel the kind of anger that cancels out any likelihood of forgiveness. The kind of anger that, like my mother before me, makes me mean. And way too honest. The level of honesty, that, admittedly, has gotten me into my share of trouble over the years. But trouble, I've decided, is sometimes a necessary side effect of having the guts to say what you really think. Funny, though, no words were required. All I had to do was give him a look.

"Sorry," he said, sniggering, but he got my point.

"You wouldn't believe how fast he got my point," I said later, describing the whole incident to Larry over dinner.

"Yes I would," he replied, too fast if you ask me.

See, Larry is worried that my outbursts of bravado (like yelling at the guys who spit on the sidewalk, the leaf blowers, parents who ignore their children to focus on their cell phones) will get me into trouble some day. "You need to just walk away," he says. "Learn to say nothing."

How does one do this?

The last couple of months he's been even more emphatic, ever since that story in *The New York Times* about a woman on the Upper East Side who, after complaining to an Italian plumber about the noise he

was making in the apartment next to hers, was killed by a pipe coming down, ever so bluntly, on her head.

So I don't want to belittle his concern.

Then, of course, there's the small matter of his being right.

Still, it's an impossible standard, to say nothing sometimes, for
someone like me.

Anyway, I chopped the whole thing down to my given word count,
an altogether less real way of saying everything, but I wanted my piece
to fly.

It didn't.

Funny, I was really good at not caring so much about this kind of
"success" in my twenties. Then, in my thirties and forties, the most
competitive years, I got really bad at caring too much again. I eventually found my way back. Now, even at my lowest, I know there is
only one way to write funny in the end, just as there is only one way
to write seriously. You try and delete and revise and delete and try and
revise, over and over, until you stand up and look out the window.

Sidebar: Don't be deceived by the strenuously funny/light tone of
my disappointment. After that last rejection, I thought maybe we *do*
lose the one thing we want most. It could be a lover, a career, a pet.
Or maybe, just maybe, it's another shot at NPR. It took me years to
get over what I perceived as my great big funny failure. I have never
really recovered from that failure. It helps to explain why I don't listen to NPR any more.

All things considered, it stinks to be rejected by *All Things
Considered*.

Selfish, Selfish Me

MAY

I'm sitting in my office, nursing a cup of coffee, trying to come to grips with the fact that, contrary to everything I (try to) believe in, I just lied to my mother.

And May is *the* month to honor our mothers. *And look what you're doing! You are telling her a lie! You are lying! Liar. Liar. Liar.*

Had someone interrupted me just before the lie slipped out, handed me a notepad with the word DON'T! scribbled in bold letters followed with, "You really don't want to lie to your mom, do you?" I probably would have found the lie harder to pull off.

Guilt creeps in. I'll have to ask Larry to drive his thumbs into my shoulders when he gets home. Larry is good at relaxing the baggage out of my shoulders. He knows it's more than the muscles in my neck that need to let go, but the trapezius; *this* is my storage space.

Right after I hung up, a part of me cowered.

But the other part, the part that actually told the lie, ran like hell.

And then I waited. And there it was. For what's a good white lie without the relief that comes after, a little shy at first, but firm, drawing near like a warm front to absolve me. To let me off the hook. The older I get, the more I need this self-forgiveness to remind me how sometimes it's impossible to be completely honest with our mothers.

Still, after fifty years of this scenario, there are still so many things I can't figure out.

Such as, is it true, as is said, that my reversal into lie-to-Mom-teenager role is what happens when push comes to shove between two grown women if one has given birth to the other, unavoidable as breathing? Because, as a rule, and especially around the holidays, it happens this way between us. We spread a little blame around, wave our hands in the air, fan the things we feel if it means being right, lie a little if it means getting our way.

A lie can fly out without warning. Lies are sudden. But once they're out, they are a door slamming behind you. *Click.*

And lies can expand to be as big as we need them to be. No matter how small we feel afterward.

And lies are always more about *why* we tell them.

Over the last decade, nearly every Mother's Day I've made off to my mother's home. The echo begins right around the first of the month: *This could be her last Mother's Day; you have to go!* If I try and ignore it, it's gets louder; it drowns out everything.

Years back, the trek meant returning to Connecticut, where my young mistakes would sneak up on me, sure, but I found it a comfort to clink glasses with a couple of old high school friends and visit the relatives on their vinyl-covered couches, which always meant I'd be slipped a couple of twenties, so I was good with it.

Then it got trickier. In order to see my mother, I had to make my way to, gulp, Bible Belt Tennessee where my mother lived for fifteen years with her second husband, a man from Knoxville (they met on an Elderhostel retreat) who used to tip his hat and call me "little lady." Once he bought me a *TV Guide* because "the articles in this here magazine are real good" which I found sort of charming, his attempt at trying to connect with me, the writer, even though he found the fact that I had an "occupation" but no "offspring" a little difficult to say aloud.

Here was a man who declared, proudly, that he never did read my "kind of books" (?), whose inner circle included no working women whatsoever other than female celebrity chefs, now that he was hooked on cooking shows because my mother was devoted to them. Of Paula Deen, he declared, "She's okay because she's a housewife from Georgia, not some highfalutin' showoff from New York."

"She's pretty shrewd behind all that down-homeness." I said. "How else could she have risen so far, so fast? She probably works day and night." I know I was being difficult, instigating. Why couldn't I just see who I was dealing with and shut up? A Southern man will resonate with a Southern cook; what's the big deal?

"Woman," he piped, "cookin' ain't really workin'."

Woman? Did he just say "woman?"

Maybe in Tennessee, men call women "woman." Maybe in Tennessee "woman" is considered an okay thing to say just before you say whatever you are about to say next, common as "excuse me" in Seattle. My patience hardened.

What I said next, I drew out of me in the same slow, deliberate way I set an open-faced feta sandwich onto the counter, right from under the broiler. I blow on it, take a tiny hesitant nibble from the corner ... hold your horses ... hang on ... then *chomp*.

"Man," I said in my best twang, "Cookin' *is* workin'. Especially when my mother is doing it for you three times a day." (When my dad left, my mother said the only good thing about it was that it beat having to make dinner every night.)

By now my mother was shooting me one of her looks that can, in an instant, cremate my nerve. I let the argument go, figuring what is the point of trying to confirm my version of the world with that of a, for lack of a better description, hillbilly.

"Would you, please, get off your high horse," my mother said to me later in the kitchen.

"He's so *coun*try."

"I prefer *rural*," she said.

The next day when he asked why I wasn't living a "normal" life, any trace of tolerance on my part ran completely dry.

We'd spent the whole morning driving to Oak Ridge and it's a long story which I don't want to go into, only that the thing about me that was the most difficult for him to swallow, impossible really, was that I didn't know who the Oak Ridge Boys *were*.

"If *normal* means I should have a couple of kids who hate me (his children don't talk to him, so I knew this would strike below the belt, which is where I was aiming, I reckon), if *normal* means I should distrust anyone who doesn't look like me, love a band that sings about their hearts on fire, well, then, yep, I guess you're right, I'm not *normal*." I paused. Simmered. "What does a normal woman look like to you, anyway? Do you think you can tell just by watching her stuff a pork chop on TV?" I started to look off to the side of his head because his eyes were so big. They were furious.

After that, we pretty much left any effort at communication out of our relationship. Which made visiting my mother a little uncomfortable.

Worse, the town they lived in, if you can believe, is still a dry zone.

"What?" I snapped at the waitress the first time we went to a restaurant. "Are you telling me there will be no wine-squabbling with my mother over dinner?"

The contradiction about the county is, and has always been, from what I could gather, one-hundred proof as its moonshine. Even my mother's Bible-quoting friends had their modern-day moonshine, the real deal, hidden under the kitchen sink. At one point, I got so bored, I called up one of the local bootleggers, a nurse around my age, a woman known for her schnapps recipe. She and I ended up on the kitchen floor, trying to keep our laughter down so "the neighbors won't wonder what we're up to," my mother said.

Is there any image more ridiculous than two grown women having to worry because they are laughing too loud? "What is this, the Middle East?" I said, doubling over.

As you can imagine, my mother wasn't having any more of my questions by then. She left the kitchen. As she turned her back, I heard her say to the cat, "My daughter, she thinks she's so *smart*." In my family, when you swing back, you throw a sucker punch. Wham!

And in order to stay in that southern town where the women my mother kept company with compare notes not only on their "recipes" but on their "happy pills" (Zoloft, Prozac, Paxil, Lexapro, except they pronounced them with a twang, so it sounded more like one of those really funny *SNL* skits), I gave my mother an ultimatum: "When you get older and need me more, you have to move somewhere I can stand to visit. I'm not coming back here."

So lately (thank you, Mom!) I visit her in the warm cradle of Honolulu sunshine. Where maybe she's only one of a handful of haoles in the hodgepodge of cultural divides that make up the island of Oahu; but at least she is not the only Italian in her retirement home who thinks walking to the dining room, instead of firing up the scooter, entitles you to a second helping of pie.

All this comes back to me as I think about what I've gained through my Mother's Day-commitment over the years. Slowly, I've come to know my mother better, or better than I knew her when I still shared her with my siblings, my dad, her endless game shows, and the friends she had babies with (only then it wasn't called a Mother's Group, just "the neighbor ladies").

Okay, the lie: "I can't make it this year, Mom, I have way too much work going on."

Which is true. Sort of. But I could squeeze the trip in. If I wanted to.

Thing is, I've been traveling so much, doing the work I love. The fact that I'm able to bring a staged-reading of one of my books to venues all over the country is a dream made real for me after years of elbow grease. Keeping all the balls in the air to make the dream a reality is a juggling act, though, where one performance leads to another in sort of a grass-roots manner that, in the last two decades, I've spent a lot of time nurturing.

Finding the balance is the toughest part.

I don't like over-working. But I don't like too much time off. Which is something of a problem, sometimes, this loving what I do so much that I can have these absolute sweeps of guilt wondering if the two people I love most, my husband and Mom, are being too nice to me when I blow them off in order to work more because they not only understand what drives me, but, on a deeper level, they know they have no other option.

And now, for most of May, I have no bookings. I'm full of greed for the privacy, the sleeping in, all the ways I want to spend my downtime. I want to do nothing but write and be with my husband.

"In that order?" he asked.

"I think so, yes: A. Writing. B. You."

"It's okay, dear," my mom said. "There's always next year." And though the great Pacific separates us, I could see her lips crimp, a smile that gives, at once, the impression of understanding mixed with utter disappointment. Anything else will always be beyond her at such moments. No wonder, when I was a kid, my dad would sit in the car in our driveway, drunk as a skunk after his weekly poker game, afraid to come inside.

"Thank you," I said, pretending I heard something more sympathetic than I had.

Still, there was no need for me to ask for forgiveness . . . was there? "I hope you don't think I'm being *selfish*."

Kill me now. Why do we do it? Why do we say the S word? I have got to stop using the S word. Slowly, my mother inhaled. Then, just as slowly, she exhaled. And her next "no" has always meant "yes" and makes it seem like no syllable should be able to hold so much guilt. So I did the only thing I could, I lied. Again. About how *buuusssy* I am. A lie like you've never heard. I could feel the guilt wiggling through my nerves, a swarm of serpents and snakes.

I sat thinking whether I should have chanced being more honest by telling her that, this year, "I need more time for myself, more than I need time with, um, *you*."

And that's when I thought about something my old friend Elizabeth told me years ago when she was eighty-six. Nearly everything I learned from Elizabeth bears repeating. Because not only do I love how Elizabeth made me feel about aging, how she skimmed off my worst fears of it, reminding me that, in fact, creases and lines make us more real; I loved her take on honesty. She was my wise woman. I don't have this kind of easy give-and-take with my own mother, obviously, so I've always been out there looking for it. My mother is a wise woman too, but the very nature of mother/daughter makes for more of a push-pull, more of a concession.

Here's what Elizabeth said: "If any part of the brain the good Lord gave you doubts you should be so honest, and you mouth off anyway, honey, it's not honesty; it's ego."

And just like that, I found myself in a place where all of my guilt trips could never take me, past all the complicated emotions, to where one can only come to with age. And whether the idea of getting to a place where you can lie to your mother to spare her a truth that would wound her even deeper comforts you, I really can't say. But right now I have the urge to stand and shout *hallelujah!* So I know it comforts me.

Even so, I don't expect this needling sliver of shame to fall off any time soon, which, now that I finally found time to get some R & R, sort of irks me.

I guess it's my cross to bear.

The upside is that I may not always tell the truth to my mother nor does my mother always tell the truth to me, but we are each the one the other trusts completely.

I don't pretend to know why.

My current theory is that we are normal.

Big Flavor

The most fascinating thing about June in Seattle is that, on any given day, a sliver of blue can peep out over your place, while rain pours down a block east, and it's completely sunny two blocks west.

My friend David puts it another way: "I never know *what* to wear."

And there are other kinds of mornings when there is no blue whatsoever, when you stand at your window, a little miffed because *this* is what the city asks of you. And sometimes you have to search way down deep to be good-natured about it.

I'm glad this morning is not that bad, dreary enough to make David say his second most favorite thing. Seattle, he will say: "rains like a mother-@#%*#*!"

David, like me, is relatively new to Seattle's charms. (The reason I like to quote him is because he's just so funny and irreverent. On so many levels, he's the woman I'd like to be.) Unlike me, however, he is from Walla Walla where, he's quick to remind anyone who will listen, there is *plen*ty of sun.

"Walla Walla used to be a wheat field," David says with a drawl. He tries, but he hasn't completely ironed it out of his voice and I'm hoping he never does.

I pretend I know about wheat fields and say, "I know." I don't know. I just don't want David going into gory detail about life on the farm again, and I can tell by the nasal in his drawl that he's starving for a target. David has a bit of an inferiority complex because he didn't go to college. He likes to prove how much he knows whenever a chance presents itself.

"No you do *not* know," he snaps back. I could be annoyed with David for talking to me like this. But I'm not. I'm smiling.

"Well, you can just for*get* about wheat anyway. Wine is everything; it's all very Cinque Terre in Walla Walla now," he says, holding up an imaginary wine glass and tossing it back. When his tone is pitched in "nuh uh" like this, it's a typical end to one of our conversations. Mostly because, compared to David, I'm slow on the uptake. I have to think hard for a comeback. I generally think of the perfect response a few days later.

David can see all this effort straining behind my eyes so we both start to laugh, catch our breath, laugh again, as if we're high, but we aren't. We're just exiles, new to a city, in want of company so badly. When he comes back at me with attitude, especially if he thinks he's losing the argument, but doesn't resort to insult, to hurting my feelings, but only seems to make everything funnier (how does he do it?), I always think *thank God for David*.

Later in the day, I find myself thinking more about Walla Walla, how, when I was a kid, it was known for its sweet onions, asparagus, and the Jolly Green Giant, the very pleased, very sweet giant, who stood in the rolling countryside with his hands on his hips. Mr. Jolly Green Giant was a friendly giant, the good guy.

Or so we thought.

But even as a kid, I could tell he was sizing up the valley for what land to gobble up next. And he could not possibly have been working, only claiming to work, because he'd never be able to bend over or raise his arms in that tight little number made of leaves. Middle management is pretty resourceful this way.

I share these thoughts with David in an email. "And what about those pointy-green go-go boots? It's a wonder he got away with it."

"He was the only man I could relate to."

Then he writes (why, I have no idea) that Walla Walla gets more sunshine than Spokane, which is important to him, I guess, because he's an even bigger whiner than I am when it comes to our short summers. I don't know why he chose Seattle in the first place.

Love, probably. Same as me.

"David," I write, "All that sun in your home town makes for more than good vino; it pulls in the Pacific, then the fog bumps up against the Cascades and that's what we have on this side of the summit, drizzle."

"I know."

"It's a little late in the day to expect things to be different, weather-wise."

"I *know!*"

"Okay, then, shut up."

"No, you shut up."

"No you." And so on.

This is what we do, the pure joy of picking on each other to let off a little steam.

So it came as a big surprise to learn that our witty repartee bothers some. Last time David and I had one of our who-gets-the-last-word contests in the elevator, followed by a slapping competition, a neighbor shouted, "Not appropriate!"

How do I explain our merciless teasing to this surly little woman, the policing Ayatollah who skulks around trying to find a wrongdoer guilty of something. Her eyes practically pop out when we call each other our favorite pet names like "bossy-bitch" (as if that's original, David, as if every woman in charge of her own thoughts hasn't been called *that*), or my favorite for him—Auntie—which is the name he used when he made his way across my tiny kitchen (I was having a party, he crashed it) to kiss me hello and introduce himself as "Auntie David." The name stuck. I made sure of it.

Hard to believe that clowning around can be seen as offensive.

Which *I* find offensive.

In any case, I'm always reminding David how much better things get by July when we all find reasons to stay outside until ten o'clock because we can.

"I don't know *how* people live anywhere else," he'll say.

Did I know, when I first met David, how much he'd come to mean to me?

Honestly, yes.

Before all this about David flew through my thoughts, I cracked open the window of my office. I like to listen to the finches sing in the maples that line Fifth Avenue, especially in the quiet stretch before commute hours, when the birds settle in the shady branches, when all you have to do is stick your head out the window an inch to hear the trees swish in the afternoon wind, mature maples I chose to live under because, as I told my realtor, "I don't have time for saplings."

I sat back down to work and there I was just loving the feeling of loving my work, when suddenly my grasp on the writing that held so much promise only moments before was not so promising anymore. Work was over for me. Just over.

All because the air filled with another sound, the backup beep of a delivery truck, the sound that may be theoretically saving a life somewhere while it's killing the rest of us. How this piercing noise, worse than car alarms, was chosen is a mystery, and will remain so until the last backup-beep dies a slow and painful death. I read somewhere that the beeps are driving the birds insane. I'm afraid they are having the same effect on me. And here we are believing we are noble for installing them. It reminds me of the early Romans, how they valued paleness so much that they spread white lead paint on their faces, failing to notice that one of the side effects was death.

Surely the beeping will only last a minute.

Wait, no.

Curious, I go back to the window, and there, just over the rooftops, is a row of re-paving trucks on Fourth Avenue. Which, in itself, is a good thing: the road is a mess of ruts and hollows, it's very Punjabi to drive in my neighborhood lately. But, shoot, how much road maintenance can a city cram out of one Stimulus Package anyway?

I started counting seconds. One backup beep. Two. Three. Another makes four. When I give myself over to aggravation, it's time to hit the streets.

Soon as I was outside, I was flying! Released from my desk, the possibility of life-after-writing enters my bloodstream and the only word for the feeling is *free*. Free to ride my bike to the top of Queen Anne and wait ... now *this* is a farmers market. I had no idea there was a farmers market way up here. Just look at all the unaffordable fruits and vegetables.

See, when it comes to food shopping, I have to leave Belltown if I don't want Doritos and malt liquor.

My longings for a real neighborhood gets pretty bad sometimes. Seattle is just so *new*. My feelings get worse if I've just come from San Francisco or New York. I long for history, for buildings that have been around for more than a couple of years and people who fight hard to preserve them; corner markets with cut flowers out front, decent food within; neighbors who look at each other, the sky, the blocks we share, instead of the lowered stare into one's own palm that causes me to feel that our culture is at an all time low, spiritually.

I like what my old friend, Shannon, said about this the other day: "I'm done with email, Facebook, all of it. It takes guts to pick up the phone." Shannon lives out on the Olympic Peninsula and we used to tie one on quite frequently, the kind of fun that was easy for us when we were in our thirties and is almost impossible now, which is why we don't drink vodka anymore. Anyway I was saying to Shannon, "You'd love all the cute little houses on Queen Anne." (I don't tell her what they sell for). "You have to come visit me. We can revel in the farmers market together."

I don't think Shannon wants to visit me. She has her own garden and, as far as I can tell, doesn't know, or care to know, this city or any other city. She'd never be swayed by the clever down-home marketing of organic food anyway because she *is* down home. She says that farmer's markets are the only way modern-day Americans take to the streets, apparently. "A decade of war in the Middle East? Nah. Fresh basil? Let's march right out there!"

All I have to do is think of the leafy-green heads of lettuce and how it feels to buy them the day they are pulled from the ground, and, well, it's hard to describe the flavor of something so alive. I want to say that it tastes green, but this word means so much else these days. So I'm content to say *flavor*.

Big flavor. Ask me why, I don't know.

But I want to know. So I call up Nash's Organic Farm in Sequim. Nash Huber and I go way back. But this doesn't sound the least bit significant any more. Old news. Ancient history. As far behind me as when I lived in Sequim. Before I realized that there were better places for an East Coast runaway with my kind of "energy" to plunk herself down. I don't know how many times I found myself staring back at someone referring to my "energy."

I don't even think "energy" is the word they meant. I think what they were trying to say is that I'm ambitious (not always construed as positive for a woman: if she admits to being so it's held against her; if she admits to not being the least bit, same deal), goal orientated, a striver, wanting of the proverbial "more" I've yet to define even for myself. But I keep trying.

Which can be a little off-putting to some people, especially if they are done with trying.

Take my old neighbor, Heidi. Last time we talked over her fence she said, "I don't know why you work so hard, Larry makes plenty of money."

Huh?

After, I thought a lot about how clueless some people are about what it takes to write, to stick with it, how it has nothing to do with the money for most of us. But it wasn't until after another so-called friend said I was addicted to my work, the idea of which I simply couldn't stomach, especially when a day doesn't go by when she doesn't light up a joint (do they still call it that? Weed? Grass?), that I knew I needed to move on. Collecting roaches was not in my future.

Plus, I found, a small town gets even smaller. Which can be a comfort in some ways, absolutely. But in others, not so much. Cities aren't all that great sometimes, either, but no one stares at you if you are different. Let's just say, for now, I like feeling as if I have my own little sea of anonymity to swim in again.

Not that I've swum all that far, really, but I've crossed a few accomplishments off my list, things that define my "energy" I suppose. Even if I no longer feel as connected to some of my old neighbors, I love to return to the Olympic Peninsula whenever time allows, the quieter/ cleaner oasis beyond me and my present hungers.

When I knew Nash, he was only talking about being an organic farmer. He hadn't planted his first seed yet. Now, talk about devotion. Have you seen his beach ball-sized cabbages, his nuclear-sized carrots?

I know the word *nuclear* doesn't do justice to produce, but in this reeling time of shrinking ozone layers and coastal regions, it's wonderful to see heads of lettuce just get BIGGER!

I don't get Nash on the phone, darn it; I get the produce manager, happy to tell me that it's three basic elements that make organic produce taste so good, the first being freshness, of course. Secondly, glacial till and good water quality.

The third?

"We choose the right variety of seeds to grow in our soil."

This strikes a chord. My father used to say the same thing about his tomatoes: "You gotta match-a the seeds to the dirt, *capisci?*"

Tomatoes, I decide, are the number one reason I love a farmers market, tomatoes that taste like tomatoes. Even if I flinch as I hand over a fortune for half a baggie (that's it? that's all I get?), my heart lifts at the sight of them. I love how people without the slightest green thumb can take part without ever having to till, hoe or ... I don't know what all. Creatively, I have to draw the line somewhere.

But honestly, I don't give a hoot about the folk music (my response when I hear folk music is to walk in the opposite direction), about organic tote bags (people who care if their tote bags are organic and I couldn't be more different), or about handicrafts (sorry). No, get out of my way. I'm here for the food.

Panniers full, I fly back down the hill to another oasis, Greenlake, where Larry waits with a blanket and a decent bottle of wine.

It wasn't until our picnic was over and we were gazing out over the lake, that the mood changed. As usual, the auto-changer was the sky. It started to sprinkle.

"So what," I said, not taking the mist personally for once, possibly for the first time in Larry's memory. "It's good for the vegetables."

He looked at me with a mildly disbelieving expression. I could tell he was thinking: "I don't believe what you just said." And to be perfectly honest, my comment surprised even me. It sounded more like someone who wouldn't mind another cool-rainy summer, and we both knew there was no woman fitting that description sitting cross-legged on our blanket.

In her place, though, is a woman who moved to Seattle without knowing all that much about it. A woman who, years later, has a better idea of what she wants from weather, yes, but she also knows sun is not all she needs from life. There are other pleasures to perceive.

She's a dreamer that one.

Auntie David again.

She likes to fantasize.

But I am (I'm convinced of this) content all the same. No grappling. No squeezed feeling in my chest when I think of lasting gray sky, no cloud-fearing. Just ordinary Seattle-acceptance. I may bend low in the rainy season, but I bounce back.

Because it is possible, to be a rain-whiner while being okay with the rain, too. Emotions are full of complicated twists and turns.

"Besides, I don't whine as much you do, David."

"Yes you do!"

"Nuh-uh."

This conversation is in my head, of course, but even so, "I don't know what your problem is, David. You are such a pain."

Loose Threads

When I pick up my new cell phone after throwing it to the floor, right away I think two things: how much I depend on it; how angry I am at it.

"Oh, all right," I said, swiping it off the floor, "but you better watch yourself!"

In the week since buying it, I still can't figure out how to answer it, see. Still, when it struck, my anger, I knew something else was up.

But some mornings I find harder than others to get to the bottom of what this *something* is. And if I start to suspect that it's big, and I don't feel like big at the time, my mind will seize on a smaller problem.

After simmering for hours, I finally understood what set me off.

See, something happened yesterday. The man who moved in down the hall jutted his chin toward my *Trader Joe's* bag as I squeezed by him in our narrow hallway, bear hug around my groceries, and said with a snort (and I think it was the snort that did it), "Cat food for your significant other?"

I thought I heard him incorrectly, but when I realized I hadn't, that he was summing me up, because, granted, not all that many women my age live downtown, I said, after a slight pause, "I don't have a cat. But I have a new dog for a neighbor, apparently."

And then I turned my back.

It doesn't sound like such a big deal, but it was. The speed at which my brain discharged a comeback was worth the insult. Worth more, actually. I've waited my whole life for this, how to stand in my own corner. How to raise my chin, the slightest bit, a tilt of the head, until I know just what to say and how to say it, the perfect thing. At the perfect time.

All along, all I had to do was say how I really felt. But as a younger woman, it wasn't only that I'd go blank inside, disarmed by my own clumsiness; I didn't know how to trust what my insides were feeling.

I didn't have the nerve, the confidence to wait a few seconds before shooting back.

I remember the exact morning, not too long ago, when I decided I would no longer take an insult quietly. I was chewing a corner of English muffin over the sink, lots of olive oil dripping through my fingers, and along with the Extra Virgin, another lipid slid in, it just did. An essential structural component that said, *All these years of faking it, taking it, smiling when I should have said you jerk-off, who do you think you are?*

I recognized his type. A straight guy who talks only about himself, who's in love with his own beefy-ness but not all that fond of women, really, who snorts when he laughs at us but lives in fear of us and masks it with rudeness, rejected one too many times (go figure), and now he likes to throw the first punch whenever he can.

And, shoot, these guys don't make the best neighbors. When you're out of town, say, he's not going to offer to bring in the UPS package in front of my door. He may bench press it on his way to the elevator. But that's about it.

Keeping the insult to myself will be impossible! For this, dear cell phone, I forgive you. Describing the putz to my friends will be fun, likely to intensify to fit whichever friend I'm talking to, getting longer and funnier depending on where I am, how many coffees I had before telling it, or glasses of wine while.

A picture comes to mind. I'm chirping along while running my errands, making dinner, bathing, laughing at my comeback again and again before catching up on the details of my friend's lives with pleasure. But they understand my cause célèbre is so fresh, so vital, that the speed I dealt with an insult is a real passage for most of us and *this* is what's vibrating through the airwaves between us. So they allow me more time than my due, before they say, "I know what you mean." Because they do know.

And if Larry is eavesdropping on one of these giddy conversations, he's bound to say something he's rather fond of saying ever since I showed him the article I tore out of a magazine so fast the receptionist in my dentist's office didn't suspect a thing. How I, alone, make true the fact that women talk three times as much as men do.

But there is another truth at play here, and there is no good way to tell such a thing to your husband. It's impossible to modify your tone to the small, suitable space on the marriage dial where a man can hear you without hearing the scolding voice of his mother. The point where love is present, of course it is, but the wand is moving dangerously close to what you could almost let yourself say if you didn't know better. "Oh, for cryin' out loud! You don't know anything about most things unless I spell it out for you."

I'm sure you've heard about it by now, how, apparently, all those stony silences we see on our husband's faces when we let our emotions rip don't mean they're ignoring us. How could you ever think that? No, according to this theory, men are actually, factually, tone-deaf to all the extra sounds we use while trying to explain ourselves. Evidently woman-speak is relayed at too high a pitch, unperceivable to the male species.

Holy cow. I think every woman should face the direction of Mecca and submit to this law of nature five times a day, head down, hands at sides, feet evenly spaced. Then drop to her knees. Because we forget this about men over and over again as we keep trying to make them more like our girlfriends. And they are totally ill-equipped for the job.

Or, wait, we don't try to make them into our girlfriends; we try to make them into *us*.

Just think of the last time you told your husband or boyfriend you wanted to "talk." Remember the look on his face? I picture my husband's face when I describe what I'm totally passionate about, or upset about, or unsure about, and how, after a minute or two, he clouds over, stops listening. Even though he promised he'll listen until I'm finished.

He promised.

The last time I read over the reader comments I've saved over the years, I saw a lot of things like "I can't follow your thread" from various men, while women tend to appreciate how I weave several subjects into one. So, in a nutshell: Loose threads to men. Interweaving to women.

Comments from men are generally pretty short, too, and go something like: *Too personal.* (Heavens!) *Wordy.* (To which I want to respond, I am a *writer*.)

In contrast, whole sentences of sentiment from women: *Your words go straight to the heart of me. You write what I'm thinking. I love how you make the tiny details into the larger picture.*

While I was eating that yummy, oily muffin, something else trued up inside: Nothing is more satisfying than writing for women who don't want another diet tip, makeup tip, or celebrity chase; women who skim the pages looking for any trace of truth, and when they find it, stop flipping and read. I thank my lucky stars I have a few of these readers who get the intimacy I like to slide into my work, who understand how the personal is really our human need to grasp our place in the world and not the self-indulgence some say it is; these readers are pure heaven for me. Because talking it out until we get to what we believe *works*, even on the page, if it's done right. It lets both the writer and the reader wind their way in.

Oh, and women use the word "love." Women love to use the word *love*.

Actually I think the word *love* separates us right down the proverbial middle.

Of course, there are always the exceptions. John, a fan in Colorado, composes beautifully penned emails, lovely letters, really, though he swears he is "just a tech-head." And there's a woman out there who constantly berates me, cyberspace allowing her rage to stay hidden from the real world where she could be spilling all that creative energy into something to be proud of.

Still, at least she takes the time to write to me.

It seems this is where my first tangle with my cell phone and all my other thoughts should intersect, no? Where my threads need to interweave or ravel out completely?

If marriage has taught me a thing, I can easily picture a group of guys staring into the drawing board, emitting *uh huhs* as they set out to make our cell phones as complicated as possible. Complicated conversations? No way, lady. Complicated gadgets? Oh, baby.

And why I swore at my cell in the first place. Yes, it's the latest big deal, more toy than ever, upgraded to me for being "a loyal customer."

And, yes, I fell for it, confusing the word "upgraded" with "free." I didn't stop to consider that I had to replace both chargers, ear buds, and headset. Not only that, I figure I need at least a hundred hours to learn how to use it and I haven't got that kind of time.

I miss the simplicity of my old phone. I loved that phone. I wish I'd never handed it over. I'm certain it would have kept me describing my neighbor's insult, perfectly, without the capabilities to download world secrets and, presumably, make frickin' cappuccino.

I yearn for simpler phones, simpler dashboards, simpler *every*thing. I love when something has one basic capability instead of an instructional booklet of directions in four languages. There is nothing within the pages I will retain. I'm a glass plate. The words slide off me.

Someone should open a boutique for people like me. Make it cool, hip, glamorous to snub technology. All the gadgets with one on/off switch. You don't have to give people another reason to shop, or feel special, but it never hurts.

In any case, it takes experience to know how to keep it simple. Confidence, too.

So my thread? Well, snags and all, don't you just love, love, *love* how the threads keep coming round in life? Never tying off completely?

And how this is thread enough.

Because it has to be.

The Newsroom

There was a time I'd reject a story that smacked of "when I was younger." Now, I get it. Memory holds every one of my strengths and frailties, successes and failures, up to the light, in the truest possible sense of the word "light," even if most of time it does so when it's dark outside, as in the early morning hours between two and three. All I can do is allow the memory in if I want to get any sleep whatsoever. There really is no other choice.

Even if thinking back on this memory, and all that followed, causes me to flinch, remembering how young and feckless and hungry for approval I was at the time.

How I managed to *react* in spite of how young and feckless and hungry for approval I was, well, I like remembering this part. I like it very much.

I have a shelf in my office filled with tiny notebooks. Pages and pages of my thoughts written down for no other reason than to know myself better. Over the years, the notebooks have grown in number, spreading to fill a basket next to my desk. No one but me will ever read them, of course, but I like to borrow lines now and again from the young hopeful I was.

This line, written in my twenties, has reigned over my work ever since I turned down my first steady writing offer: *I think following through my way will save me from a lot more serious unhappiness down the road. Which will probably get me next to no money, but it'll make me happy.*

Look at these words. I want to hug the writer who wrote them, the woman who was me *when I was younger.*

There's something about nearing completion of a book that always makes me think of my beginnings. Like the first time I faced a bookstore audience, or, worse, a college reading (I could barely see over the lectern), or the newsroom I held in high esteem but couldn't allow myself to enter.

Ah, the newsroom.

The last time I was in a real, live newsroom I was briefly—momentarily, really—writing for the Job Market Section of the *Seattle Times*. This was at the height of my career-search phase, before I knew where I'd fit into the newspaper world, or if I even wanted to. When I was, somewhat desperately, in want of any writing that would pay me something. I didn't yet know the real difference between a job and a career that would sustain me.

All I knew was that there was writing that made me want to get up in the morning. And there was another kind of writing, the flat, factual copy I was asked to produce for the *Times* that made me want to burrow into the blankets deeper.

It took me awhile, sitting here, to find out why this all feels so important to bring up again, but it comes to me now. All my seeking, blind faith, and cluelessness about the world of print media were the fits and starts, tries and failings, that led me to where I am now. Writing poetry led to writing essays which led to writing journalism which led to writing memoir which led to writing the novel that is killing me. The difficult task was paring life down to the single-mindedness it took to wade through all the decisions, good and bad, any eager young writer has to face if she doesn't want to end up waiting tables, even when it breaks her heart, and breaks her heart again, until she cannot imagine why she chose to write over doing just about anything else with her life.

Especially once she discovers that writing what she wants won't steer her as quickly forward as she thought it would.

Little has changed in this regard.

Most days were nothing but pure determination. Granted, I started in Seattle's newspaper biz before the *Seattle Post-Intelligencer* folded, so there was less of a moral dilemma in the newspaper circles I skirted. In fact, my editor was only too eager to show me around and bring me "on board." Silly me. I never dreamed it was because *I* was so eager, i.e., willing to work cheap. Still, what the words "on board" really meant was not even close to being clear to me yet.

What I remember most about my one day at the *Times* headquarters — I was given the grand tour, ending with a wall of award-plaques that made my editor sigh with envy — was the way I felt right after he asked, "So, can you see yourself working here?"

Emphasizing the word "here," he spread the length of his right arm to sweep over a room full of expert competence, but to me it was just a nightmare. Too many people in too many partitioned spaces, too many conversations at once, too many monitors blaring, too many phones ringing, too many deadlines pressing, just way, *way* too much noise. I thought I'd be thrilled by such an invitation. I'd gone expecting it. But I felt the thought of having to block out all the noise and distraction set quickly, like super glue, on my nerves. *I cannot write in this room.*

"Me? Wow!" I chirped, trying to fake it.

It was false enthusiasm, like cherry blossoms popping out pink in February. "But, if it's okay with you, I'll keep writing my stories from home," I said. "But thank you *so* much!"

There was silence to his end of things. I was a little terrified of the consequences of rejecting his offer, that instead of being allowed to continue to write from home, I'd be fired altogether; but I was even more afraid of accepting, of rearranging my whole life to make something I didn't want to happen, happen.

I was out of that office in ten seconds. The relief was all-over.

Back on the streets, the city was as busy as ever, but I was so relieved to be on my own again that it seemed as if there was a special calmness in the air. The calm was inside my head, of course, but in any case, it belonged to the writer I was determined to become now that *that* decision was behind me. In a moment of clarity, I decided to write my pages my way, rather than another word about unemployment statistics.

Maybe it was just an idea at that point. A wish. A prayer. But I remember thinking if anyone had just been through the fear-of-fitting-into-a-newsroom that I'd just been through, even briefly, anybody with half a heart would understand.

"Face your fears!" my friend, Gina, said not long ago. (I doubt she knows how much her infinite good humor works as a terra firma for me. I need to tell her.)

So that's what I did. Yesterday, I faced the newsroom again, the *Peninsula Daily* newsroom, where I've contributed my column for years now. I wanted to see if I was made of hardier stuff, if all the immediacy, distraction, and tough-mindedness huddled together in one room would spook me the way it did once.

You know what, it didn't affect me like that.

I walked up to the familiar chaos and the most appreciative feelings came over me: *To be able to write my stories my way is fantastic.*

The *Peninsula Daily News* allowed me to stop seeing myself as a writer on the rise and get back down there in the trenches of my own vision where I belonged, on my terms, no one else's.

For me, its smaller size never felt like my relevance was on the wane, but just the opposite. The *Peninsula Daily News* allowed me to grow in all the ways I longed to, my ideas growing into column inches I was proud of, my independence granted in a way that a larger, corporate entity would not have allowed as they went about the business of branding me, letting me write on one subject only, which is slow death to a writer and goes against the grain of everything basic I believe in.

I stood in the wings watching the team of reporters work, forestalling the urge to clap my hands. It's hard to say what my feelings were about. Pride?

Definitely.

Straight ahead was Paul, my first editor. I walked over, said hello. We shook hands.

Back when Paul and I worked together, we were each other's quandary for a while. As with most editor/rookie relationships, I could pretty much count on the fact that ten seconds after I submitted my column, he'd call my cell, chew me out, make me both mad and afraid at the same time. We yelled at each other. We goaded. We took turns pointing out who was right. I made a little fun, called him up-tight. He sighed, called me cocky. But I think we always knew we were in the same boat, that our mooring would hold, that our particular push-pull was not a disrespectful thing. Our conversations (his questions and my growls, or the other way around) used to go something like: "I don't see the connection between these two points, Mary Lou."

"Well, I *do*."

Then we'd make up and go our separate ways. We got pretty good at it, too.

Before I walked away from Paul's desk, I reached out and touched his arm, something I would normally never ever do in a professional setting, especially in the Northwest where everyone requires S P A C E. Where people talk about the time they went to Italy and gained ten pounds, things like that; but, I've said it before and I'll say it again because I'm insufferable sometimes: the Italian right here on the shores of the Pacific, full of her hand-waving, touchy-feely-ways, can unnerve the natives without so much as trying.

But all that doesn't matter to me anymore. The real me, the woman no longer desperate for a job, touches people when she wants to. The real me doesn't know from Adam what it feels like to go through life with her emotions on hold with office protocol dictating her actions. The real me touches a man she's argued with for years. It's the least I can do.

To my left, I could see the publisher, John, behind glass. Still, even from where he sits, the entire newsroom in view, nothing makes a powerful man seem more unthreatening than a smile like the one he wears.

The first time John called me "kiddo," I suppose my feminist leanings should have toppled over. Instead my heart swelled. He reminded me how nicknames are okay sometimes. That before PC-ness ruled, calling someone a fatherly endearment wasn't inappropriate. Not for anyone with any memory whatsoever of Ed Asner. Actually, the kind of bantering we share remains, in my mind, one of my greatest pleasures, professionally. We pull it off. There is never any puffery of his role as the man-who-could-fire-me with two simple words, "I'm sorry."

From: johnbrewer@peninsuladailynews.com
To: marylousanelli@marylousanelli.com
Subject: Your Column

Hey Kiddo. Not bad.

That's it. That's the entire email.

Incidentally, the last time a reader expressed respect for my column in the *Peninsula Daily News*, I felt his compliment reach in and pat my shoulder. On the same day, I was asked by another why I bothered to write for newspapers instead of writing a blog? Didn't I know, she asked, that people don't read the paper anymore?

Wait. Didn't she just read my column? Wasn't she, in fact, people?

"Papers are doomed," is what she said. "Get out now."

Now that bothered me. No way to pretend it didn't. Especially because I agree with her on one count, because if I were a big city newspaper, buying into my own failure is not how I'd sell myself. Copying everyone else in order to be *myself* makes no sense. I'd draw the line on simulating a blog page, aim toward giving people creative reasons to read me again, be what I read another writer wished about the paper he writes for: "Please, let's be better than, not an imitation of." Because the world has shown me far too many times how the larger an entity grows, the less creative it becomes, the more imitation it practices, the more it sits with its shoulders slumped, less at home in the creative world, confidence gone. "I like to think my column is a creative reason for you to read the paper," I finally wrote back.

On the bright side, the *Peninsula Daily News* isn't a big city newspaper, thank goodness. They still run stories about what the neighbors are up to, the kids' baseball games and ballet recitals. And readership is up, I hear, even when a lot of us have let go of any number of things we have to pay for.

Best part (I think, conceitedly) is that it still runs my quirky column. And no one at the paper gives me a hard time anymore.

Having said that, I don't love everything about it. Good pay? That'll be the day. And my editor gives me 600 words, not a syllable more. I've exceeded that by well over a thousand words here so most

of this will be cut.
    See. I hate that.

Breathe In, Breathe Out

If you are anything like me, that is, grown up in every important way, you are old enough to read this story. But I warn you, your mascara may run.

You see, when I wasn't paying attention, something shocking happened. My mother got old. I went home to visit and I was stunned. In a year, one year, she'd grown smaller. She *shrank*. It scared the hell out of me. Worse, her fingers, once nimble enough to paint porcelain figurines were twice their normal size and crooked.

How easy it is to neglect someone when you only talk on the phone. I felt a little sick from realizing it.

To see your mother grow old is just the toughest thing. I found myself squinting, aching to see her, every part of her, as she used to be. I felt as if I'd do almost anything if she'd just come back to me in the same way I knew her before. But no amount of want changes reality and my face must have shown my dismay.

Of course, my own face reveals aging, too, and that's what I could see in the way my mother's brows lifted, how she was studying me in the same way. I think, right then and there, we both took tacit vows to say nothing about aging, hers or mine. Love *is* silent sometimes. It has to be.

As the days passed, I tried to hide my concern and be good, positive company, but certain self-concerned thoughts kept horning in: *How will I handle this? How will I turn my life around, the one I worked so hard for, in order to be there for my mom?*

It didn't take long. Directly behind my questions, guilt sidled up, very specific guilt, left over from adolescence that is still, and will always be, part of our continual mother/daughter evolution. We will always be a work in progress.

I don't want you to do this, Mom. I pleaded (again, silently). *You can't get so old! I'm not good at this kind of thing! I can't do this!*

There, I said it.

None of this matters, of course. I did it anyway, I became the guardian, the protector, in the same way I take in water and food.

I began by cleaning out her home of old sheets, towels, books and dishes, every shelf and closet jammed with our mutual past, way too many memories until my entire emotional state was out of whack and the lines between Mom and me were so mixed and muddled and scrambled, just like all the clutter I was sorting out, that at the end of Day Two, I felt utterly not cut out for any part of it. *This sucks!*

Actually, now that I think about it, my crash came on Day One, right after the huge dumpster arrived outside my mother's door, the one that couldn't care less about my mother's stuff, let alone our nostalgia for it. When I gasped at the size of it, Larry said, "It's big enough for the lawn ornaments, at least."

But I knew, the way I know everything about my husband, that he was overwhelmed by the size of it too, that nothing was really funny about disposing of a woman's keepsakes, even the chintzy, chubby gnomes with their stubby legs, objects of my teenage obsession (every time I smoked pot they came to life) so that the number one question of my entire life for days became: *Do I keep this or pitch it, keep it or pitch it, keep or pitch?* Meanwhile my mother watched TV.

I knew Larry was as confused as I was, holding it in, as men often do. I put my arm around his waist. It was the nearest feeling to crying together. And we got on with it.

We found a smaller home Mom could move to. Which is not as easy as it sounds, believe me. I'm a boomer, remember, the most self-indulged generation ever. I've always thought about the future in relation to my own fulfillment, not with respect to what my mother needs to assure she'll live the good life into her eighties and nineties.

Consequently, Larry and I went in search of the perfect sunny independent-living retirement community, rather than a larger house to buy with a separate room for her.

I told myself I was doing the best I could: *I'm doing the best I can.*

Still, I couldn't help but compare myself to other ways of handling the same transition. Only to feel even more guilty because, unlike my friend Rachel who moved her dad into her spare bedroom, I was relieved, excited, *ecstatic* when my mom decided to spend her last years in Hawaii rather than next door to me.

Then, as if on cue, another emotional crash, crazier than before. Which is only fair. I certainly sounded crazier than ever every time I asked, "Mom, are you walking enough, sleeping well, eating enough fruit?" exposing my desperation with its never-ending concern that, say the experts, is more about me than the person I love. Because I know there is no cure for age, no diet, no exercise that can save my mother, even as my so-called love pours out of my mouth.

Besides, I am such a hypocrite. All I can think lately is, *Oh, crap, it's come to this. I'm the middle-aged daughter wheeling her feeble mother through Macy's, staring straight ahead instead of at the clothes racks, rolling my eyes with exasperation because my mother is complaining about everything, griping to cover up her fear neither of us knows how to bring up, talking to the saleswoman as if she's my best friend because I'm lonely with only my mother to talk / argue with.*

Which reminds me, last week I went to visit my friend Bon. From her backyard, I could see the house her mother lives in now, ever since Bon moved her from Minnesota to right next door.

"I'm in awe of you," I told her. "I'm more selfish."

Selfish? Untrue. I didn't mean to use the word again. What I meant was *I'm too ambitious to forfeit any part of my work life right now.* Because I still apologize for ambition in a way men rarely feel the need to and this irks me.

Why do I do it?

Easy. Because no one knows better than me how ambition works as a window *and* a shade, allowing me to see into all the satisfying possibilities of my work while it screens out just about everything else. Just so I can do the one essential thing my work demands: hear myself think. A couple days without doing so, I start to pine for it the way a young girl pines for a boyfriend, for the inner discussion, the frankness, for the work that defines me, even when I know there is other, greater, life cycle work (i.e., Mom) to be done.

I realize I wrote that last paragraph without exhaling, which means only one thing: that instead of writing about my mother, I *should* be visiting her.

And yet, last time I did visit, a surprise I planned for Mother's Day, she dropped heavily into her recliner and said, "What are *you* doing here?" so loudly it made me jump.

In some ways, I get the feeling my mother couldn't be less interested in having a visitor, even, gulp, *me*. Any intrusion sort of throws her off, turns her routine upside down, and I see how difficult being taken unawares is for her now. Family can need so much from each other, reminding each other of too much history along the way. The last time I went to a family reunion, I felt like I'd been trampled by a heard of elephants, only the elephants were memories and I suffered every stomp, in amazing ways and overwhelming ways, all at once. It took me weeks to feel like myself again.

When I moved in to kiss my mother hello and give her a squeeze, she let me. But she gave back more of a half-hug, less muscled than what used to join us. I was so embarrassed. But it left me with another message, too. One I considered a blessing, really: *Whew, I am not yet so needed after all!*

Still, for the life of me, and just to prove how potent denial really is, I allowed myself, after that visit right up until now, to think there was still plenty of time to get everything in order (she's been after my husband to "see to the paperwork" for years) because I can't allow myself to think about life without her. I'd rather imagine another world completely, even when she irritates me/I irritate her/she irritates me. To no end.

The experts also say (they have plenty to say) my denial is a kind of "psychic numbing," a mental deadening that works as a coping mechanism to keep us from exploding with grief.

Well said. But it's also a deficit. One I'll surely be paying huge consequences for soon.

Because there is still lots of work to do, learning to exchange our appreciation of each other instead of all the silly, useless gifts we buy one another to fill in the gaps of what we don't know how to express would be a really good start.

And I am, well, no, admittedly, *Larry* is just now learning what all needs to be done, legally, to ensure my mother's estate is handled as she wishes. He and I, the proverbial blind leading the blind.

This is all such new territory for me. Seeing myself as a mother. Mama to my mother. Mom to my mom. Which, I've decided, is nothing more than recognizing a ferocious need to protect the people we love the most, the turning your insides inside out, like a wet mitten, every mother knows.

Cleaning out my childhood home? Oh man, piece of cake compared to this.

Breathe in. Breathe out.

Perfect Solution

"Let's have Thanksgiving at an inn this year."

"An inn?"

"An inn."

"Why not?"

My husband's idea is the perfect one. The most I'd have to do by way of preparation is dress, comb my hair, comb his, and make sure his socks match.

And there it was, all the turkey we ever wanted. A set table. Real cranberry sauce. Champagne. Three desserts! Dishes swept off, bed upstairs, faux fire burning, tiny chocolates on our pillows.

When was the last time a chocolate was left on my pillow?

With vivid clarity, I remember the one and only year I tried my hand at a formal Thanksgiving dinner. Before then, I'd never dealt with Thanksgiving in the traditional sense in my own kitchen, not on my own. Not on my life.

It was a fiasco.

The gravy, anyway. The rest was pretty much okay. No one had too much wine and got too upset about something that happened a hundred years ago; no one stormed off and left the rest of us at the table in what you'd call "uncomfortable silence."

There was, at one point, a lot of whispering going on in the kitchen and, from what I could tell, tears. Naturally, I wanted to know who'd said what to whom because it was sure to be juicier than my turkey. I got as far as the doorway and was waved off with a flick of my mother's hand which was fine by me. Beyond that, nothing out of the ordinary, emotionally speaking. *Salute!*

All day long I tried to act competent, capable, wanting more than anything to please my mother in ways that count, i.e., cooking, because my being able to cook means more to her than all the books I've published. If it's true that our work is how we define ourselves, my mother defines herself in the kitchen, always has, always will. And whatever anyone might say about a woman's right to choose in the modern world, mostly what she sees when she looks at me is a daughter who can't cook—tsk, tsk, tsk—and that her powers of influence have failed.

And, given that I'd do just about anything to make my mom believe that the holidays won't vanish in her impending absence, I got out my list of ingredients, the sum of what it takes to both pull off a holiday and avoid a guilt trip. Here goes nothing, I thought. I'd made it this far without ever giving in to the whole idea of stuffing my forearm up the anus of a vertebrate, but time had caught up with me.

I suppose in any family there's always the one who cares more about carrying on tradition, the foods and customs, than the others do about making it all go away. In my husband's family, the holiday steward is his sister, Cheryl. In our family, it's always been my mom. Now it's Mom à la me (through default), or another way my mother has managed to make her problems my problems.

Here is what I learned that day: You can't fake gravy.

Up until then, I thought making gravy from scratch would be like the recipe I use for giving a good reading: my readiness will kick in. It'll work.

"Larry, holy shit! I can't serve this. I don't know what happened. It didn't come out right!" I was mortified. All the giddiness that came from my edible turkey debut dissipated when I was faced with lumpy gravy.

"Are you joking?" he asked. I know this voice. Larry-disappointed.

See, Larry loves gravy. And not once have I made it for him. If you are reading this and want to please my lovely husband, invite him over for mashed potatoes and the real-thing gravy. Some men stare at boobs. Not mine. If we pass one of those restaurants with glossies stuck to the window and one of the photos is of mashed potatoes and gravy, Larry gets all goo-goo eyed.

"Joking?" I could barely contain myself. "It's not like I planned to screw this up merely to deprive you of gravy. I whisked, I used that stupid wiry-thingy!" At which point, all I wanted was to sit on the floor with a bottle of wine to myself, tell everyone to go home, good riddance. "Don't you dare laugh!"

"Never." Quick exit.

Plus, I didn't want everyone missing gravy at my inaugural Thanksgiving table, but that's exactly what happened. Before I slinked back in there, I rehearsed my tone. I wanted to keep things up, lighthearted, no matter what anyone said.

I even tried to be positive about the fact that I hadn't written in a week in order to carry off the whole thing. True, I would have felt like a rotten daughter had I sidestepped Thanksgiving, but, honestly, that kind of guilt doesn't make me feel half as guilty as not writing. I remember thinking that, no matter what, I'm going to feel like I'm not doing what I should be doing, which is a bad way to pull off a holiday in the first place.

Or, for that matter, a page.

So you have to cut me some slack when I tell you that when I couldn't take the gravy-ragging anymore. I yelled, "No goddamn gravy, got it?" I even pounded the table, all Italian macho-like. I had learned from the best. Which hinted that no one should say one more stupid thing like, "What? No gravy with these weird mashed potatoes" (yes, I *meant* to leave the skins on). "What? No gravy and biscuits?" (Do not tell me I was supposed to make biscuits. No one said a *thing* about biscuits.)

But that's not all I yelled. "As if any one of you *needs* gravy."

The room went dead. It was sort of like being in a blackout where the silence is anything but silent.

Luckily my insult made everyone laugh. It didn't fall flat. It worked. It saved the day. All my years of performing, of finessing, of working on timing and delivery—good for something, apparently.

My mashed potatoes ran out in seconds. So did my salad. As we cut in closer to the middle of the turkey, it was evident the bird was still alive. By the end of the meal, my mother was in the kitchen defrosting frozen vegetables and firing up the pasta pot.

Afterwards, after everyone went home and Larry was asleep on the couch and I was wrestling with a backed-up kitchen sink, I felt two things: That I never want to reach a point where food matters so much. A few eggs in the fridge, a block of feta, a bowl of fruit, salad fixings, and I live without want. *And* that it wasn't a mistake that I chose to live so far from my mother's food expectations, which are: you cook for an army no matter how many you are feeding. And everyone goes home with a plate full of leftovers under aluminum foil.

Consequently, the entire day was pretty stressful for me.

And there is only one thing that releases that kind of stress from my body, and I couldn't exactly excuse myself from the table to take to my bed, close the curtains, lock the door, and prop my hinny up to accomplish the one thing that calms me completely, now could I?

I sat there staring at the turkey. And I kept thinking how women used to take up their entire lives with cooking like this pretty much every day. Maybe it's why so many women of my mother's genera- tion, hell, of my own, claim to never have experienced the slow-to- ripple, time-taking, big luscious roll of our body reaching its ultimate consummation.

Now we do make time for our own pleasure.

Hence, pre-stuffed turkey and store-bought pie.

"Clearly, you have no children," my friend Jennifer said when I told her Larry and I were taking off for the holiday weekend. Jennifer is always reminding me, sometimes as a friend, sometimes as a foe, that when a woman has children, she can't be so im*pul*sive.

As if I didn't know.

And it's weird to watch a friend turn into her twin. You begin with your pal, someone to share a laugh with, then you tell her about the inn you'll be spending Thanksgiving in and she thinks about the kids she waited until she was forty to have and, just like that, you aren't laughing together anymore.

It's not surprising all this is making me remember how much time Thanksgiving used to take when I was a kid, when, like it or not, we'd sit at the table around three in the afternoon, and stay seated until seven or eight. The men stayed seated anyway. From the antipasto to the minestrone to the lasagna to the turkey to the *frutta* my dad would polish till it shone like my grandmother's linoleum before paring it in one, continual spiral. Then the grappa with espresso, the cannoli, the torrone in tiny picturesque boxes, what with the serious eating behind us a couple of courses ago.

Then there was the year I sensed a change in the air—1970, I think. Nothing too dramatic: I was sitting at our Thanksgiving table with all my aunts and uncles and cousins stuffed to the gills, telling myself I'd never waste *my* life staging such extravagant meals, when my mom stood to clear the table. And because my dad just sat there puffing his cigar, instructing my mother to take away this plate and that platter, as if she'd never done it before, in my rebellious, teenage mind, red flashed. I was a tiny inferno by the time I yelled, "Jesus, Dad, *help* her already!"

I was, by Seattle standards, a minnow challenging a sea of King Salmon.

Even so, things changed pretty quickly after that. My dad started taking us out for Sunday supper every now and again which was like a fault line for our family. It split everything open. For the first time, we saw dinner through the eyes of other American families. It was weird to think the day didn't have to be spent with my Uncle George asleep in a recliner, my mother in tears about some unflattering thing her sister said about her meat sauce. It seemed extraordinary that my mother, instead of rushing around, could sit back and let a waitress do the work.

How did she do it for so many years, feed so many of us so often, so selflessly? How on earth did my mother pull it off year after year after year?

The answer seems simple enough: She was really, really good at it. True.

She didn't question everything . . . *like I do*.

Um, true again. She complained, but I'm pretty sure if my dad ever showed up in the kitchen, she'd have complained even louder.

She liked to cook for an army.

Now, that's not entirely true. It's a lovely lie people like to spread about good old-fashioned mothers on good old-fashioned holidays, but when I think of the nervousness that came streaming out of our holiday kitchen, "liked to" is not what I remember. "Was expected to" works better for me.

She wanted to?

So she says. But there is so much more to the story of a woman's wants, especially once she is married, more so in my mother's day.

Regardless, she did it.

Yes, she did. And I'm going to end here. Before I start to question just how good all that holiday cooking really was for our family.

In any event, when Larry suggested we skip all the fuss and take off by ourselves, I could not imagine what kind of drug-induced state of consciousness I'd have to be in to not jump at the chance.

Sacred

DECEMBER

If you ask me, December rolled around a little too early this year.

But I'm surprisingly okay with it. It's perfectly *fine* to feel nothing this month but resigned. No worrying about who gets what.

Still, in my family, it's no easy thing to take the no-fuss view of Christmas. But in a process as slow and complex as maturing, I've had to get real about just how many of the endless male icons I'm inclined to promote, even if everyone else is so willing. I'm not referring to Santa; he's all right. Any man willing to bring me presents is, at least, trying.

But Jesus? I've never cared for the way he's been inserted into all the best things, until we're expected to let guilt trump joy most of the time. Yet, I've had to pretend as if I do care. And celebrate his birthday along with everyone else. Not to say I don't believe he existed. I'm sure he did, but so did a lot of other people with good advice. Or that I haven't enjoyed parts of his annual BD party; I have.

But this year the holiday season seemed to head, nonstop, away from yellow forsythia directly into evergreen wreaths, set into motion by the first Christmas card to show up. Aunt Connie's Christmas card. It's always the first to arrive, the biggest, most ornate alongside all the others, a sort of competitive ritual. Aunt Connie is not really a competitive person. She just likes to have the upper hand once in a while, never having had it while my uncle was alive. Too old to rely on her perfect olive skin and figure my dad used to say could stop traffic, her beauty has been relegated to her ever-religious, glittery Advent calendar cards heralding the countdown to Christmas.

And just to be sure the man behind each pop-out window—Jesus in the Nativity, Jesus parting the Red Sea, Jesus on the cross—walks right into her niece's home without knocking, puts his feet up on my sofa and stays through New Year's, she encloses fifty bucks.

Miracle is, it means my very devout, very generous, beautiful-always, optimistic, recently widowed aunt still doesn't mind spending a little extra on irreverent me.

It's an instant delivery of love.

"The holidays" are two words that, for my mother, start to buzz in late August. It's not at all unusual for her to Christmas shop before Labor Day ("in case I die before the holidays"), every gift wrapped before Halloween.

And then there's the next generation (me) saying, jeez, the hours we could get back if we didn't have to worry about the holidays.

Still, it's hard to let it all go.

It's really hard to let it all go.

Even if I try, all I have to do is think about all the gifts my mother used to stack in her bedroom closet, and all of a sudden I'm hurled into Christmas past. Which should make me appreciative, happy, pleased. But it doesn't make me feel that way. The other stuff, the stressful stuff, takes up residence like Jesus over there, snoring now.

I swallow hard.

If I'm honest with myself, this is what I would shout from the rooftop: "Christmas is so tedious! I should care, but I DON'T!" Which isn't the worst part. This is: Even though I swore I wouldn't give in this year, as the month progressed, my subconscious boomed louder and louder: *You better make it happen. Mom is too old to make it happen but she still wants it to happen.*

Until a decision was made. In order to make things easier on me, I'm asking (telling!) Larry to deal with the gift-buying this year. I've done it for the last couple of decades. It's. His. Turn.

But come on. We both know he'll put it off. Until it's too late.

We also know it will be me who is blamed for the neglect—by his mother, by my mother. Because this is our story, isn't it? This is what it is to be a woman/wife/daughter whose job it is to pull off Christmas, whose job description, other than not complaining about it, includes making sure the sentimental side of the holiday is met.

I'm having trouble sleeping because of it.

Besides, it's a really bad year to feed the inner-shopper in me. Larry is changing careers, setting up a new office, and things are a little tight. I can't go out there filling my brain on dopamine, leaving the store in a rush of credit-card happiness because I don't have the cash to buy the gifts I just bought. Believe me, if I'm not super careful, my no-shopping bravado can collapse pretty quickly. Instantly, really.

And you know what will happen next? I won't be able to pay our property taxes come spring without a lot of shuffling. Just like last year.

Besides, there is another thing I can count on like the sun rising: just when I think I can really do it, finally let go of the holidays for good, the holidays won't let go of me. Especially when Aunt Connie's Jesus is sitting straight up again, projecting himself into my living room with two squinty eyes that say "buy the gifts and then we'll talk."

Which means now I have no choice but to join the rush of shop-pers, hordes of them at Ross Dress For Less, looking for the last-minute gift, with stories that may vary, but for all of our differences, the central theme is that we are desperately geared up for the hunt, lists in hand, shopping at the last minute in hopes of shrunken prices and store labels we can peel-off.

So here I am, headed like a lance through the doors, passing the weary husbands who wait by the entrance, corralling old dogs and young children, their babies past and present.

Anyone who has watched last-minute Christmas shoppers can attest to the fact that there are a few of us who look pleased by the effort, and more who look absolutely miserable, lost, winding slowly into the hubbub. And there are some ... who would rather forget about gift shopping altogether and just hide out in the shoe racks.

Last year I started early. Early for me anyway: in the second week of December. I foraged the racks for an hour before walking out of that store with every unchipped scented candle there was to be had, enough to please every woman on my list, all for the cost of one can-dle elsewhere. Easy. I was so happy, I think I skipped to the register.

But this year, there's no time to forage. My reason for entering the store is simple: *Scarves!* Perfect for my girlfriends. Even David. Draped just so, they are still one of my true beliefs in beauty.

Maybe I should have started here, tell what happened when I was rifling through the bin, searching for any fabric that didn't feel especially cheap.

When I saw the woman swaddled in a burka, I immediately thought what I always think: *enslaved!* And when I let my gaze linger over every part of her body hidden beneath those ridiculously heavy black layers of cloth, my stomach, my muscles, my brain just totally rebels. I am incensed, infuriated, and, honest-to-god, I could just scream, *Please stop! You don't need to dress like that here!*

And, please, do not tell me it's her culture. Because does she have a choice in the matter? Look at her husband over there in Tommy Hilfiger Polo stripes while it's nothing but funeral drapery for her. No, sorry, burkas are not culture. Burkas are control.

I was thinking all this, so it was hard to tell, but I think my outrage sort of showed. And by showing, I mean it had a little pull of its own. Because the woman in the burka walked closer, looking both ways first, which made me want to say, sweetie, the Taliban doesn't live in Seattle.

Does it?

"Do you like this one?" I asked, holding up a scarf.

"Yes, I do," she said, "It is very hot."

A voice in me screamed, "Freeze this moment, go back to what she just said!"

"Hot?" I said with a laugh, nervously.

"Yes. Silk is very sexy."

I'm telling you her words knocked the breath out of me. The reels started turning: *remember this, remember everything she says.* Which obviously showed on my face, too, because she tried to hold my eyes a few seconds longer.

I let her.

Then, I swear, I felt something come into focus for me in a way it hadn't before. You have to imagine her saying "sexy" with an accent, the shape of her mouth hidden, her bright eyes blinking. All of which made me lean in closer. As if I might make sense of why she lives in hiding. If I could just get in close *enough.* I stared straight into those cutouts-for-eyes.

She didn't seem afraid. Or even surprised.

Closer ... closer. Lashes caked in mascara, smudge of coal underneath, dark purple instead of the black I imagined. She blinked. She smiled. Or I had to imagine her smile. But you can tell by a person's eyes when they are smiling.

I heard myself gasp. Because I got it. Even if I didn't say anything because I felt so out-of-body. Stunned by her eyes, I felt a shudder, a shiver of redemption even Aunt Connie would sanction holy *enough*. All I could feel was how grateful I suddenly was to live in a country that lets me be me if I have the courage to be me. To speak up and be me.

I looked back at the woman. "Wear it well," she said. Then she turned away.

"Thank you," I said, wishing it possible to convey that, because of her, I could for the first time in a long while imagine women in burkas all over the world waiting patiently until the perfect time, and then rebelling, throwing off their robes like wigs they can't bear to wear a second longer, circling them over their heads like Samantha in that *Sex In The City* episode before pitching them as far away as possible.

Which, strangely, put me in such a good mood my Scroogeness sort of petered out.

On my way out of the store, a handsome man (early twenties, military uniform) hobbled in on crutches he was obviously just learning to use. His right leg was gone from the knee down. But here's a miracle for you: he had a smile on his face, a grin so full of childlike anticipation it makes you go completely soft inside, when he has every right to feel sorry for himself from now on.

Still, I'd forgotten how quickly my emotions can tumble down. Stricken does not begin to describe me at that moment. The slightest thought of war makes me want to boycott the holiday all over again. While our President accepts the Nobel Peace Prize with one hand and sends more troops off to the battlefield with the other, all I can think is *wait just a goddamn minute! Thirty thousand more troops? I am dead inside. I'm still breathing, working, carrying on; but inside, my hope has collapsed. Now what? All I ever wanted by voting for you was peace.*

But this is not the kind of thing you want to talk about this time of year when everyone is breaking out their cherished boxes of ornaments.

I know this voice. It is the voice of the woman who wants to be happy, who knows how much work it is to decide to be happy, how much acceptance and vigilance it takes to even come close, the voice of a woman who is now thinking two incredible things: I might never have known how much appreciation a woman in a burka could give to me.

And I would never have guessed a soldier's smile would remind me that I have no right to pout.

People say the more you know of the world, the more fearful you become. But that's only true if you pay too much attention to politics. If I pay attention to people, no matter where they are from, I am less afraid. Holiday "spirits" may have come to me inadvertently this year, accidentally, unintentionally, but they did come.

And they were sacred.

Part Three

"The only way to avoid being a miserable writer is not to have enough leisure to wonder whether you are a happy writer or not."

—GEORGE BERNARD SHAW

The Big Question

Picture yourself huddled under the covers.

Now, picture an idea coming to mind, moving through you, your whole body suddenly awake; not the first of hundreds of times you've felt this way in your life, yet, still, it feels different every time, fresh; so you close your eyes until you and your idea fit together like two halves of a magical whole.

And because it's good to present both sides of such an idea, picture trepidation creeping in, collecting, the queasy other possibility, of failure, of everything not working out as you planned once you remember what your idea will demand of you, when you must face it head on, knowing how much discipline it will take, how much attention, because it's impossible to give it anything less. Because no matter how experienced you are, no part of the process allows for a short cut; you'd never allow it; it's such a great big incredibly long course over and over and over again.

And why it's so important to get started right away.

Picture yourself facing the page, or the canvas, or the mirror if dance is your composition. The first quirky turn to your stream of thought, the first sweep of color, the first plié, and, oh, the charge, the exhilaration! How focused you feel. How centered. You are immersed!

Finally, picture energy, effort, fatigue, and afterward the sense of accomplishment: how work should feel but rarely does.

Is this not the true definition of work?

For many of us it is. And, yet, it's become practically my mission in life to get people to recognize that what we "creative types" do is, indeed, work. Hard work. Our job title is: "worker." Albeit, with no contract or health insurance, but still, "worker."

Not that any of us like being reduced to what we accomplish; that's not what I'm saying. Still, I don't think artists/writers/dancers are ever made the least bit weary by being called by the work we do. It's not like being called, say, a housecleaner, even if we clean houses for a living, a fact I was reminded of when I called my friend who *is* a housecleaner just that. Never mind that she *is* wonderfully thorough not only for others but, like me, after her work is finished for the day, she settles her inner mess with half an hour of dusting, fluffing, and vacuuming her own space, repetition that doesn't drag us down, we agree, but gets us out of our heads.

And never mind that she runs a housecleaning business. Or that I was introducing her to an elderly bachelor who needs her services in the worst way.

"Do *not* introduce me as a housecleaner," she scolded. "I'm an artist. Who cleans houses." Reminding me that my faux pas was just about the most unkind thing I could possibly say, to leave her essential work out like that. Because artists don't have two lives, even if we split our work time in two, our lives and our work are one. Our work is who we are, no matter what else we do to pay the bills. And we are pretty quick to tell you so.

That is, until the Big Question comes: "Do you work? I mean at something other than your writing (art, dance)?"

"Sorry?" As if I didn't hear.

Sometimes I shake my head but say nothing. *God, I'm tired of this question.*

Sometimes I put my hand over my mouth to be sure nothing mocking squeaks out.

Sometimes I just rub the side of my thigh pretty hard. I've lost the will to try and explain, so I just go around with my hand again.

Why this question? This time, from a woman who lives down the hall. (This is what I get for running to the trash chute in my baggy sweats first thing in the morning when most of my building is scrambling to get to the office.) Sometimes I say something that moves us quickly past the subject of work altogether. A dodge I've pretty much perfected to make it seem like I'm not only part of the real working world but, I've made it b-i-g. I brag a little, say something like, "I work in my pajamas because my readers can't see me," which usually makes a corporate "team member" perk up with envy no matter how much money he or she makes. I think it's the notion of being your own boss, of not having to do everything by consensus, the feeling of freedom all that money is supposed to bring but generally doesn't.

I'm sure I'd be lucky to find even one artist that hasn't fumbled for an answer when faced with the same question. I've decided I don't struggle with the question because of its pointlessness, or what feels like pointlessness, or even because of its implications. I struggle with the question because I still haven't been able to come up with a response I'm especially proud of. I haven't progressed past what I call my 3-D defense:

1. DENY the assumption I'm hyper-sensitive to: *You can't possibly make enough money to live on by writing, can you?*

Because it's true what they are thinking. I am paid poorly, next to nothing sometimes. So I absolutely know what the next question is, whether or not they bother to ask it, *So what does your husband do?*

2. DEVISE a comeback that brings the asker to heel.

3. DUCK out of the conversation as soon as possible.

I don't know when this woman inside of me will finally find the balls to surface, but I really, *really* want to be poised in the face of the Big Question next time. I want to say the perfect thing not in defense of myself, or my work, but in praise. But, for whatever reason, a part of my confidence still goes missing when the question emerges, especially if I have to endure my work referred to as, among other things, a hobby, an activity, or the word that makes my hair stand on end: fun.

Fun? That's right, lady, I write for *fun*.

In the beginning maybe. Back when I was just beginning to understand how many choices and compromises it takes to follow one's true desire rather than bow to the unending obligations one is supposed to live up to, how hard it is to even know what your true desire is if you're distracted by the million other things calling your name, how disciplined you have to be.

I never expected any of it to pay well or be easy. All I knew is that I wouldn't have to suppress myself, what most people mean, I think, when they use the word "fun."

So in this sense, yes, my work is fun.

I've certainly had my share of fun. The first time NPR aired my commentary, there was full on unrestrained drunken revelry in my living room. Motown music broke the sonic barrier. The cops were called. It was the best party I've ever thrown. It was the best party I've ever been to.

Anyway, to say that artists and writers are just working people, a daily grind of our own, nothing especially fun about it on a daily basis, would be an understatement. We are *unquestionably* just working people, a daily grind of our own, nothing especially fun about it on a daily basis. Still, when all sides of it are going well, which happens occasionally, I would describe it as exactly what I'm looking for in terms of work. This makes me one of the fortunate few, I know.

Oh, in case you were thinking all artists and writers are cut from essentially the same cloth, we aren't. Not even close. All we have in common is the need to hold our thoughts and ideas up to the light so we can take a closer look. Other than that, I can still be taken aback by how little some of us can identify with or even like one another. What we share is discipline and routine, which is absolutely nothing like the media-driven overnight success stories for 99 percent of us. My reality is more like making sure I hit SAVE before I exit the page so I can take a minute to remind Larry to do whatever it is I already reminded him to do a hundred times, "Get to the bank before it closes, k?"

And given that I still don't have a clue what I'm supposed to say when someone asks me the Big Question, I've made up my mind to try for a reply that makes me sound (and feel) both wise and funny, without having to have a cocktail first. A response I will still be proud of at three in the morning when my mind riffles through, without mercy, all the mistakes I made in the last twenty-four hours.

Like, for instance, Numero Uno for today was when my friend Sandy called this morning at ten a.m. and said, "Hey, sweetie, what are you doin'?" in her in-between-careers, carefree voice, like a girl talking to a boy she likes, and I was taken aback. Every time I hear her voice, it reminds me how serious I'm getting, especially when I'm working.

And it's not just that Sandy is chirpy and friendly and girlishly positive most of the time; it's that no one calls a dental hygienist (her line of work) at ten in the morning to have a chat. And yet, somehow, the fact that I'm working doesn't register in the same way with my friends. Not at first, anyway. Which is why I have to remind them.

But it's hard to find the right tone to remind them, even harder to keep friends once I do. Because what I sound like is someone who doesn't have time for friends. I wish I'd given more thought to how to answer Sandy before saying, in a voice straining to be warm but coming out rushed instead: "Sandy? It's ten in the morning. I'm working. Just like the next guy."

"So why do you pick up the phone if you can't talk?"

Now I guess we're tied, Sandy and me.

Because Sandy's question not only makes sense, she's absolutely right. Normally, I don't let much interrupt my work. And, yet, I answer the phone when I'm writing.

Why so?

Well, hmm. I don't know. I guess it's just another one of the many things I'd better be up to admitting I'm a hypocrite about, terribly embarrassed about, no good at; things I never saw before but once they are looked at through a friend's eyes, I suddenly can see nothing else.

So let's be sure I'm seeing this right. Since writing is so isolating, I think I'm triggered by the sound of someone perceivably reaching out to me.

I'll drop Sandy an email. Her question became the pivotal question this morning, and I want to thank her. It made me forget all about the other Big Question I thought was so important but now seems silly in comparison to all the issues the word "isolating" brings to the surface. *Why* I pick up the phone when I'm writing just never came up before.

And it's a Big One.

Ferry Line

FEBRUARY

Everyone needs to escape now and again.

And in Seattle, a quick escape comes in the form of the Washington State Ferry system, and right now, I'm sitting in my car watching two women sitting in theirs, side by side in the ferry line.

The wind finds its way in through my cracked open window, making a whistling noise. Last time I waited in this line, a homeland security dog stuck its nose right in and sniffed and sniffed, and I went numb with fear remembering how my friend Suzi Seagull (it used to be Susan Segal, but there is such freedom in moving to Seattle!) used to light up a joint every time she rode in my car, but not today. Today the dog sniffs once and moves on.

Ah, the city of which I speak. As far as the inner neighborhoods go, we have Belltown, the residential part of downtown. Queen Anne, which looks after the well-off; Greenlake and Fremont; where the more liberal flock; Capitol Hill, the most liberal; the trendy University District; and the Central District where Madison Avenue divides it from higher tax brackets just like in New York.

But everyone comes down to the same level at Pier 52—idling, bumper-to-bumper. I find these little gathering places in a city protect me from more serious bouts of urban disconnect, relieve me from the lonesomeness that creeps in if, say, Larry and I have had a row and I don't want to call and say it was all my fault. I want to call and say it was all his fault. But it will pass. It always passes.

The women in the car next to me are eating grapes. One holds up a bunch and tilts her head back to swallow it. Like Cleopatra.

Writers stare. We stare too much. We stare until, in ways that matter to us, we click with some new Meaning of Life in some new Meaningful Way. We stare until we forget we are staring. We don't know when enough is enough. We forget to say *when*.

We eavesdrop, too.

I'm beginning to think I write too much, as well. Writing can be a substitution for other things, important things. I have to literally force myself not to write. You can glamorize writing all you want, but it's not about inspiration; it's about *doing*. Actually I have no idea what inspiration is really, other than a good idea, but that's the easy part. Carrying it through a couple hundred pages, plus a hundred more, is just a lot of hard doing.

Still, I don't want to look back and say, "Man, I missed traveling to Greece, hiking in the Grand Canyon, or watching an Olympic skater who just lost her mother win a medal because I had to write." Which is me in a nutshell right now.

There is so much time to think in a ferry line.

Before I was a full-time writer, I was a full-time dancer, and before I was a full-time dancer, I was a competitive skater. So my mother just can't *believe* I missed the ice dancing last night.

But I can. There is so much about ice dancing that always makes me kick around a few things in mind I'd rather let go of. I try to watch the competitors, without feeling competitive myself, but I can't. I get sucked into the world of competition and by Day Two I'm living there. And it's not a "gold" feeling by any stretch of the imagination. By that I mean it's not pride I'm feeling in my chest, but more of a molten goo running over my exposed nerve endings. All I can think of is the buildup of tension behind all the sleek costumes and feigned smiles.

Which gets me thinking even more about my own life as a dancer. And I can't think of this without thinking of my dance partner, L.

For years we danced together. After rehearsal, L. was my confidant; our conversations settled me down inside because one thing there is no shortage of in a young dancer's world is insecurity. I often felt floored by how much of it was whirling inside me. When I think about it, it may have been the strongest source of my determination to dance in the first place. To prove to myself that the world I was the most intimidated by, which at that time was the dance studio, could be my world. *Watch me.*

Even when I got to the level of directing my own studio and my own dance company, there was still this niggling part of me that felt like I was faking it. I know how common this niggling is to people. I knew it even then, but knowing it never lessened its load. I was lithe on the outside, moving with the kind of ease and grace only years and years of discipline can instill, but inside there was a lot of lumbering. I carried a lot of self-doubt. It was like carrying a load of bricks.

I always knew that writing would eventually ask more of me than dancing (I was right) and that I'd better stick with dancing (a workout I am never bored by) as a way to stay fit enough to handle writing's demands. No one ever talks about how much stamina it takes to write. Double for speaking in front of an audience. You can't be sweating and gasping for breath between the points you need to make.

Now I can see how L. and I short-circuited way before we quit performing together. It was the kind of defeat that makes the real world of dance, not to mention the cycle of friendship, even more baffling because nothing is ever how it appears on stage.

When I was dancing, I thought real sorrow was made of a dance partner who hurts your feelings; that real disaster was defined by dance heartbreak, like missing a move you mastered in the studio but couldn't carry off under pressure. All of which now seems like the most measly of heartbreaks. But it doesn't keep the startling reality of how quickly closeness can fade, how little it takes for two partners to become strangers again, to cut into me every time Bob Costas spins an Olympic dancer's life into a cozy sound bite.

Like hell, I scream back. *Like you know.*

Back in the ferry line, I turn my head to watch one of the women get out of her car and look both ways as if waiting for another friend to join her. She waves to someone in the walk-on passenger line who comes running over. Before they climb back into the car, she looks right at me. We both look quickly away when our eyes meet and then

she turns to talk to the other woman again. Then they *both* turn to
look right at me. I am so embarrassed. I can hardly move.

Not that I'd admit to anything.

Well, well. What it takes to shed three layers of clothing in the front
seat of a compact is nothing I would ever shove aside, visually. I'm just
glaring out of the corner of my eye into the car next to me, pretending
I'm not about to watch how one woman will manage to change her
clothes. And that the woman wears a lacy demitasse bra under standard Seattle-issue fleece is like witnessing both sides of the coin, is it
not? This, I say to myself, is what a writer is ultimately looking for:
the world, and all its sides, at once!

Which brings me to why it hardly bothers me when all three wom-
en's eyes are suddenly glued on me, exaggeratedly so, chins jutted forward. One folds her hands into binocular-fists. I look away slowly,
simulating I'm scanning for who on *earth* they could be looking at.

The ferry slides forward.

I stare at a new house in Magnolia that is just hugging the cliff.
The architectural skill required to hold such a tiered weight in place
is amazing, what with the sea moving closer all the time. I'm fanning
myself with the ferry schedule when my cell rings.

Mom.

I lie back on the headrest and gear up for a good long talk because,
as with most things Mom, before anything else, before any warm
greeting, there's trouble in her tone that I will need to get to the bottom of.

"You *have* to watch the skating tonight. Joannie Rochette, from
Canada, is an only child and her mother died on Sunday," and I know
this is my mother's way of saying, "*I* could die on Sunday!"

"But wait, it's only Tuesday, how can she be skating so soon?" I
say this because I can't imagine regaining such mind-boggling focus
only two days after losing my mother. Following her death, I'll cave.
I know this is true as much as I know what my mother will say next.

"That's what I'm saying!"

I sit for a while, maybe five minutes, waiting until I can figure out what else I need to say here other than I forgave Larry before my mother even called.

And finally it comes.

"I forgive you, L."

And, after a minute or so of one-sided forgiveness, I nod to myself.

"I forgive *me,* too."

Hands

As of today, I officially think in terms of "how it used to be."

It's like having someone slap me across the face and say, "There is no going back. What's true is true."

"You know where it is," I heard myself say to my neighbor. "It's right *there* next to the nail salon that used to be a hardware store that used to be that funny-looking art gallery that used to be a video store, remember? Surely you remember."

And even if not one other "how it used to be" ever popped into my mind again, I could write for days just by reliving the "used to be" that really threw me recently when a friend told me, quite out of the blue, that she used to be a man.

You used to be a man?

For all intents and purposes, a person's sexual preference, to me, has never been even close to being the most interesting thing about them. Even after a sex change, she still better never lie to me, come on to my husband, be late one too many times, or not return the money she borrowed.

In any case, she used to be a man and that's that. Nothing about our friendship really changed after that. She's still someone I'd call for an honest opinion. She's interested. She asks questions. She wants to know.

Besides, there are always "used to be's" behind everyone's story. Hers. Mine.

For example, I know that when I walk into the kitchen to pour myself another cup of coffee, I don't want to stand at the counter too long staring at my mother's floral pasta bowl, I can tell you that. It's mine now, the bowl, which means it's propped up in a frame stand and never used. But when I look at it, I mean *really* look at it, I have to be sure I have the heart for being swept back into the 1970s.

Even if, and I'm just being frank, I was pretty cool in the 70s. In my yearbook, there's a photo of me sitting on top of my locker flash-ing a peace sign. It was my first sit-in. (Little has changed. Peace is what I long for and war is what we get.)

Anyway, my mother used to fill the bowl with pasta and ring the dinner bell to gather my sisters and me up from wherever we'd wan-dered off to. The bell was loud, too, embarrassingly loud, but it never stopped her from yelling "supper!" She could see us running for our lives toward home already, but she'd yell it again, louder, drawing the syllables out this time: "SUP-PER!" sounding as if, before we even sat down, she needed to speed things up.

This is how she used to mother us sometimes, as if she was late for her other life, the one she needed to get to after the dishes were stacked in the dishwasher and my father was stationed in front of Archie Bunker.

And the silk flowers that sat in a vase in the middle of our table? They used to be plastic, and before that, real, straight from my father's garden. It was my job to move the vase back from the Formica coun-ter that used to be tile, so the pasta bowl could take its place. I did this very carefully because I knew if I broke the vase that used to be my grandmother's, I'd be a goner.

Tile has come around again and vanished. Now we say our granite counters used to be tile. And I wouldn't be a goner, either, I'd be *wack*.

I counted four more "used to be's" in my conversations today alone after I found a photograph of Larry tucked into a book. *Ah, there you are, love*, I thought, *how you used to be.*

I thought about shoving the photo back into the book it fell out of before too much history reared up on me, which always happens whenever I stare at Larry too long. After all, we fell in love when I was twenty. Larry: so self-directed, so handsome.

And, sure, I could try and sway the way my memories will go, but sometimes surrendering is just so important. I wound up focusing on the photo until all my thoughts found their way into the deepest, most tender places, kindling the most lovesick feelings. From my ears to my knees, paralyzing nostalgia. One memory after another. Our whole story.

I took it in. And then I stashed it.

I didn't chuck it or anything, of course not; but I hid it away.

I could frame it, but, unlike most of my friends, I don't have dozens of framed photographs adorning the shelves of my home. I will one day again, surely. There used to be photos everywhere. But right now my life requires a lot of mobility and too many photos sort of short circuits my flow.

It wasn't that long ago, maybe a year, I tried letting my photo folder revolve as my screen saver. One by one, my past came at me in two-second intervals. It drove me nuts. I'm quite proud of my achievements, the lives I've lived, but, I swear, every time I passed my monitor, I had a little heart attack. All that emotion really slowed me down.

I'll forget half of what I saw in Larry's photo if I don't get to it: Specifically, his hands. Knuckles swollen from building the sailboat we used to live on. Our first home.

His fingers used to be the color of old wood; new skin grew right over the dirt; callouses grew a good half-inch above his palms and when nicked, drew no blood. And just look at his mop of curly hair. No wonder my dad said he looked like Charles Manson.

About a year before the photo was taken, Larry picked me up hitchhiking. I was on my way to the Olympic Hot Springs. We wound up soaking in the warm water together. I moved in with him a week later. We lived in an old milking barn in Sequim, Washington. It was the 80s.

Back then, in total-lust stage, Larry, always the gentle lover, wouldn't cup my breasts with the tips of his sandpapery fingers, but roll his hand to one side to let his thumb do the work. Neither could he let his hands rub my legs covered in nylon tights without making a crackling sound, or lie in the dark with me on our double sleeping bag, unzipped and opened flat, with hands that prowled easily, without catching on each lofty seam.

Rough. That's how Larry's hands used to be. I study such things.

Which brings me to Larry's hands today. Smooth all right. Nickless as a slab of marble. Around the age of forty, like many the boatbuilder before him, he left his "sail around the world" dream to find work that 1: paid, and 2: let him use his mind more than his hands.

Now I call Larry's hands white-collar pink. And this used to be funny between us.

Either way, then or now, Larry has never wavered from being the kind of man who would never, not on your life, drive a bent nail deeper into the grain of mahogany just to get the job done.

Rare, don't you think?

And why, I believe, there is more at work in our marriage than two people trying their best.

So thank you for letting me reveal Larry how he used to be. If I didn't think my "how it used to be's" were connecting us, and to the big-picture I love, I'd have stopped sharing right after the pasta bowl.

And I can't quite picture leaving Larry out like that.

It used to be something I was capable of, in the same way I was capable of thinking that lifelong marriage is not possible.

But not anymore.

Pet Stylist

MAY

I'm not going to tell you her name, only that, by trade, she's a pet groomer.

"Pet *stylist*," she corrected, pointing at me with dog scissors. "And go ahead, print my name; I could use the publicity."

"Okay," I said, but what I was thinking was that I wasn't at all sure she'd want to be my friend once she reads this. It's a risk I take. People will see themselves in my story no matter what, even when I'm *not* writing about them. Something jumps out and catches their eye. Regardless of the story I tell, from that point on, they see another story. I can see it in their eyes way before they ask me. Or they don't have the nerve to ask me.

When my friend told me she'd stopped writing poetry and teaching poetry to pursue her new profession, pet styling, I couldn't think of anything to say at first. Which is so unlike me.

The truth is, I seldom watch television (hotel rooms, maybe; when I visit my mother, definitely). I know this sounds snooty, but I really don't care much about forensics, interns, celebrities (especially celebrities), lawyers, more forensics, more lawyers, younger and younger celebrities, and more and more grotesque reality situations. They make me afraid, truly afraid, that the future of our culture belongs to hateful, horrible, obnoxious people. And voyeurs. And why I completely missed the fact that pet stylists have been all the rage for a while. I did see an infomercial about pet stylists once, at the gym. My reaction was to stand on my tippy toes and turn the set off.

In the spirit of friendship, though, I said, "Wow, good for you! What a fun way to milk the rich!" not wanting to remind my friend she has a master's degree in literature, loves to teach, and writes the finest stanzas I've ever read, because it's pretty tough right now since her divorce, and that's what was written on her face.

"Not the rich," she retorted, "the *lonely*. And I should know."

I gaze at my friend whose husband moved to Santa Fe with a woman half her age, trying to imagine what her life has been like since he left. This helps me remember how, soon after his exodus, she visited the pound and came home with a dog. Now she has three. Last time I ran into her on the sands of North Beach, it was like she was being led by a team.

Her flyer is beautiful. And, in a way, poetic. Much more elaborate and well thought out than my writer/speaker throwaway. It reminds me of what a woman in front of Metropolitan Market said to me when we were both picking out a few potting plants: "My mother said a good window box needs a filler, a spiller, and a thriller."

My friend's flyer has it all. A cover image of a dog wrapped in a plush bath towel is a good filler. An ellipsis trails off the end of "pet stylist...," nudging you to open the flyer and read on is a bang-up spiller. And the cost of her services is quite the thriller, if you ask me.

- Style cuts
- Summer cuts
- Puppy cuts
- Nail trimming
- Nail grinding
- Teeth brushing
- Teeth whitening
- Bathing
- Blow drying
- Undercoat removal
- Specialty shampoos
- Conditioning treatments
- Ear cleaning
- Ear plucking

I didn't even know my friend had changed professions because I don't see her that often, don't own a pet, and, frankly, I had no idea such a job exists outside of Los Angeles. I thought Seattle was too, I don't know, unstylish to care much about style, pet or otherwise. I can't help but think how a lot of men I know could benefit from my friend's services, especially the ear plucking.

"People who haven't shopped for new clothes in years will spend a fortune on their dogs," my friend says. "You'd be surprised."

I settle into nodding, supportive friend.

"Yesterday I sold a Doggie Dryer to a woman who feeds her dog leg of lamb every day."

"When did the word *stylist* replace *groomer* as the official name of someone who does what you do?" I asked, imbued with the kind of curiosity that comes from hearing about someone else's obsessive behavior. I get so tired of my own.

Big mouth me. She looked back at me with eyes that said, "You are such a snob."

Please, don't think *that*.

But maybe she's right. Maybe I'll never be the kind of person who sees this kind of money lavished on pets as completely sane, politically corrected enough to say something like "If leg of lamb is what she wants to feed her dog, who am I to judge?"

Still, I want my friend's business to grow beyond her wildest dreams, just to prove to the worm she married that she is able to support herself, so that when the pretty young thing he flew off with has had enough of his saggy butt, he will know who has the better life now.

What is more, I want to be filled, spilled, and thrilled with easy encouragements and not think twice about extending a compliment. It's the way I want to see myself, the way I want to be a friend. I tossed and turned all night figuring this out.

In the nick of time, apparently. Because on other sleepless nights, I'm beginning to imagine myself, with more and more frequency, as a woman alone, hair the color of January, and, if I don't stop writing about my friends, with no one to love me back but a couple of dazzlingly lustrous, spoiled beyond belief, well-styled cats, halibut cheeks in the oven for their dinner.

Wait. I wanted this to sound like the most lonely way to live, but it doesn't feel that way. It feels like a luxury of sorts. It was just one of those things that pops out just because, for a joke. But when I read it again I see nothing I've ever written is more telling.

To which I say, *wow*.

Totally Unexpected

JUNE

Something totally unexpected happened. My friend had a heart attack. She is forty-two years old.

A *heart* attack.

Before you think she should have quit smoking, tossing back the vodka, or laid off the fries, I will say that none of this is true. Even when it's happy hour and the booze is only three bucks, she never has two.

When we walk the rim of Greenlake, it's she who wants to go twice around. Halfway around, I want to stop and have a drink at any one of the lakeside bistros. I don't care which. Pick one. And bring me the wine list.

When we order dinner, she's quick with her standard fish and salad. I'll have the mac and cheese, thanks.

She says her heart attack is a fluke. "An unlucky fluke in a string of flukes I've had to get a grip on lately."

I watch my friend try and fold her heart attack neatly into the layers of other recent setbacks, but I'm not buying it. Trying to convince herself that a heart attack is a fluke? It's as if she decided to cope by sewing a rock into the hem of her skirt. And every time the rock hits her leg—*ouch, ouch*—she bears it.

We cried, naturally, she and I. We cried and cried.

Now, my friend's stoic coping skills have left me questioning my own. Like, how, exactly, do I explain that I'm having a few attacks myself. Well, maybe not *attacks*, but little spasms in my sleep. I think I'm trying to come to terms with what's important to me now, which to me means trying to appreciate the good rather than worry the bad. Unlike my friend, I can't carry my rocks too close for too long because they will sink me if I let them.

Like the wars we're still fighting. *Ay caramba*!

Like the oil spills. Major payback from Mama Earth. She's tired of turning herself inside out, of giving, giving, *giving*, and getting nothing back in return. This is my spill spasm. Black sludge. I'm unable to breathe. And then I wake up.

Like our planet heating up. *Jeez*!

Like too many people living beyond their means, and thinking it wouldn't catch up with them eventually? Wouldn't that be something? It's like my cheesy Cousin Mario who lived like nothing unusual was happening while he tried to cheat my dad out of beaucoup bucks. He ended up doing jail time. (The family doesn't like to talk about it.)

Sure, my friend's husband decided he was bored and moved out. And, yes, her cushy corporate job with health benefits was swept away with all the other cutbacks of late. But I don't think either of these setbacks brought my friend to her knees in pain.

Women can handle men leaving; it's an old story. It was knockdown drag-out ugly, but she regained her equilibrium by donating everything he left behind to Goodwill. (When she told me he was storing his stuff in her garage until he could come back for it later, I said, "Oh he thinks so, does he?" We got out the Hefty bags.)

Women can handle losing jobs, too. We have amazing life-balancing skills. I'm reminded of our poise whenever my husband thinks he can work himself into an early grave, and I have to call his office to inform him that oh yes he *will* be cashing in on vacation time this year, every single deserved day, because I found a house exchange on Lake Como and WE ARE GOING!

As for my friend, time away from feeling "unappreciated, micromanaged, and unable to work creatively" (her words) will add years to her life, not lessen them, may even force her to find work she enjoys. Even if the pay stinks *because, my friend, a bottle of wine doesn't have to cost fifty bucks; you'll get used to it.*

But can a mother, whether she admits it or no, handle her son's returning to Afghanistan for another tour of duty? This asks an awful lot of a parent's heart.

Her attack continues to alter things in me, too, fundamental things. I finally let go of a lot. After I realized that I didn't have to understand *why* my friend's attack was righting my own life, that sometimes we just have to accept what knowledge comes our way and not question it, the changes elbowed in. They pushed.

For example, expecting more from others than others can give? I'm done with that. I've been way too idealistic. Others can't hurt me anymore.

Or, if they do, so what. Next?

As to my work? Another book will be great. I'll celebrate! But I'm no novice at this business. I know what it takes to sell a book to a publisher, the humility; then to travel from point A to point B ten times in a month in order to sell it afterwards. The honeymoon ends. After a while, questions like, "Isn't it exciting?" make me want to fake enthusiasm for my Motel 6 room by the freeway.

Honestly, I wish I could just sit here writing forever and never move.

Mostly, I let go of lying to my friend. I no longer agree with her about why she suffered a heart attack. I don't nod my head in agreement about why her fragile heart can't take much more of this crazy, good-for-nothing war, and the even crazier men who start wars or let them go on. "And," I said, "until we find out what's making your heart twitch, I am not going to buy anymore it's-just-a-fluke bullshit from you."

"Okay," she said.

I feel the need to repeat myself here because, for whatever reason, my hard drive is full. There is no more room for Middle East anything, other than its people and its food. I'm not sure what else is expected of me now in terms of understanding or sympathizing with countries that still stone women to death. And I swear if I have to try to remember which province we are fighting in now or how to pronounce one more name like Kandahar, Jalalabad, Mazar-i-Sharif, I'm going to crash.

And . . . and I don't like to use the word "liar" lightly, but when I think back to the last election, a straightforward pledge to pull us out of war was the clincher; so, dammit, the word does seem to apply here.

And, yes, I know our president did not start our current wars. So I'm not blaming him alone.

Still, next presidential go-round, I'm going to vote with something other than hope.

Problem is, I don't quite know what that something *is*. I guess I'm still waiting for someone to come forward with enough of something to appeal to my ... what?

I resist getting too sidetracked here, but I think my point is clear: I'm stuck with the fiercest thing I feel about my friend's heart attack. Which boils down to the fiercest thing I feel about the world: We need more women running it. Men have made such a mess of things. We need to get in there in big, big numbers with big, big sponges and clean up the mess. Just like after our brother/husband/son uses the bathroom. We have to roll up our sleeves after yelling for the millionth time at whoever left a heap of wet things on the floor that we don't leave heaps of wet things on the floor, and then we have to get down on our knees and mop it up. (Remember, you will be called a bitch for yelling, and, no, you won't be thanked for wiping the hairs out of the tub.)

Clearly, my heart can't take much more of the way things are going, either.

Crow

Lying still, I wallow in the image that comes to mind.

I throw off the covers, pull on a robe, and head to my desk. I want to write about her, finally, the crow that comes to me in a dream now, the crow that, last June, made her nest right outside my window, an urban glove of weeds, sticks, strips of plastic, and a fistful of my own frizzy hair.

There was no mistaking the frizz. That's how close to my window the crow made her nest, working with her mate, wings fluttering, beaks jabbing, a devoted couple who built a pocket of warmth that would hold, midair, even in a windstorm.

I like to think the nest was thanks for my remembering to throw my loose strands of hair out the window whenever I clean my brush. "Birds love hair," I read. "They use it to fill in the gaps like a boat builder seals with caulk."

Crows mate for life "although adultery is not unknown," says the Bird Facts website. Funny, that's exactly how a few of the men in my family would define marriage, too.

For weeks and weeks I watched the crow sit in her cradle. Every morning I'd get up and immediately look out the window. And there she was. So beautiful and patient it *hurt*.

In my dream she squawks at me. Just as she did the day I tried to peer into her nest. As soon as she flew off, I leaned over my balcony and tried to see the eggs hidden deep within and, out of nowhere, she dive-bombed me. I never tried to snoop inside her nest again.

After a few more days of proving I could be trusted, she let me near enough to see her dark eyes blinking. And, really, that's what I loved most, *her*.

And once, I swear, as soon as she saw me, she briefly shut her eyelids, held tight, and then quickly opened them again as if to say, *there you are!*

It takes about a week for a crow to build a nest, another to lay two to six eggs, nineteen days of incubation, a month before fledgling, then two months of feeding her young. That adds up to four months start to finish, instinct driving her all the way.

When she'd screech at her mate even though he works his tail feathers off to bring home the insects and worms, just to unburden herself of, oh, I don't know, one of a zillion frustrations that can befall a female any given moment of any given day, I completely understood.

And her desire for a perfectly tidy nest?

Yes, of course.

Her diligence?

I get it. Food, water, and right back to work? Oh, lord, yes. How else do we get what we want? There is no other way.

Then there was the day the maintenance man came with a massive leaf-blower. I couldn't stand it. *If only he could identify with something other than power.* That's how I felt. Like the crow was trying to remind me of so much *other* knowledge. I ran outside and made him stop. I have my ways.

Maybe that's what the crow was squawking about in my dream, expressing gratitude for my being so bold, for trying to make a gas-guzzling man see there are living things in his path, that before men wanted to be called landscapers (land*scrapers*, I roll my eyes) women were content to be gardeners.

Or was she squawking at me because I couldn't do more to save her flock?

Either way, it's unsettling to have a crow squawk at you in a dream. Stranger still, to talk back. "I will strangle a squirrel with my bare hands if it comes close to your eggs," I promised.

I would like to be able to tell you I kept my promise, that I saved the eggs.

But I didn't.

One neighbor swears it was a raccoon. Another blames a stealthy cat. "A cat?"

"The feral ones," she said, "rats with fur."

Total despair. I didn't even try to hold it back.

To this day the nest is still in the pouch of the tree outside my window, but lopsided. Every once in a while, I squint to see her shelter as she would. If I stare too long, tears well up. If I try not to cry, it's just impossible. I've never understood the point of *not* crying. If there is some other lousy thing going on in my life and I look at her nest, that's it: major bawling. Like this morning. If someone looked up from the sidewalk to my Juliet balcony, they would have thought I'd lost a loved one.

My husband thought I cried so hard because, together, we'd watched the last combat troops leave Iraq. "You hardly reacted," he said. "I knew sooner or later, you would."

Somehow I found the good grace not to tell him how wrong he was about this. Nothing about men and their need, want, lust for war surprises me any longer. I watched it all: the convoy crossing the border into Kuwait; the soldiers giving the thumbs-up; the reporters reducing the scene, the very war, into short *excited* clips for the nightly news; the cameras clicking. *Click. Click. Click. Click. Click.* There was nothing new to see and I knew it. I sat there asking myself why men do this?

So no. Nothing I saw on the screen touched me like watching the crow.

Even now, I can't stop thinking about her. I can't get her out of my mind. The image of her sitting so patiently in her nest helps me make new efforts to live more patiently in my own.

If, through reading this, you feel the need to pay more attention to the feathered black circling above, if you feel that, however far out this sounds, it's your *privilege* to take in the crows, to really see them, you simply have to do it, if only for a few seconds a day.

Until you can say, at least, "There, I've taken the time to look up. I've taken the time to be *moved*."

Rose

Rose, your email came to me at just the right time.

Because here it is December, and I'm at a loss. What can I possibly say? Everything "holiday" has been written before. I have serious doubts as to whether I can find a fresh angle.

When you become a writer, Rose, you'll understand this dilemma. I promise.

Your writing to tell me that you read my column is the best present. How many fifteen-year-old girls even read the paper? Which makes your gift even more precious. Sure, your mom and I know each other. Still, knowing her, knowing *you*, I infer no female in your home is deciding what the other female reads, period.

What I need to say, readers, is that Rose wants to be a writer. But when she shared this with her guidance counselor, she didn't get the reaction she was hoping for. In Rose's words, "My counselor says I need a back-up plan."

Rose, hear me: Trying to do the jigsaw of maturing is no easy feat for any young person. But trust me, if you have already found work that makes you happy, a huge piece of you will not go missing. I will go so far as to say your passion for writing may turn out to be your truest love in life. This might not be an easy thing to hear in your young romantic world, but no friend, especially no *boy*friend (doubly hard, sorry), will be able to fill that place inside you that longs for so much. Only you can fill it.

And writing will help.

Boy oh boy, was I thrown into a tizzy of remembering after reading your email, Rose. See, once, in the seventh grade, I called my Home Ec teacher by my English teacher's name and, humiliating me in front of my classmates, she yelled, "Get your head out of the clouds!"

Clouds? I was mortified. I imagined *not* suffering in silence but walking right up to her desk and slicing her head off the rest of her body, like when two tomatoes are conjoined, one plum smaller than the other, and all it takes is a single swipe to make the smaller one go rolling across the counter.

Because I know how important names are to people. I'm just so bad at remembering them. But ask me anything, anything at all, about her physical details—what she wore, the ever-changing color of her bristly hair, the squiggly little lines around her eyes, her lips of coral-colored lipstick that bled into even finer lines around her mouth (scary to a twelve-year-old)—and I knew, baby; I *knew*.

Even then, I was obsessed with the details. Noticing them was my best, possibly my only, skill. I just didn't know how to apply it yet, how to make use of the fact that not only could I itemize, specify, describe, interpret, and elaborate; I loved doing so. To anyone who would listen.

But retrieve someone's name right after I meet them? To this day, I go blank. I soak up the visual, the single hair growing out of a mole, the untied shoestring, the green toenail next to all the blue ones; but I'm resistant to names the way some people are to colds. In this area, I have what my mother would call "a strong constitution." Until I get to know someone better, I'm porous to the name. It leaves me. I'm a sieve.

Maybe this is why the old cultures christened people with names like, "Girl With Mole Over Her Right Eye," or, "Boy With One Arm Longer Than The Other," names that described something obvious.

Rose, what I'm trying to say is just think how much time I could have saved if my guidance counselor had picked up on my wordy, descriptive babbles and leaned me toward creative writing instead of laying the secretary/nurse option on so thick. Insecure, vulnerable me might have left high school with a feeling of *I'm going to be a writer!* Instead of the vague *I don't think I want to type for a living . . . or draw blood;* the *I have no clue how to fit in* feeling that made me face my immediate future with phony confidence, while my insides knew better.

See, the thing about my guidance counselor, the thing about my guidance counselor and *me*, is when I look back at the two of us sitting there face to face in her office, trying to come up with what I should do, who I should be, with fifteen minutes for concerned-looking her to make a stab at my future, all I could see was what she was able to help me with, which was . . . absolutely nothing, that's what.

Here's what she said: "You can make more money as a secretary. But nursing offers better benefits to your family."

Benefits? Family? Death to a seventeen-year-old.

I inhaled. All I could exhale, given my age, was a nervous giggle.

She certainly said nothing that helped me perceive my peculiarities as the very traits a writer needs. Gradually, gratefully, through the years, I learned this on my own.

To be fair, there are amazing guidance counselors; I'm sure of it. Just as I'm sure the word "guidance" affixes to the word "counselor" for a good reason. But, Rose, what you have to understand is that I knew, even then, that the woman before me, a full-fledged member of the adult working world, was going to be of no help to me whatsoever.

I did suspect that her lack of help was warning me of something, though, something important: that you don't have to be crazy to do stupid things that screw up your future for good, just young without any imaginative guidance whatsoever.

High school, for me, bristles with so many of these warnings.

In time, all the lost little parts of me came together, together enough anyway (there are still plenty of holes) to make me see how I really had no choice about what I was meant to do because I was already doing it.

Just as you are, Rose.

And it's not hard to see how the rest of my life fell into place around me in all the determined, common-to-writers, obsessive ways it needed to eventually: notebooks full of ideas, pages and pages rejected, or rewritten and then published, some of them. Every surface of my home shining because I believed if I could just keep my nest clean and organized, I could keep my goals in order, too.

I still believe this, by the way.

And as the world around me grew more scary and chaotic—in other words, as I got older—I sat, for longer and longer intervals, trying to make sense of it all, trying to hold on to some of it. Which, when I think about it, especially as a college freshman, was way better than drugs and alcohol, or dividing a tomato into a day's worth of calories. Or too much eating dragging me down.

·

So, Rose, I advise you to keep following the swerving road onto your very next page. Write about what stirs you to laughter, to tears, what stirs you at all.

Above all, promise me, promise your*self,* that you will be utterly, totally, completely selfish about making time for your work. Remember the word "selfish" is rarely applied to self-disciplined men.

And be open. To all kinds of writing. Try them out.

More than anything, Rose, promise me that you will absolutely insist on two things: Reflective silence. And passion.

Because without them, there is only numbness. And numbness — also known as using technology not to gain time, but to consume it, leaving no time for introspection, a writer's greatest tool — is very acceptable these days, very *in.*

So, more than anything in the world, *insist.* Because you will need to.

Again and again and again.

Part Four

"I write to become myself, more so day by day."

— EPPU NUOTIO

January Second

A windsock? Really?

This was my first thought this morning, early on the second day of a new year. And when first thoughts turn to bad gifts received, I figure it's time to raze the season for good, starting with the tree, a chore that presents me with an unmistakable truth: No part of carrying on with "the holidays" is still possible.

Perhaps I knew the season was officially over even before I made another round of New Year's pomegranate martinis in hopes that I'd stop worrying that alcohol would prevent me from writing the next morning and started hoping that it would. My tiny kitchen was crowded with vodka-happy friends, but still, I was having a little identity crisis, something that always happens if I haven't written for a while. I needed it, those couple weeks of slumber. *But now,* I remember thinking as the blender ripped, *I just want to get back to work.*

There's something about pulling ornaments off a tree that stirs my sense of fleetingness. It's a temperamental task. I'm hardly new at it, but somehow it doesn't get easier to deconstruct a living thing while there's still life in its limbs. I can smell it, my tree; it's still alive. It seems impossibly cruel to hermetically seal it in a giant plastic bag and send it off to be shredded.

I keep looking over at the tree as I write this, and what seems funny to me now is how I used to strip it bare the day after Christmas, no problem. But I was younger then, in more of a hurry to move faster on all fronts. Larry, oblivious to tree sentiment, calls the tree a fire hazard. "It's finished," he says.

I remind him that for an entire month the tree was our private celebration of light in this city of darkness and that no one over the age of fifty should use the word "finished" so indifferently.

Besides, I have my standards for putting down a tree, my demands. I want them carried out as carefully and attentively as ... okay, for example, the demands of my work. Before I accept an engagement, I want the programmer to have some understanding of what it is I do, that in no way do I require a lectern. Second, I want her to know I prefer a lapel mike, not a hand held, because I absolutely need my hands to talk. And, I'm sorry, but there must be some kind of mistake because, yes, actually, I *do* expect to be paid. Nothing but a check is going to fly with me. Having lunch with your group is a perk, I appreciate the grilled chicken and mixed green salad, but it's not payment. You can't offer your dermatologist grilled chicken and mixed green salad. You can't offer your hairdresser grilled chicken and mixed green salad.

Tonight's the night. But before we slip off the first ornament, we will linger, at my insistence, in front of our tree's mini-light glow to go over what we believe will make the next year a better one, everything we are grateful for now, and things we hope to be grateful for in the future, a ritual that used to involve personal accomplishments. Nowadays it's the worldly feats that impress us and I'm always reading between the lines for new ones, for proof our species is, in fact, evolving. Especially after Larry read somewhere that we may very well be evolving *backwards*. "We are the first generation living a shorter life span than our parents," he says, "thanks to obesity and diabetes."

"Really, Larry? This is what you want to say tonight?" Well poo on you, I think. I can't figure out what to do about obesity and diabetes right now. So I am relegating both to the back burner because my gratitude list is ready and I don't want to wait another year to share it.

Thank you EPA for pressing ahead on greenhouse rules! I jump for joy!

Thank you Interior Department for reinstating wilderness protection!

And thank you, sweet hallelujah, thank you, nuclear arms pact. Anything to assure I am not incinerated before my time is up definitely helps me sleep sounder. I haven't completely lost my faith in mankind's ability to stop us from detonating ourselves, far from it.

I just need to wean myself off C-Span, is all. To listen to a roomful of men talk about bombs is totally, unbelievably, surreal. When they carry on about which nations will arm this or that rebel group in order to get this or that ore or oil field, the lifeblood flows right out of me.

And the repeal of "Don't Ask, Don't Tell"? Why, thank you!

On December eighteenth, the day the repeal was passed in the Senate, my friend RJ (Richard James, but don't you dare ask him what his real name is because he won't tell you) came over and sat with me, all choked up and deliriously happy. I kept looking at his eyes when he was talking because his lips were quivering so much. RJ has so much compassion. He wields his chin around like a magic wand but never tries to force his version of things, nothing like that. He just blows kisses and says things like, "Have you ever noticed, dahling, how the whole world talks about peace on earth, but they aren't willing to make it happen?"

When I say I have noticed, he says, "They mean well, the masses; they just don't have the right *masseuse.*"

What I love most about RJ is how he can talk about totally serious things like war with appropriate respect and make me laugh at the same time. I don't have another friend quite like him, fully aware on some level *exactly* where fear and fluff meet.

Ever since the repeal passed (because I swear RJ has grown a little taller since), I've spent a lot of time thinking about what a repeal really means, what evolving *is*, and what it takes to finally shift a country's collective mind set so that we keep progressing, starting by rescinding ridiculous, intolerant laws.

Anyway, there is enough hope in the air to make me believe the year ahead will be splendid … short of North Korea going off the deep end, Afghanistan becoming a war without end, China demanding we pay up, or my dear friend, Shanta, marrying too soon again because her biological clock is about to burst into a non-stop relentless reminder of fertility. *Tick. Tick. Tick.*

"Keep a little mystery going, dahling. What I don't know about you is *fasc*inating," RJ said. We were talking about Facebook and selfie addiction, how boring it is to know too much about people, how drunk everyone is on voyeurism in the same way the Russians guzzled the vodka. "And look what happened to *them*."

Just the other day while waiting in line at Whole Foods, I was chatting with the guy behind me. We were talking local lettuce, fruit in season, that kind of thing. Except, as we talked he kept looking at his phone.

Few things irritate me more.

I tried to overlook it, be cool, be current, but it felt like he was rubbing my nose in the fact that one conversation, one person, one reality, is never enough anymore. It's like being put on hold. In the middle of a sentence, you have this sudden feeling of being canceled out, disregarded, worse than when someone puts their hand up like a traffic cop.

Even now I think of him nodding, talking to me, and scrolling at the same time, and I see a rude, cowardly way to communicate. I think it's time to remember that we do, in fact, exist without our phones. Because we *do*. We really, really do.

At first, I had to take a wide detour around coming right out and asking him what is so important that he has to be in on it even as he lays carrots on the conveyor belt. Then, I did ask. "I ask because ..."

But before I could come up with whatever ridiculous thing I was about to say next like, "... because I'm a writer," his girlfriend (wife?) jumped in, "This is just how it is now."

As if I knew nothing.

At any rate, she reminded me that since I do have more years behind me, I've attained more success, too, more independence. So I can enjoy a little harmless chitchat, and, okay, a little harmless flirting, without checking in.

My flesh may be softer than hers, but my attitude is firm: if I have faith in one thing, it's in eye-to-eye exchange, in the way one idea, opinion, observation, or secret shared can lift us out of ourselves, create a conversation that feels true, and make everything seem more alive. Why settle for less when you could be listening to the secret of a perfect marinara sauce as told to you by a lovely stranger by the avocado bin, her secret (dash of cinnamon, tablespoon of sugar) now yours as well.

And, yes, I may very well be hoping for a miracle. But if we're shopping in Whole Foods we are certainly paying enough for a miracle.

So I say thank God for RJ, who still knows how to leave the rest of the world out for however long it takes. Life may be going on at a hectic pace around the two of us, but RJ looks into my eyes when he speaks. He makes me feel that he'd never want something as big as his love for me to be shared with something small as a phone.

I hope to hell he's right about the masses, too, that a good massage may help work the tension right out and evolve us with a little more flexibility. I can almost let myself see this image it in front of me like a mirage, my eyes squinting.

Because I want it so badly.

The corner in our living room will feel unbelievably naked for a few days.

Mom. Me. (& Oprah)

Part I: Mean Streak

FEBRUARY

When I told my mother I was about to finish my new book, she answered with what she believes is the perfect parental response: "You'll be on *Oprah* some day!"

I wince. I shift my weight to the other foot. Mom's closest companion and all-around reference point these days is the television. I know that.

Come to think of it, this was true even when I was a kid.

So the real problem isn't my mother's TV habit; it's that I think I may have become another writer who is insanely jealous of anything Oprah. The words "Oprah Book Club" can make my face turn two shades of red. Envy giveaways, these cheeks of mine.

Which sort of negates any pleasure I may have found in my mother's compliment, though I know it's not her fault. She doesn't come right out and say so, but somewhere along the line, in spite of how many books she reads by authors she's never met on television, on another level—television level—she's come to feel that if you (if *I*) haven't been on *Oprah,* you aren't (*I'm* not) really a writer. If she sees an author on *Oprah,* "Someone's going to sell a *lot* of books right there!" she'll sing. It's a bit of pressure on the 99.9 percent of writers who never got the chance.

What I do is smile, swallow hard, take a deep breath, sigh. Try not to let my big, touchy, easy-to-press buttons get pushed.

And that she thinks I'd be read by Oprah *personally* is pure maternal pride, so I'm careful not to belittle her naivety. I know anything I try to say about the Great Big Publishing World is sticky business, that my mother's hands-on involvement in my work life sort of peaked when I stopped studying the catechism, that she'll take any explanation of my work at this point as more of an insult. Even I know better than to talk about agents, editors, and digital files at a time like this. There are just some things that drive mothers and daughters apart and do nothing other than lengthen the silence. If a wedge is what I want to drive in, there's no better way than to expound on a subject my mother knows little about.

But I haven't completely mastered shutting up. Sometimes I try to spell out the complexities of my working world, snarl by tangle, to my mother. When she says, "So, what did *you* do all day?" I want to say, "I don't know where to begin."

But I do. I do begin. I talk about my day with the heat I feel.

It takes only a few sentences. She's already looking away. Her eyes are moving from one corner of the room to the other searching for a world she understands. And when she finds it, usually with two tiny ceramic hands in prayer, she closes her eyes and gives a little nod as if she's listening to me; but she's not; she's found comfort in one of her figurines instead. Figurines are a lot easier to deal with than a daughter whose life is so *complicated.*

This is when "informing" my mother is still my worst habit. Blame it on a lifetime of competing with the fantasy my mother prefers: Religion; Disney; the Lifetime channel; romance novels; anything painted with religious, bird, kitten, or puppy scenes.

I'm not trying to win my mother's approval; that isn't my problem. It's more like I am trying to be seen as *is.*

Even so, I really should learn to say nothing. *Say nothing. Please, just say nothing.* Or sparks will fly.

It's tricky talking about work with anyone, let alone one's mother. Unless one does the same work you do, no one really gets the intricacies. With moms, though, there comes a point, there always comes a point, when buttons are pressed, re-pressed, held down, sending me into a tailspin until I need to speak up, say something, shield myself my way.

Especially when faced with—how can I say this without feeling horrible for saying it—my mother's mean streak. It's not hostile, never materializes into force, though it's pretty aggressive. It's more like a series of intonations, emphasis, and declarations that, in the end, are loud without being flagrant, leading nowhere good for either of us.

As in what she says next. "Al*though*," she takes aim, "Oprah wouldn't read your new book anyway. Not after what you said about her in your last one."

I'm sorry but a span the size of the Pacific rises between my memory of what I wrote about Oprah and what my mother remembers. What could she possibly be referring to? But it hardly matters, because there it is. The little stab that accompanies a compliment. She gives and takes back, almost in the same breath.

The warning sign is there. How she says the word "al*though*" as if she's been storing it up, knowing the word will wound, but choosing to wound anyway. Half of my life I've been describing my mother to my friends as "Edith Bunker with a knife."

"A knife?" they'll say.

"A knife of . . . frustration, disappointment; I don't know for sure."

I'm not entirely convinced trying to explain my mother's mean streak to my friends is a good idea any more. The thought of trying to put into words what I *mean* without sounding mean myself, well, it's my least favorite topic of discussion.

I do realize that what I may be interpreting as meanness could be no more than an everyday mixture of age-related ills that are stowed in the nooks and crannies of eighty-year-old limbs: discomfort, irritation, old resentments, anxiety, loneliness, all of the above.

Still, no amount of sympathy for aging makes a stab any less startling, even though I've dealt with them over and over. As a writer, I should be used to all kinds of injuries. But, somehow, my mother still has the power to fill the air with an electronegative jolt. *Prick. Pang.* And then it drops like a bombshell. *Boom.*

I don't mean to suggest that my mother doesn't get around to saying something kind and more encouraging after the knife goes in. It's not generally the first thing out of her mouth is all, even when she can see by my expression just how far her dig went in, fully aware by now what effect her stabs have on me, but most of the time before any admission or apology crosses her lips; she's too busy saying, "What?! I didn't say *any*thing."

Because she knows she said *some*thing.

Where does this come from?

Let me think. Now that my mother lives alone, silence gathers. Thoughts pile up. By the time I arrive, she's pent up. My husband says she needs the release and that I'm the valve. Which, I'm sorry to say, can feel like she's sort of blaming me for something.

What something?

I think she blames me for the fact she's old. Who else is left?

And so I wrap my arms around my waist and just listen for however long it takes for her to vent. The real test is to try and force myself to hear without paying too much attention to any one thing she says. To stay in the big picture. I try not to lose patience and blow up.

This is my problem: I've been known to blow up.

On another level, my mother's mean streak is just an Old World Italian thing; or so I've been warned by another Italian, Flo, short for Florence, my mother's closest friend. "We turn into real cranks," she said, crankily. "We're like varnish, we make things *hard*."

I think here of an artist friend who attributes everyone's imperfections to their artistic relevance. She put it like this: "Meanness is common to people who haven't directed their inner lives creatively. It's passive aggression in its simplest form."

"What's so passive about saying mean things?" I say.

"To your own daughter? *Every*thing."

I suppose she's right. Any one of us can define our life by what it is we are making right or by what's going wrong. And people get stuck in the wrong. There are days I have to work pretty hard to climb out of the pothole myself. I can fall in pretty deep. It takes every bit of my energy to crawl back out.

And then there's my mother's "new life" in Honolulu. She likes to think of this time as separate from "who I was before." She describes her retirement home as "a new start" without "old baggage." And it is. It's a world of landscaped gardens, swimming pools, movie nights, field trips, shopping trips, activity rooms, reading rooms, *music* rooms, dining rooms (with rolling dessert carts!), even a dress code. "It helps, psychologically, for the residents to dress for dining," the professionally pleasant manager said.

I've overhead my mother tell friends on the phone how beautiful her new apartment is, how daily sunshine warms her aches and pains, how friendly the staff is.

They say that to be an effective writer, you have to get past the pretty and explore the shadows. Okay then. There may be huge urns overflowing with tropical flora in every common area of retirement upscale splendor, but behind the hibiscus, every imaginable loss awaits. I'm getting used to complete strangers sharing their lung problems; heart problems; gut, bowel, and bladder problems; every procedure; every surgery; the fall everyone fears; the broken hip that could well mean the end.

And there's no quantity of sunshine, no activity, no adjustments or changes to your past that can buffer anyone from losing neighbors and friends one by one by one on almost a daily basis. Or prepare us for the depth of depression that continual condition-comparing can bring to the mahjong, poker, and bingo tables.

My mother has made the inevitable crash landing. She isolates more so she can direct her thoughts her own way. Boredom has set in. I believe boredom will be the symptom my mother will struggle with most.

But wait. As real as all this is, this is not the sole reason for the mean streak. Here I am trying to entwine my mother's new life with her old bad habit of being sort of mean to me while claiming she loves me, and I feel hugely mistaken.

Honestly, I'm not writing this to be all *me the victim.* My stabs have bled some, sure, but they've managed to heal. My sense of self hasn't been damaged or wronged in any significant way by the scars she inflicted. I don't look to my mother's flaws as a source of my own failings.

No more than you do.

Throughout, for as far back as I can remember, even when my mother was young with a houseful of kids, a home to run, friends visiting all the time, she wielded the same streak. Until now, I've never been able to say exactly why it's been difficult for me, over the years, to converse at any length with my mother about most things dear to me, but if I had to come up with the biggest thing, I'd say it's this need of hers to take a stab.

And if I stop to think about it further, her inability to curb it drove much of our family life, and not in the best direction. I have put off saying this until now in the same way my mother's meanness put my sisters and me off, before we found the nerve to challenge her, to make her take it back (which never worked). Still, to this day my mother denies she is moody and swears she's always been the most caring and kind person. So there is the little matter of how hopeless it is to try and talk with someone about a problem that, in their mind, doesn't *exist*.

The good news is I realize, on every single cellular level, that my mother has done the best she can with her own set of insecurities and fears. I have officially surrendered trying to remake her into a mom with a more positive temperament, more to my liking.

The bad news is, in order to pull this surrender off, a new problem has surfaced: I have been protecting myself by holding back. It happens more and more frequently, almost every day since I realized the basic equation of our difficulty: My mother's stab plus my reaction equals Mom and me, separate.

By holding back, I figure I can't hurt my mother. Plus, *I* won't be hurt. In other words, our sum whole has become something I can add to only by withdrawing, a lot like our deficit economy. Because this streak in her is so deeply ingrained that she doesn't even recognize it when it's occurring, or she refuses to. Either way, we now live in an atmosphere of holding back.

And yet, and *yet*, according to my friend Jeane—who has listened and re-listened to my trying to explain what this meanness has felt like my entire life—in the same way that some mothers can't help but blame us for their dissatisfaction, their aging, "Don't we, in our own mean ways, blame our mothers for getting old, for leaving us, how looking at them, we're forced to see our own frail bodies down the line?"

Without talking about it further, without asking Jeane to go on, I turned to her and gave her a kiss on the cheek. I heard her question. And I knew she was right.

~⌒

There is an old Tuscan proverb that says, "When I die, the world dies." I want to remake this proverb. Mean streak or no, stabs that stab or no, holding back or *no*, what the simple truth will be for me, regardless of our mother/daughter intricacy: "When my mother dies, the world dies."

Who was it that said the greatest journey can be the distance between two people? I think the distance may even be farther if the two people love each other.

In the name of the Mother, the Daughter, and the Holly Molly Spirit, amen.

Part II: I Am Mother, Hear Me Roar

And now we embark on this whole new phase, where, in the last couple of years, particularly since my mother entered her eighties, I've become (if not officially) a parent, mother to my mother, the one who fusses over the other.

And with each passing year, our role reversal intensifies.

If I were a philosopher, I'd say this is one of life's greatest trials. Like no test I've yet to face, it requires an almost daily reconciling of the past with what is in store for me now.

So far, I've been up to it. I like to think so, anyway.

But who would have thought the day would come when a certain childless someone would sleep in the disturbed way parents sleep when they know their only child is unhappy, even if the unhappiness pertains to one little skirmish on the playground (i.e., Mom's retirement home game room) while the rest of life at "school" is going pretty well.

That someone is me.

For instance, tonight, instead of sleeping, I'm thinking about the bully at my mother's poker table, the man who called my mother *fatso*, the man who made my mother cry.

There was no question what I had to do.

I pinned the bully against his walker. "Listen, I said. "You, call my mother fat again and you've got me to deal with, buddy. Got it?"

It felt justifiable. It felt *right*.

Part of me wanted to rewind, take it back. He's old, after all, and *skinny*.

The other part stood her ground. Said nothing. Walked away with an eye that could melt a glacier. And let us not forget the impact of melting glaciers.

A mother can only pray her instincts are right. If I were a man, I thought, the only harm that could come now would be if I turned around and apologized.

I heard a Japanese woman click her tongue. She thinks I went too far. I doubt that it would occur to her to act unladylike. But on the way out of the game room I turned to look at myself in the mirror, expecting to see my face full of righteousness, triumph, *verve*. Instead, I saw something that totally threw me. All I looked was ... afraid.

I'm also thinking how I must make sure the kitchen staff at the retirement home knows when it's my mother's birthday this year. Last year they forgot to bring her a cake so the entire dining room could sing to her and she was upset for days. Weeks, actually. I can't let that happen again. It would kill me.

And this morning I woke with a jerk. For the first time I understood how the word "never" doesn't apply to life after a certain age. When I was a girl and, I admit, right up through last year, I would wince at my mother's bingo addiction. "How can you waste your time like this, Mom?"

"As opposed to doing what?" she said.

Now I see how time swallows the word "never," chews it up and spits it at your feet out of pure necessity, not out of mockery. In my twenties and thirties I swore I'd never be a soccer mom. But now that I show up every week to watch my mother *call* bingo after her *promotion*, I know exactly what I am.

I am a bingo mom.

Because there's something about my mother's eyes at bingo, her appetite for bingo, the way she acts at bingo, that makes watching from the sidelines an absolute essential primal thing for me now. I'd do just about anything to see her smile like that.

Still, none of this role reversal is easy. But I'm learning to laugh more than I ever thought possible. When my mother swanks her little mean streak, I keep it light, keep the frustration to myself most of the time; do whatever needs doing at her place (wash dishes, empty trash, do laundry, clean out the spam file, walk the dog), and that is the most important thing right now.

And what a relief it is to nod my head while my mom shakes hers at all the modern ways (ahem, *my* ways) that disturb her. Even after things like betrayal and divorce blew her whole perfect, post-war, Rockwellian version of marriage/house/family right out of the water forty years ago, she still wants—with a visible vein running through her temple that throbs whenever I say I never regretted not having children—an easier way to explain to her friends a childless, sort-of-successful daughter. And her being able to say I was on *Oprah* would solve this problem for her in one clean sweep. We both know this.

And, really, I wish I could help.

I also know there's really no point in going over it again: that my golden rule about my work, in order to save myself, is that I absolutely have to find joy in my writing career as it is, in each small success as it comes, versus any mega-success story she sees on television.

"Mom," I say anyway, "I looked up what I wrote about Oprah. All I said is that a woman who chooses not to have kids of her own, yet continues to say things like, 'Motherhood is the greatest achievement for a woman,' is pandering. I was just being *honest*."

It doesn't take long (forty, fifty years) to realize that there are mothers who would remember what their daughter wrote about Oprah, who would understand, be sensitive to how it might feel to a childless woman to hear such a thing said by TV's most celebrated female, thus continuing the message that no matter what we achieve it is not enough, will never be enough, if we haven't reproduced.

And there are other kinds of mothers.

Mothers who would not remember what their daughter wrote about Oprah, only that it was not a glowing compliment. Because, forget about it, Oprah is *Oprah*. And no daughter of hers would be crazy enough to swim against a tidal wave, not in her mind, not in her experience, not on her watch; it is out of the question.

And that's what mothers are for, I guess, to try, to the best of their ability, to keep us afloat in the waves as they see them, as they define the waves. And I suppose this hidden compliment, this disguised lifeline, is the one I look for now, the love and concern within the mean streak, the words I want to keep alive when she's gone.

Even after she looks at me with the smirk that precedes the streak that precedes the stab, the roll of her eyes before she says, "You and your honesty. When will you ever learn?"

I close my eyes and pretend not to hear.

Because I am finally, at last, able to shout back in mind while keeping quiet. People call this a paradigm shift these days, but really I think I'm just growing up.

And when I heard myself saying to my friend Diane, five years younger than I am, "Sweetie, never say *never*," I shook my head.

Repeating adages is nothing new to friendship, but I'm always a little surprised when I rely on them, even when others are not; and Diane was not. She says I'm always acting the big sister. This makes me smile.

I may not know all that much about what it feels like to be a mother of any, or a big sis to many, but something tells me as Mom and I get older, the word *never* will slip from my lips less and less.

Until I can never, and I do mean never, *ever* use the word "never" again.

Part III: The Weight Issue

For all my talk about never getting the chance to be on *Oprah,* do you want to hear something funny? I *was*!

Ha! Got you.

As part of the studio audience.

The concierge of my hotel, to my delight, scored me a ticket. I shared a cab to Harpo Studios with another woman about my age. And when we pulled up, a queue already wound around the block. It seemed as if all the women found deep pleasure in just being able to *wait* for Oprah, but I wanted to slink back into the cab and ride back to the hotel.

And that's when, in a confident, unmistakable Noo Yawk accent (always less about what is said than how), my cab mate turned to me, slapped my shoulder with the back of her hand, and said, "Yu'd think dey'd nevah seen frickin' Oprah befah!"

It might as well have been the official slap of my youth. The real thing, passed from one East Coast woman to another. I fell in love with her instantly. In one sentence, she reached out across the continent and brought me home. Where is it written that we can't slap one another in Seattle? Which legislation says so? Because I sure had to learn that a backhanded shoulder slap doesn't fly on the West Coast. It may have been my first, truest acknowledgment of just how far from home I'd ventured. If you only knew how much trouble this familiar, sociable slap got me into my first year in Seattle.

"Well," the woman added, "I have no idear wad is up wit dis line, how lawng doze people are gonna stand ovah dar, but I turn fifty today, frickin' *fifty*, so I'm goin acrosst da street to have a scotch and soda. You comin'?"

I followed her, naturally. I would have followed her anywhere.

And right now, in retrospect, I am not only remembering the woman from Lawng Eyeland, but I see something else. Right out of the blue.

Thanks to you, Rhonda.

I'd almost forgotten that I promised my friend Rhonda, also turning fifty, that I'd consider her question. She wants to know how I, and a handful of other friends (there were eight of us cc'd) stay thin in our Fabulous vs. Frumpy Fifties. How do we, she wants to know "manage to live life to the fullest, not the fattest."

Do we drink? What do we eat? Do we snack? Do we exercise?

I've taken over a month to answer. My sweet time.

Because I didn't feel up to it.

I still don't.

I feel a lot of dread seep into my stomach every time I reread the email, but I can't avoid it any longer. I try to keep the dread from spreading by telling myself how much I love Rhonda and, on top of that, how *interesting* it will be to write about this particular subject.

Right.

Another week goes by. I'm still not sure I have it in me to face your question, Rhonda.

But a part of me needs to. You are not the first to ask how I stay thin, nor is this the first time I've evaded going back to the root of why I chose staying fit as a way of life in the first place.

But, you see, I do have some issues.

On the other hand, I've been writing a lot about Mom and me anyway, so what's the big deal? Haven't I wanted to remember us *deeply*, on so many levels?

Still, I have this feeling the whole weight thing will flesh out a wave of family history like none before. A big, big wave of what came before me: a long chain of fat women.

But the thing is ... your tone, Rhonda, like *you*, sounds positive and upbeat. But how my practice of thin began is not, I repeat, *not* a positive, upbeat matter.

I say to my audiences all the time how fear has been the stepping stone to insure my growth, how challenging my fears is a large part about why I write in the first place. Still, what strikes me as really odd is that this writing-about-being-afraid-I'd-end-up-fat feels so much more weighty than all the other fears I've pinned down.

Until now, it never even crossed my mind that I've completely bypassed writing about this issue. I've teetered on the edge, skirted the entry into fat-writing, but I never dove in, figuring there's enough, more than enough, emphasis on the subject already. Like most women, I'm sick to death of the whole weight-loss industry. My god, it's not rocket science. Eat less (especially less sugar) and move your ass. I suppose not writing about it, now that I think about it, has been kind of a consolation for moving my ass.

And isn't it just so right to begin with Oprah? Because here's the most amazing thing. What I remember most about the live show I witnessed was how, at intermission, Oprah sat down in front of a cloth-covered table of snack food.

I can't remember who the guests were or what they talked about, but I watched breathlessly as Oprah gobbled a handful of potato chips while searching the other bowls and trays; how she suddenly, as if a switch was flicked, paid no mind to the audience she was so in touch with when the lights were up. We ceased to exist. Everything but the food fell by the wayside. She was mesmerized. By the food.

And that night, trying to sleep in my hotel room, all my thoughts turned to the image of Oprah eating chips, the look in her eyes, the way the food, just looking at the food, brought her into another dimension.

How well I know that look.

And so my thoughts turned, as they do now, to my mother, how the same look comes over her, has always come over her, from as far back as I can remember, when food is present. How her weight has forever been the biggest issue and failure for her, even in her last years, and how much this saddens us both.

Oh, it hits me! Could this life-long weight frustration underlie her mean streak?

When I was a kid, she'd weigh her food on a tiny scale, count each calorie, then, while cleaning up, stuff food into her mouth, chew, spit it into a napkin, or (gulp) *swallow*. Always the next new fad diet, the next promise of slenderness: the bulimia; the laxatives; food hidden in the clothes hamper, under the mattress; candy tucked in her dresser behind girdles and bras (nothing escaped the young writer); the endless cottage cheese containers; the food hoarding—a fridge and freezer in the kitchen, two more in the basement. Every nook and cranny overflowing with food.

We gauge so much of our own lives in relation to the choices our mother made. My mom's desire to be thin and the methods she chose never worked, of course. But this isn't what gets me most; it's what the sight of a cottage cheese container brings up for me to this day, namely, my own persistent fears of being fat, fears that, even though a lifetime of dance and bicycling has made me firm, are still so easily reawakened even though I thought I'd suppressed them for good.

Because we overlap, Mom and me. We are completely looped and entwined. We are a *wreath*. We reflect one another so deeply, though we never say so. But we know how much of the other there is when we look into each other's eyes. And when I look into the mirror, there are still some days when all I see is *her*.

And then, lord help me, all I see is *fat*.

You know what, I can barely take all this in. I'm finding it a little hard to breathe. I'm going to open the window even though there is already a chill in my office.

My mother who couldn't stop eating, my family of fat women. The subject of exercise always one I couldn't find a way to talk about with any of them. And, honestly, I was never sure it would make a difference anyway. It was safer to say nothing.

But I had plenty to say. Exercise had become my scripture. Like any dancer, I was capable of saying all kinds of unkind things about fat people. Instead, I let my aunts pinch my cheeks, say I was "too-a thin-a" with a sorrowful look. I let them eat their sausage and cheese in peace.

(Strange! The headline this very morning reads, "Jack Lalanne dies at ninety-six, a man who exercised every day of his life." "Billy Graham was for the hereafter. I'm for the here and now," he told *The New York Times*. My father thought he was a nut, but I adored him.)

I grew up thinking, *Was I next? Could I escape being fat?* This was the eternal question of my girlhood. It overshadowed any pleasure I might have found in food.

Today I eat with a joy I never allowed myself as a younger woman when I knew so little about the women in my family: my aunts who never left the kitchen (so it seemed to me); my grandmothers who couldn't speak English, who seemed so distant, so old-fashioned. It didn't matter because, sadly, all I cared to know was that they were fat.

And I didn't want to be fat.

I'd rather bury my head in sand, smother it, rather than remember this next thing on top of everything else. But here goes: When my Aunt Margaret, Nanny, my mother's sister, moved her head, her cheeks swayed. When she laughed, they flapped. While my mother had round, full cheeks, my aunt's face, by the time she was forty, had slackened into jowls. When Nanny had a heart attack in her fifties, the doctor told my mother, as I listened on with horror, that he couldn't cut through the layers of fat fast enough to save her life.

The very morning before, I'd sat next to Nanny while she ate breakfast cereal out of a mixing bowl. A mixing bowl. *This is how much cereal it takes to fill Nanny,* I thought, *Nanny needs so much food.* It astonished me, the size of her bowl. I was spellbound. Fascinated. Repulsed. I felt shaky and scared to death.

And, see. Now she's dead!

Watching my aunt eat, I decided I would go to college and reach for a life as different from hers as I could possibly find.

My own life.

All this was going through my mind and yet my aunt had no idea I was watching her. I don't think mothers, aunts, sisters, friends, any of us, realize how closely little girls are watching for clues about how to feel about themselves. And wouldn't you know it, while my aunt was spooning the cereal up, she had that *look.*

The look that comes over my mother's face. Oprah's potato-chip look.

I was in the studio yesterday, going through my dance practice, when a woman from China knocked on the door to ask if she and her daughter, maybe four years old, could watch. Later, we talked about classes for her daughter and, in front of her perfect in-every-way little girl, she said, "I don't think my daughter is thin enough to be a dancer."

I decided not to pay any mind to what the woman said, not to call more attention to her ridiculous, damaging remark. I knelt down, looked directly into two tiny brown eyes and said, "You have the loveliest body I have ever seen. You will be a fine, smart, beautiful dancer."

There may be some old Chinese tradition about not complimenting children directly, but to hell with it. All I could see was this beautiful little girl who could not flee from her own beautiful body, ever.

Saying this makes me remember how it was that I dealt with not wanting to be fat. I *fled*.

One coast to the opposite.

One way of life for another.

Where people talk more about what they don't eat than what they do. I married a man from California. We stir-fry vegetables. My new tribe runs in marathons, bicycles to work. A whole new universe. Strange and green and wholesome as the artichokes we buy loose and fresh, not suffocating under plastic, the perfect metaphor for my new way of life.

Rhonda, what choice do I have? I have to work my way through to the end of all this. You started it.

It comes as no surprise that my sisters who stayed behind didn't fare as well, weight-wise. "Well, she certainly is your *big* sister," Larry joked at our family reunion. We laughed.

But behind my laughter, so much hurt had collected over the years for my older sister, the former beauty queen who struggles with her weight to this day

My other sister smokes a pack a day. "To keep my weight down," she says. Her voice is so gravelly, I hardly recognize it.

But it wasn't only the fear of being fat I was running from, but fat-expectation. My mother still swears: "We come from fat genes. I've tried. I've really tried. It's *hereditary*."

Luckily, thankfully, dance became my vice, bicycling my favorite pastime. I believe I have become what I wanted: thin enough to wear jeans without flinching.

I remember when one reviewer called me chic. *Chic?* I thought. *My writing? Or me?*

I didn't know. I didn't need to know. Because either way the word made me proud. And while I know it doesn't take much in this city for someone to call you chic (a little lipstick and a good haircut, and, presto, you're chic), still, it made me happy to read the word in print. I gloated. Take *that* heredity.

I realize eating as an emotional response to being unhappy was not the popular theory back in my mother's day. People of my mother's generation may have lived through a war where there was famine, but I believe my mother's hunger over the years became of another sort. Losing her dad as a young woman, a man she loved desperately, is, I bet, when the overeating began.

Losing her husband to her best friend? I can't imagine.

And now, older, weaker, in lieu of always cooking, always eating, my mother watches cooking shows with the same look in her eyes. And she still hides food. When I clean her apartment, food wrappers litter the floor, her bed, fall from her pockets, her purse. There is never enough food in her fridge even though she pays through the teeth for three full meals a day.

It's her way to make up for the fact my sisters avoid visiting, her way of trying to fill the loss of losing her second husband to cancer, a man she was devoted to. There is always some new wound to feed with another trip to Safeway.

In a nutshell, Rhonda, I rebelled. Growing up in a house stuffed with food, if I now have a dozen eggs, a bunch of bananas, enough salad and fish for dinner, I live without want. When my friend Pam opened my fridge, she cried, "Christ, there's nothing in here!" (People assume, because I'm thin, that I have all this will power. Nope. If it's in the house, I'll eat it. So it's not in the house.)

Okay, that's enough. I'm going to excuse myself now and wrap this up.

But before I do, I just want to say something that suddenly feels very important: More often than not, after I write about whatever subject preoccupies me, I forget most of it. I really do. I forget what I wrote, why I wrote it, how I wrote it. I choose a subject. I spend hours with it. But when I stand to stretch, it slides off. I've written so much over the years, I can't possibly retain it all. All I remember when I turn off my laptop is that I've faced myself again and it didn't defeat me.

So, Rhonda, when I sat to write to you this morning, I intended to share with you a few simple secrets to my thinness, pass it on. Like a recipe.

Sorry it didn't turn out as simple as that.

Yet one thing is as simple as ingredients written on an index card: I will not forget how your question forced me to go back over my life, see how things were, how I felt about them, how I understand them now.

And can I just say that you are gorgeous. My god, do you even know how many heads you turn? No couple of pounds up or down will make one bit of difference in your life unless you swear they do.

And just so you know, I've gained a few pounds myself. And for once, I don't care, or not in the way I would have once. I'll take them off. Or I won't.

But I won't obsess about them. I may obsess *writing* about them (thanks to you) but I won't let the pounds haunt me.

Other than that, I'll continue to fill up, absolutely gorge myself, on all the things that really matter to me. And, knowing myself as I do, I'm sure to bite off more than I can chew now and again. And then, sleeplessly, I'll have to find a way to prove that I didn't.

Oh, and Rhonda, I've added swimming to my routine. Less cheese. No meat. Unless my mother makes meatballs.

Then, screw it, my fork is the first one in.

Mr. Wong

While it was happening, I didn't realize how relevant it was. I certainly didn't realize that leaving my wallet behind could turn out to be the enlightenment of the year for me. It's amazing how we can sort of stumble into the truths we are looking for.

Before dipping in to Mr. Wong's shop for a quick wash and blow-dry, I had no idea what it would cost, didn't care to ask, because when you live in Seattle and your husband lands mid-winter work in Honolulu, you go with him, regardless, and then you find a way to deal with 80 percent humidity. And my way of dealing with it was Mr. Wong, whose name I am terribly fond of.

"You got frizzy; come come, I fix for you, yah yah; then you pay me money, okay?" Mr. Wong said, pulling my arm in a way no one pulls anyone's arm in Seattle without someone calling 911. I hadn't been prepared for such a pull, but somehow it didn't startle me, either. Clearly, this was a pull that needed pulling.

When in Honolulu, the smorgasbord of all melting pots, it is strangely incomprehensible, when you're in the middle of such a pull, to not read it as anything but excitement, the near childish way new immigrants display eagerness, those who haven't been told it's rude or uncustomary to talk openly and ravenously about money, or the possibility of making money, and are just so happy to make money that they don't even try to hide it. Like kids on Christmas morning.

"Okay," I said.

"And I do extra good for you so you come back next time, yah yah!"

At once I felt the relief of having someone to talk to after days of being on my own, while my husband, a marine surveyor, was working twelve hours a day. (The tsunami that devastated Japan left Hawaii with a few problems. Unbelievable what the surging swell of a tidal wave will do to a marina 3800 miles away. East of Pearl Harbor, floating docks broke away with 120 boats still tied to them, and that's just one of the emergencies Larry was dealing with. It's incredible what my husband does.)

And so I told this complete stranger the first thing that came to mind about my hair, how many hours I had lain on my back as a child, on a twin bed next to my sister's, staring at a picture of Cher, touching my finger ever so desirably to the black straightness of hers as she sang into a microphone, sang with a smile on her face that even I could tell had nothing to do with Sonny and everything to do with the spotlight shining in her eyes.

"Who dat?" Mr. Wong asked, not really listening, running over to a table to grab a stack of magazines. "Here, dis," he said, pointing with his brush at two frayed copies of *House Beautiful* he'd thrown on the counter as if to say, "You are a haole with enough money to sit in my chair rather than struggle with frizz in the bathroom of your hotel room."

"*House Make Nice,*" he said, pointing with his comb this time.

But before I could flip through all the throw pillows perfectly aligned on couches that always make me think that this cannot be a real couch in a real living room, he pulled me again toward the back of the salon and pushed me into a black vinyl chair with a stack of newspapers covered with what looked like a dishtowel for a seat. "Yah yah, sit!" Then he dipped my head back under the faucet. I am always grateful for a situation that doesn't make me to do all the work of communicating. Doubly in foreign cultures.

And communication in the local dialect of the Hawaiian Islands is trickier than you think. While pidgin may sound like English, or something close to English, it's not all that easy to speak or to understand. It's a chop-chop, rapid-fire of English mixed with Chinese, Japanese, Filipino—any combination until a transaction is carried out.

Suffice it to say, I was grateful for Mr. Wong's take-charge attitude.

The other reason for my visit to Mr. Wong's was that we were bound for Seattle in the morning and I'm one of the last remaining few who still likes to look her best on a travel day. When I stride up to the checkpoints, I want good hair; don't ask me why.

The wash and blow-dry Mr. Wong gave me, minus the hairspray

overload, was terrific. "Yah much good! Hair many many bettah!"

"Okay," I said again.

I wanted to say, "Yah yah, tank you, tank you!" because I'm pretty good at accents, all in all; but of course I couldn't do that.

Later in bed, Larry sleeping beside me, I was beginning a new column. I thought that the most interesting thing I had to say about Mr. Wong was how his forcefulness somehow allowed me to easily trust him. Between thoughts, I began organizing my handbag for travel, when suddenly it dawned on me that my wallet was missing. In it, cash, credit cards, my license. Wondering what I had done with it and fearing I wouldn't be able to find it, I got up, dressed, and proceeded to retrace my tracks, starting at Mr. Wong's. (Larry never heard a thing: not my panic, not my dressing, not the door that snapped behind me. God, I envy the way he can sleep.)

People in Mr. Wong's neighborhood went into fear mode. "Cancel your cards!" is what they advised.

"I no have Wong's number," said the woman at the Korean BBQ next door to Mr. Wong's. And because I'd already checked the phone listings where there are pages and *pages* of the surname Wong, I looked to the other woman behind the counter with pleading eyes. "No worry, Wong no steal your money," she said. My spirit perked up. "He steal your *Visa*." And the two of them laughed.

The African American security guard said, "You know, lady, Wong is a *Chinese* name; you're screwed."

Two local boys, meaning Hawaiian born, biceps like smooth brown mounds of earth, said I'd never see my wallet again because, as one of them pointed out, "Immigrants steal you blind."

After returning to the hotel and calling the airport to change our flight, I lay awake, more upset about the smear campaign I'd listened to than about losing my wallet. God, the prejudice!

I was also thinking: *medical card, library card, voter registration.* What to do first?

The next morning, standing on tiptoe, nose up against the window, I could see Mr. Wong in the back room of his salon. I pounded on the glass, all very crazy haole lady, because the racial slurs had affected me from the outside in, much to my horror. Overnight they'd infused me. I had become suspicious.

Another stylist came running: "Mr. Wong have wallet for you!"

My wallet was handed to me wrapped in delicate rice paper, flower petals pressed into the grain. A braided ribbon made from Ti leaves tied the bundle together.

I didn't need to scan the inside. Like my first instinct about Mr. Wong, I trusted everything was fine.

Now I look back over this story and see how the whole of the world's problems were exposed for me at Mr. Wong's salon.

This is how it is.

This is how it's always been.

Maturity

Last week I was taking a walk through Seattle Center when I came upon a gutsy young woman holding a neck-to-toe signboard with the words "BIG BUSINESS RIDES THE WAVE OF WAR" written in caps across it.

There were other words, too, like, "WE'RE DROWNING IN DEBT" and "I HAVE A SINKING FEELING ABOUT WALL STREET." Words we've all heard, wondered ourselves, and, on a personal level, have all had to find ways to cope with through the last unbelievable years.

But here's the fun part: to tie in the whole water theme, she wore a wet suit. With Tevas.

I like to think the best part of being human is acknowledging each other, especially our courage and creativity; so how could I *not* acknowledge her sign?

Or, for that matter, her wet suit?

Not a political remark, mind you, something less heavy to shed some light on the dimness of war and government, no matter what side of the issues we cling to.

Now, sitting here, I keep coming back to the words I said with a smile on my face and what I remember as laughter in my voice: "Sweetie, you can share my lifeboat."

My words bounced right off her wet suit and fell flat on the sidewalk. Her mouth writhed sideways. In no uncertain terms, she said, "I am *not* your sweetie."

Oh come on. Why would the word "sweetie" trump my obvious support of her? When did using an endearment become offensive, the kind of thing we can't say anymore? And when, pray tell, did we start to believe that using humor, even about something dire as war, is disrespectful? Because that's what I read in her face, that I lacked respect.

There's an elderly man who sits in his wheelchair in front of my corner market who served in World War II. A few others from the

Vietnam era join him every once in a while, and I've heard them joke about the things that happened in those wars, jokes that can make my hair stand on end. Still, anyone can tell it's their way of coming to terms with the horror they faced. They make me see how if they can laugh at all they went through, *sweetie*, we had better, too.

"Oh, sorry," I said, and skedaddled away, thinking that there is so much give and take that needs to occur in this country if we are ever going to mature past head-butting. I was inspired by the woman's sign, her courage, but her reaction to my reaction came off as intolerant, small-minded, especially when she seems to want spectators to believe she is so very progressive.

Meet the Progressives's worst enemy: ourselves. Because you can't call yourself progressive if you've lost your sense of humor, not in my book. Because how far does it get us if we have no humor along the way for things like, oh, I don't know . . . one woman's wet suit is another woman's haute couture? If we can't share a little laughter what is the point? Isn't open-mindedness the very thing we say we are about?

Maybe meeting this daring woman was just another example of how my Back East sense of humor can ricochet and come flying back to thump me in this city.

Or maybe it's that some people, even in their twenties, are just what I think of as fuddy-duddy, not about to laugh at anything, especially themselves.

Because a woman wearing her politics on a signboard over a wet suit is looking for a reaction, no question. Otherwise she'd wear a short black skirt over black tights like everyone else. So why not have a little fun with the effect? The awkward responses?

Because it *is* awkward to come up against my greatest fear—that war will sink us—on a reasonably warm Sunday in the middle of a busy park when some of us are feeling fairly hopeless already, too let down to believe anything *but* laughing will save us.

The whole thing reminds me of a boy I encountered on the ferry once. His hair was a purplish Mohawk that stood inches above his scalp. When I turned to look he said, "What are *you* looking at?" in the knock-down drag-out tone teenage boys with a lot to prove will use.

But here's the difference: he's a kid. A baby, really. Which, in itself, makes his lack of humor more forgivable as he struggles to figure out if he is this, that, or the other enough.

The thing is, I was going to compliment his hair. But I weighed the likelihood of any remark made by me against the likelihood of his getting my try at lighthearted connection, which I completely doubted once I turned ever so slightly around again and he flipped me off, asserting that under no circumstances should I even *think* of speaking.

So, of course, I said, "Mohawks are *so* over." And then I ran to my car so fast my favorite hairband slid free in the stairwell and I didn't stop to get it.

In challenging situations like these, we all have a choice. We can look the other way or choose delicacy, finesse, tact, which I did by excusing myself quickly from the gal in the wet suit.

And there are other times we push back with all our adolescent might, left to deal with the consequences best we can.

It's amazing, isn't it, what a lifelong process maturing is?

Keith & Mike

"The way I see it," Keith says, "I'll have to plan the entire wedding my*self*."

I've seen Keith in action. He's a professional choreographer. I'm pretty sure he'll compose his wedding much like he would a dance. He's not going to measure the stage; he's not going spend big on costuming; he's not going to mark the lines of sight with stage tape. He is going to choose the most amazing music and *believe.*

"Because you know how Mike is: *bor*ing."

I laugh out loud. It's like a one-liner vocalized by Nathan Lane.

Mike is a lot like Larry. So neither of us mean boring in the usual sense of the word. But you know, would-rather-read-the-paper-than-go-dancing. I married a fourth-generation Californian WASP of Scotch-Irish descent.

"All I ask is that he find a decent pair of earrings for the ceremony. Fourteen karat gold balls," he winks. "At *least.*"

Again I laugh.

"But if I know Mike, he'll come home with a faux silver hoop from Forever 21."

I nod, a little more eagerly this time remembering what my friend David said, "WASPs are bred not to get too excited. Like cattle." I laughed and laughed.

Always the writer, I like to think of Larry and me like ... well ... like: I am the exclamation point and Larry is the comma. Unless a tragedy occurs, then, for whatever reason, we switch. But normally, I don't expect too much emotion or exaggeration from my trustworthy, responsible comma. (Oh, the words I've used over the years to distinguish between us. Does the whole world, gay or straight, or *what*ever and who cares, fall in love with their emotional opposite?)

Keith and Mike, like hundreds of other gay couples, are off to their home state of New York to wed in the first weeks of legal, unrestricted, same-sex marriage. They'd stay right here and get married on Alki Beach if they could. But, like Keith said, "Washington State has some *serious* catching up to do."

It's like a reprieve for me, writing about Keith and Mike, two men who are part of something much larger: making history. I suspect I am still somewhat of a journalist at heart, in want of the perfect story: A little love. A little politics.

"And I ask you, why does it feel *so* important to say those two silly words anyway? 'I do.' I mean, *really.*" Keith says, his cheeks red from the wine. "Because if you've been together as long as we have, everyone knows it's more like I do *not,* especially when it comes to yard work."

We clink glasses. When Keith is finished telling me all about the wedding, I hold his two hands in mine. He gives me another wink and says, "Bella." And every time he calls me this, I think how easy intimacy is between us.

Maybe because I've watched Keith and Mike work it out for so many years that their marriage feels more like the great BIG check mark for our country that it is. And watching Keith now, after New York became the largest state to pass gay marriage, how differently he carries himself compared to how he used to pass through the lobby of his rather posh, if a little staid, sea-front condominium, has been an impressive lesson in politics for me. It's made me see how civil law plays a huge part in all our lives, in how we view ourselves. Before, it was as if Keith seemed not to notice his neighbor's sidelong glances.

But I noticed.

Or maybe he received their stares but from an emotional distance he'd gotten really good at through the years, his entire life. But there's a new spring in his step. He addresses his neighbors cheerfully, directly, by *name.* His thoughts are not focused on the rejection he used to feel, but moving right to his neighbor's eyes with a grin. Like, yesterday, for instance. He addressed one couple in the elevator by saying, "Isn't the sky just lovely today? Positively *breath*taking!"

This instead of the mute, aloof man he used to feign, not wanting to call attention to himself before saying something like, "Honey, stuffed shirts for those two only come in extra-large. Did you see the size of their tooshies?" once we are alone again, feet up, goblet in hand, each of us completely frank.

And now? Well, the same couple who used to shun my friend with a downcast nod, whose biases have dominated this particular condo ever since Reagan, smile at Keith. *Ah, here's our Keith now! Let us shake your hand and smile and smile because we don't know what else to do. Or say.* It makes me think of the way a puppy will follow you anywhere if you run ahead playfully, wanting the same playfulness because they've been cooped up too long.

And get this, after two decades together, Keith and Mike still hold hands. Even at the grocery. Every couple should be so lucky.

⁓

Same-sex marriage became legal in Washington on December 6, 2012. Keith wrote me an email: "Thus far, I have refrained from sending the governor a bill for our airfare."

Show Me

Every now and again, my subconscious knows just how to make sense of things.

For instance, I had no idea my thoughts this morning held the very things I've wanted to say since . . . since forever. Mainly, that I'm too in love with books to look at them through the eyes of the future.

Too lovesick, in fact, to download a book at all.

I admit I have a romantic's sensory system. I cannot envision a world where books and bookstores are not valued. Books are the only way I know how to live. I would haul water jugs from town on my bicycle and live in a 8′ × 11′ foot trailer in the middle of nowhere again without electricity or heat, if I had to, but I cannot live without books I can hold in my hand until all the pages are turned.

Let's say you are walking down the sidewalk and you take a look, and then a double look, and that's when you notice it's gone, one of your favorite bookstores. And if, like me, you are more than a little wary of corporate development lately, you say to yourself, oh, no, I *loved* that bookstore.

Eventually the image of the bookstore recedes as you get used to the Starbucks or TCBY that took its place, but not entirely. Every once in a while, the bookstore still comes back to you, a familiar feeling that has to do with memory, obviously, but even more to do with longing. I don't know how to explain this feeling except to say that it's real. And it comes up a lot.

You could live Anywhere, USA. But in this instance, the bookstore is, or was, Fremont Place Books in Seattle. Henry Burton, the owner, wrote, "We have reached the point where the business is no longer sustainable."

And there it is again, *the* fashionable word: *sustainable*. Four syllables just about everyone likes to throw around these days. It's all sustainable this, sustainable that, despite the fact that in most neighborhoods independent businesses (bookstores, hardware, coffee, you name it) can no longer sustain, thanks to us, the sustainable-loving public.

Actually, we don't say we are the sustainable-loving public so much as the word *sustainable* is the current catchphrase; so it's more like we mostly pretend we are a sustainable-loving public. While, in fact, we want to buy everything for as little as possible.

And the real trouble isn't that we aren't really doing all that much to ensure any sustainability for our own economy, or, at least for the part not owned by multi-national corporations or technology giants, but that we think, we really do think, we are doing something, something big and sustainable, by recycling our bottles and cans.

Oh, I'm so heated right now.

So I'd better stick to books here, what I'm *most* passionate about: my world. Or I won't be able to make my way back.

And yes, I know I run the risk of sounding hopelessly passé, that I belong to a vanishing species, but that's the least of it. I acknowledge that reading is good, no matter the method. Still, I can't help but want to be respectively read between two tangible covers. I don't think this is too much to ask for years of hard work. Writers want to be read between book covers. We are *supposed* to be read between book covers.

Still, I'm no technophobe. I rely on my laptop and cell phone as much as the next person. I just need to find a way to say that no matter what technology needs from "consumers" (I hate to be called a consumer, don't you?) to ensure their own continuance, that is, that we keep buying the next new iWhatever as fast as they can turn them out, no questions asked, nothing is uncool, unsexy, inadequate, unhip, out of style, unsustainable or non-green about holding a book in your hands.

Don't be fooled.

It's time to come full circle on this. Because contrary to the overload of advertising for green this and sustainable that, PCs are not green or sustainable.

Books are green, or greener than anything your PC, large or teeny, is made of.

When I searched for a list of raw materials used to make up PCs, I had to stop reading after the words copper, lead, aluminum, platinum, tin, gold, silver, bromine, mercury.

I've read about gold mining in Africa, platinum mining in Russia, bromine mines in Arkansas, mines that blow away mountain tops and pollute the surrounding land so horribly it is nearly impossible to imagine. You can spin modern mining practices however you want, but I would think that the only people who should be able to own multiple PCs without some shame are the ones who crawl through those mines. And now the same mining companies are dividing up the rights to our ocean floors. I don't think we will be able to get over a loss like this. Maybe there are some losses we really do get over, but sacrificing our seas to mining is not one of them.

I didn't even get to lists of polymers.

When I researched modern-day book materials, here's what I found: rags, wood pulp, wood bark, ink. Another site read: recycled clothing, recycled paper, cellulose, plant-based dyes. It seems the modern-day book is a reused garden. And get this, the number one industry that still logs trees whole is housing. *Housing.* For China, India, the United States. Trees are no longer felled for the making of paper and books. Paper and books cannot *afford* whole trees. Paper and books use the leftovers in the yard once the planks are cut.

I hope you feel fantastically consoled.

So go green, readers. Buy a book!

In fact, I hope what you are doing right this very minute is lying in bed, a book propped on your chest. Or better, and deliciously more decadent, reading in the tub, candles burning.

And even if my harping on this issue is met with no success, I will continue to say that books don't belong in huge warehouse stores soulless as the pavement that surrounds them, but in close, cozy, intimate rooms where you just might meet another booklover and get to talking about the books and authors you love most, which is what happens pretty much every time I visit one of the last remaining independents.

After all, the strongest argument for religion is not that it is in touch with a Supreme Being but that it puts us in touch with each other. I think the same can be said about independent bookstores.

I may be a novice when it comes to understanding all there is to know about the hard laws of big business where profit is all that matters, but I have a handle on the basics: No one is making out like the guys who make the software.

It may be a small thing—buying a book from a humble store, talking to the owner, recognizing ourselves in someone else's story on the back of a book jacket—that causes such strong feelings you say *wow* out loud before hugging the book to your chest. And yet these are the strongest connections, sustainable only if we are committed to sustaining them.

And the best part is you are making "community"—the other four-syllable, fashionable word everyone likes to say but more and more of us know only in the abstract. No one in your pseudo-world will drive you to the emergency room when the tip of your little finger ends up in your first and last try at making bona-fide French Onion Soup.

My friend from India, Amargit, said the other day, "Americans seem lonely, is this true?"

"Yes," I had to say, "I believe it is."

I said so remembering a woman at a reading I gave in Port Angeles the night before. She sat in the first row and looked to be in her late seventies, maybe early eighties, if I had to guess. And later, when we were talking in the foyer, it took her a few minutes, because I think she wanted to be certain I had a car first, to ask if I was driving back to Seattle or staying the night on the Peninsula.

She was really only half listening when I told her about my need to get back to the city, but at some point after my explanation, she managed to work in that she had over a thousand Facebook friends.

"Well," I said, "you must be very well cared for then." She looked out the window at the rain for a moment before she turned and asked me for a ride home.

And for the entire ride, I thought about how we can delude ourselves about how many friends we think we have in a way no other people before us ever could, but the truth remains: "You are alone. Without a ride home."

And maybe something like this has happened to you: You stand to address an audience, and there is the one person, the one rude, oblivious person, who won't put away the phone.

At Village Books in Bellingham, a young woman sat in my audience, third row back, looking down at hers. Every time I looked over at her, a too-bright light rose from her lap against the more subdued lighting of the bookstore.

Why had she come?

After the reading, she approached me, and I'm not kidding, told me how much she enjoyed my talk. I found my nerve and asked her why she'd come to a reading if she didn't want to listen to one.

"Oh, I *was* listening," she said. "But I wanted to share with my writing friends what you were saying."

Friends. That word again.

For reasons not easy for me, but necessary under the circumstances, I smiled. But I wanted so badly to say, "You weren't listening. You were looking down. You wrinkled your nose when there was nothing to wrinkle your nose at, smiled when I'd said nothing funny, and you didn't laugh, you little shit, when I said something clever. You were busy elsewhere, your thumbs were *flying*."

And thank heavens, I thought, because if she'd not come alone, if she'd come with others instructed by their English teacher, say, she and her extra-credit pals would likely have sat in my audience texting each *other*.

But even harder for me to swallow than her bad manners was her parting question, one that left both the coordinator of the reading series (dependent on book sales) and me speechless, "I can download your book from Amazon, right?"

We, all of us, need to protect what we love. If you say you love the independents (bookstores and otherwise), buy from them.

SHOW ME THE LOVE. Four exceptional syllables.

Big this time, big, BIG syllables, the biggest.

But not big enough to accommodate good intentions if we don't carry them out.

PS: I loved Henry. If only because each time I was in his store, I could see how much he loved books. And because I can only guess at how much he'd supported authors and books and other bookstores over the years to arrive at such a love, I spent the rest of my afternoon writing an email to Henry.

Then I rode my bike to Queen Anne Books (now the Queen Anne Book Company, long story) because I needed to be in a space I want the next generation to value, to inherit, to *get*. It was just something I needed to do. I can't help it. This is the world I want to live in, the one I will support to the very best of my sustainable ability: the world of books. Reading them. Writing them. Books I can touch and hold and *smell*.

It would be so much fun to be able to do so in hardcover.

But I'll settle for a paperback.

True Love: An Afterword

Each December I reread *Gift of the Sea*, by Anne Morrow Lindbergh. It is my most comforting holiday tradition. One chapter in, and I immediately feel at home.

I'm familiar with every paragraph by now, but, still, the book becomes new to me all over again, as if the author and I are alone together, catching up on old times; this is the best part, and I'm a little overwhelmed (in a good way) to be in such skillful company. But I'm not intimidated, and I don't feel awkward. This kind of ease matters more to me than just about anything nowadays.

I am abruptly changing the subject here, but last night I woke with a start because Larry was snoring again, which is also overwhelming (*not* in a good way). This is our interminable night-tussle: He snores. I wake. He snores. I wake. Come morning, it's a wonder I can write anything at all.

Though some nights he sleeps silently for hours, just breathing. Just like I remember. I have no idea why.

Last night, no such luck. Oddly, for once, this was okay with me. I wanted to get back to my book. So I propped up the pillows and read from Chapter 5: *Oyster Bed*. I came to the end of the first page when, in the margin, I saw what I had written last year in sprawling blue letters, "Call Shanta. Do *not* ask if the Irish boyfriend has proposed yet!"

Shanta is my daughter/friend. Our bond is to love and be loved. What is the point of anything else? Anyway, I mention her because love is really the point of this month, right?

So, this year, firm in my new approach as a conscientious objector to spending, eating, and drinking too much, I am my own Secret Santa. My gift? Reading for hours, day and night. Book after book. I know what makes me happy. Reading makes me happy. Books are what I want to open.

The only other applicable thing I have to say here is that I know that you don't necessarily have to be a writer to know what a mixed bag of emotions it is when your own book is near completion.

Book finished? It's impossible!

Eventually, though, it sinks in.

Still, I can't believe I'm here again, where all the things I still want to say whirl around in my head while I'm also fully aware that a book, any book, can go on indefinitely, revision after revision; when I not only spend my days improving and clarifying (my favorite part), but I bask in the process. Honestly, I could easily, happily, joyfully make refining these couple of hundred pages into another year's work. Two. Three at most.

And not to drag things out, but I could linger in this Afterword forever . . . .

Because after I hand over the manuscript, here we go again, what next?

Out of the corner of my eye, the morning sun creeps across my chaise and everything about the way the light catches the cloth stirs me until I think, *hmm, maybe I can write about this?*

Because I know there are only so many non-writing days in a row of non-writing days before this writer needs to go at it again. When I will do anything, anything at all, if only I can get back to work.

Yet, I have to choose my next commitment carefully, be sure to pick a subject I can stomach for the long haul, which is not easy. I'm not always sure at the beginning, or even toward the end, who or what I'm looking for, exactly, other than there has to be some kind of serious connection between us.

Once I find whatever it is I'm looking for, I'll begin.

Because, after Larry, writing is my only true love.

And I have a sneaking suspicion this will always be so.

Acknowledgments

Some of the pieces in this book originally appeared, in shorter form, in the *Seattle Times*, the *Seattle Post-Intelligencer*, *Seattle Metropolitan Magazine*, *Crosscut*, *Belltown Messenger*, *Alaska Fishermen's Journal*, *Alaska Magazine*, *Honolulu Star-Advertiser*, *Port Townsend & Jefferson County Leader*, *Queen Anne News*, *Signs of Life* (Facèré Jewelry Art Gallery literary journal), as commentary for NPR's *Weekend Edition*, KONP News Talk Radio, as well as in the publications and radio stations I want to express extreme gratitude to below.

While writing this book, I learned to surrender (and "surrender" is the only word) to the writer—the smarter, more sure-of-herself writer—within. Every writer talks about this unique otherness, this voice inside that just *knows*.

Then comes the day when there might be another way of saying something, a better way, and you agonize, because you know you should ... you shouldn't ... you should ... try and fix it.

It was only when this other voice insisted I give it up, that I knew it was over.

"It's time," she said. "Pop the Prosecco!"

So, first and foremost, I want to thank her. Our relationship has evolved over the years, though, like most couples, we still bicker about a thousand little things.

For believing in me again, I'd like to thank Aequitas Books.

A hundred thank-yous to the know-how that is Valerie Brewster, for designing this book with such patience, hard work and brilliance. It's an immeasurably better book because of her.

To all the readers of my last books who took the time to write to me, thank you. Your comments are pure heaven (most of the time).

My mother taught me early on how a good book can be your only relief sometimes. This one is for you, Mom. I miss you every day.

And because so much of the writing here was first published as a shorter print column or radio commentary, I owe much to my various editors and producers who've supported me over the years: First, I want to thank John Brewer, publisher of the *Peninsula Daily News*, for returning my phone call with all the kindness one could wish for after I left a message that went something like: "Mr. Brewer, I deserve to write for your paper." I was relatively inexperienced in the newspaper world, but I wasn't going to admit that.

To the editors at Seattle's *City Living* magazine who invited me, that's right, invited me to write a column. *What? You mean I don't need to go begging?* Totally new concept. Vera Chan Pool, honestly if you only knew how much you have raised the bar in terms of graciousness from an editor.

Debbi Lester, you have given so much to so many artists over the years. Your energy for art and *Art Access* magazine remains an inspiring teacher. That you've allowed me to come along for the ride for so many years, I offer my sincere thanks.

Christy Korrow, when I sit to read about all the amazing things people are doing to make this world a better place, it's like moving from one glowing ember to another. And that you grace my column with an entire page of its own, holly cow. What makes *Lilipoh* magazine even more amazing is the fact that you have children, a husband, a *farm*! Clearly, no free time. How do you find the hours to enliven us all like this?

Ed Bremer host of KSER, FM who allows me to record my commentary *and* to read live on the air, a test of voice and skill like no other, I thank you with affection for our years together and for your trust in me.

Not too long ago an interviewer asked if I like reading on the air more than I like performing live. I thought I was answering honestly by saying I like each equally but for different reasons.

Even if I wasn't fully aware of it at the time, my answer was a flat-out lie. Since my first commentary aired on Seattle's NPR affiliate KUOW and, later, when recording for NPR's *Weekend Edition*,

I've been in love with radio in a way I've never loved the stage. I like drawing from my words all of their—absolutely *all* of their—depth and resonance in the way radio demands. It's far harder than I first expected, not only the skill involved, but also finding stations that let me write commentary my way. Stations that are truly committed to unique programming are a rare thing nowadays. There is a continued move toward branding, the take over of all media by bigger media, so that every public station sounds like every other public station. If you take local radio away from your community, a real connection with the programming is gone.

Ed, never in my whole life have I enjoyed radio more than with you.

And to the essay within this book entitled "Among Friends," thank you for launching a whole new book of the same name. Who knew there was so much more to say?

About the Author

Sanelli is the author of nine books including collections of poetry, essays, and a memoir. She works as a columnist in the Seattle area and is invited to read from her work to audiences throughout the country. Her commentaries have been on NPR's *Weekend Edition*. Please visit her website at www.marylousanelli.com.